CHAMPIONS REMEMBERED

CHAMPIONS REMEMBERED

Ray Fitzgerald

THE STEPHEN GREENE PRESS
Brattleboro, Vermont
Lexington, Massachusetts

Arthur G. Miller, Consulting Editor

First Edition

This book is manufactured in the United States of America. It is designed by Irving Perkins Associates and published by the Stephen Greene Press, Fessenden Road, Brattleboro, Vermont 05301.

Library of Congress Cataloging in Publication Data

Fitzgerald, Ray, 1926–
Champions remembered.

Includes index.

1. Athletes—Massachusetts—Boston—Biography—
Addresses, essays, lectures.   I.   Title.
GV697.A1F53 1982   796'.092'2 [B]   82–12051
ISBN   0-8289-0483-9 (C)
ISBN   0-8289-0517-7 (P)

Photo on page 116 copyright Ray Lussier. All other photos are courtesy of the *Boston Globe.*

The thumb nail sketch of Carl Yastrzemski on page 220 was written by Dick Bresciani.

PUBLISHED OCTOBER 1982
Second printing December 1982
Third printing January 1983
Fourth printing, first paperback edition, May 1983

CONTENTS

CONTENTS

═PREFACE═

To begin with, picking the very best of anything—songs, movie stars, restaurants—is a presumptuous, subjective, and arbitrary endeavor. One man's mediocrity is another man's superstar. And while it surely is safe to say that none of those chronicled here was a mediocre athlete, to state unequivocally that they and only they represent the very best in Boston sports history is to build a house without any doors.

But that's the fun of any list, isn't it?—to start an argument, promote discussion, bring out differences of opinion? What fun would it be if it were decreed by law that chocolate chip was the absolute number-one ice-cream flavor? Where would that leave the butter-pecan crowd?

Now then, concerning the ground rules. There aren't many. One concerns the time span. With two exceptions, the athletes chronicled within these covers had their days of glory in what might be termed the modern era, from 1940 to 1980.

This excludes such obvious choices for athletic sainthood as John L. Sullivan, Cy Young, Babe Ruth, Hazel Wightman, Francis Ouimet, Tris Speaker, and Clarence DeMar, whose accomplishments took place before the specified period. The exceptions are hockey player Eddie Shore and marathoner Johnny Kelley, and there are mitigating circumstances for each.

Shore, though he started with the Bruins in 1926, didn't finish until 1940, and his influence in hockey was felt long after that. Kelley, though he began running in 1928, won a marathon in 1935 and another in 1945, and was still running in marathons as this book went to press.

To be eligible for this book, an athlete could either have been born in Massachusetts and made his mark elsewhere, or vice versa, or both have been born in Massachusetts and made his mark there. In most cases, it was vice versa: the athlete was born outside of the state and became a star here, although Brockton's Rocky Marciano fought everywhere except Boston, and Lynn's Harry Agganis reached stardom close to home.

When I made my last painful cuts from a list of names longer than Wilt Chamberlain's arm, I realized there wasn't a Patriot—or any pro football player, for that matter—on the final tally sheet.

No doubt about it, there have been some outstanding Patriot players over the years. To name just a few—Gino Cappelletti, the team's all-time leading scorer; quarterback Babe Parilli; running back Larry Garron; fullback Jim Nance; linebacker Nick Buoniconti, whose best years were with the Dolphins; center Jon Morris, and the defensive line of Houston Antwine, Bob Dee, Larry Eisenhauer, and Jim Hunt. Still, I felt that none quite measured up to the required caliber of greatness.

It was established early on that no one who was still in the prime of his career would be dealt with at length. It is good, I think, when doing a book such as this to stand back and take a long look. Sometimes, when the athlete is still in an active status, we are so caught up in enthusiasm that we go overboard in our praise of him.

And, since longevity is a big part of the qualification for inclusion in the book, today's contemporary superstar may be playing for another team before the ink is dry on this book. A few years ago, Fred Lynn was tabbed as the best pure hitter to play with the Red Sox since Ted Williams. Now he's with the California Angels.

Certainly if events follow a normal course, several athletes currently performing in Boston will qualify for future greatness. Larry Bird of the Celtics has already established himself as one of the greatest basketball players of all time. Marvin Hagler of Brockton is the best boxer to come out of this area since Marciano began his career in the same city.

John Hannah of the Patriots is the premier offensive lineman in football and Stanley Morgan is a great wide receiver. Jim Rice, in his first five seasons with the Red Sox, has had offensive totals to rival Williams's. Cincinnati Bengals tight end Dan Ross of Everett and Northeastern University is one of the most promising young stars in pro football. Rod Langway of Randolph has become a leader of the Montreal Canadiens, the glamour team of hockey.

These names are legends of tomorrow, names for another book. This one deals with those who have already done it, and done it remarkably well for a long time. This book is a reminder of a thousand glorious sport yesterdays.

Ray Fitzgerald
Boston, Massachusetts

PART I

=BASEBALL=

Babe Ruth was once a Red Sox star. So were Cy Young, the winningest pitcher of all time, and Tris Speaker, the marvelous center fielder. But in the modern era, **Ted Williams** and **Carl Yastrzemski** are the two names that stand out among all the great ones who played for the Red Sox.

Ted and Yaz played the same position—left field—in Fenway Park, the gem of a ballpark in Boston's Back Bay, built in 1912 and remodeled in 1934. The park's chummy left field wall, nicknamed "the green monster," became as well known as the Bunker Hill Monument. Home runs came easier at Fenway than they did at spacious Braves' Field, whose most memorable characteristic was a brisk breeze blowing off the Charles. Braves' Field also featured a set of seats in right field called "the jury box," where a regular coterie sat in judgment on the often hapless Braves.

The list of memorable Red Sox and Boston Braves players is almost as long as a Williams home run. The following modern-era stars deserve special mention:

JOE CRONIN—Slugging shortstop . . . Played for Red Sox from 1935 to 1945 . . . Best average, .325 in 1938 . . . Terrific clutch hitter, with lifetime average of .301 . . . Managed team from 1933 to 1947 . . . Later general manager, then president of American League . . . Elected to Hall of Fame in 1956.

BOBBY DOERR—Became Red Sox second baseman in 1937, at age of nineteen . . . Played fourteen years, had 233 home runs and .288 batting average . . . Steady fielder and fan favorite . . . Retired prematurely because of back injury . . . Later was Red Sox coach.

1

JIMMY FOXX—Nicknamed "the Beast" because of muscular forearms... Came to Red Sox in 1936 after eleven seasons with Philadelphia As... Averaged 37 homers a season in more than five years with Sox... Hit .349 with 50 homers and 175 runs batted in in 1939.

JOHNNY PESKY—Line-drive-hitting infielder from 1942 through 1951, with three years lost because of service duty... Had over 200 hits first three seasons, with averages of .331, .335, and .324... Along with Dom DiMaggio, was table setter for Ted Williams (who, more often than not, cleaned up)... Red Sox manager in 1963–64... Later coached team.

DOM DIMAGGIO—Fleet center fielder of Red Sox from 1942 through 1952, with three years in armed services... Terrific fielder and consistent hitter, with lifetime average of .298... Small (5'9"), wore glasses, and was nicknamed "the Little Professor"... Brother of Joe D.

MEL PARNELL—Smooth left-handed pitcher from 1947 through 1956... Has more wins (123) than any other southpaw in Red Sox history... Pitched well at tough Fenway Park... Had no-hitter against White Sox in 1956... Won 25 games in 1949.

TOMMY HOLMES—Right fielder with Braves from 1942 to 1951... Favorite of fans in right field jury box... Lifetime average of .302... Held modern National League consecutive game hitting streak at 37 until broken by Pete Rose... Had 28 homers and hit .352 in 1945... Managed Braves in 1951–52.

LEFTY GROVE—Pitched last eight years of career with Red Sox after first nine with Athletics... Won 105 games for Boston, including 20 in 1935... Won 300th game of career in Boston... Led league in earned run averages four times while with Sox... Voted into Hall of Fame in 1947.

JOHNNY SAIN—Right-handed pitcher for Braves from 1942 to 1951, with three years lost to service... Won 20 or more games five times, including 24 in 1948... Beat Bob Feller, 1–0, in 1948 World Series... Later became highly respected pitching coach.

WARREN SPAHN—Teammate of Sain with Braves until franchise was transferred to Milwaukee in 1953... Left-handed pitcher with big motion... Won 20 games four times with Boston Braves... Won World Series game in 1948... Slogan in 1948 pennant drive was "Spahn and Sain and a day of rain"... Member of Hall of Fame.

FRANK MALZONE—Red Sox third baseman from 1956 to 1965... Sure hands and strong hitter... Had 133 home runs, lifetime... Rarely missed game because of injury... Named all-time Red Sox third baseman.

Two great hitters: Yaz and Ted.

JIMMY PIERSALL—Colorful, fleet, fearless center fielder, who made some of the greatest catches in Boston history. . . Overcame mental problems to play eight years with Sox. . . Big favorite with crowd.

PETE RUNNELS—Spray-hitting infielder who won two batting titles with Red Sox in '50s. . . Hit .310 or better in six of his seven seasons with team.

DICK RADATZ—Pitched only four years for Red Sox, 1962–65, but was phenomenal in relief. . . Won 15 games and saved 25 in 1963, won 16 and saved 29 the next year with weak teams. . . Six feet six inches tall and 235-pound right-hander with wicked sidearm motion. . . Nicknamed "The Monster."

JACKIE JENSEN —Clutch-hitting outfielder in the '50s. . . Led league in RBIs three times during seven seasons with Sox. . . Averaged 25 homers. . . Fear of flying bothered him more than tough right-handed pitchers.

BILLY GOODMAN—Another lefty spray hitter. . . Hit .354 in 1950 to win batting title. . . Over .300 in five other Red Sox seasons. . . Never batted below .290 in nine seasons with team.

TONY CONIGLIARO—Outfielder whose career was cut short by tragic beaning in 1967. . . Schoolboy slugger out of Swampscott High who became youngest player ever to reach 100-homer plateau in majors. . . Made comeback from beaning and hit 36 homers for 1970 Red Sox. . . Retired for good after second comeback try in 1975.

CHAPTER 1

"THE KID"

TED WILLIAMS

"I wanted to be the greatest hitter who ever lived. A man has to have goals, and that was mine, to have people say, 'There goes Ted Williams, the greatest hitter who ever lived.'"

—from *My Turn at Bat*, by Ted Williams and
John Underwood

A few others hit more homers. A few had a better lifetime average. But you would have a hard time convincing anyone who saw him swing a bat that Theodore Samuel Williams was anything less than what he set out to be—the greatest hitter-of-a-baseball who ever lived.

Ted Williams at work was an art form. You'd swear he'd been born with a bat in his hands, had been created solely for the purpose of smacking a baseball.

The stance, the concentration, the swing, the follow-through—all were out of a textbook. He made hitting seem so natural, so fluid, so easy.

That's the way it looked. Reality wasn't that simple, any more than the sweet perfection of a Menuhin violin solo or the beauty of a Van Gogh painting came easily.

Nobody worked harder at his craft than Williams. He studied pitchers, remembered how they got him out and how they didn't, watched for trends and giveaway quirks—anything that would give him an edge.

And he practiced. Oh, how he practiced. "Ask anybody who had anything to do with T. S. Williams," he once said in a *Sports Illustrated* interview, "and they'll tell you he practiced more than anybody."

For nineteen major league seasons he exulted every time he won what he

5

called the little game between batter and pitcher. And a quarter century after his retirement, he would still remember home runs hit off so-and-so, or how such-and-such fooled him in April but not in July, or what the count was with the bases loaded and Jim Bunning on the mound.

He could remember the weather conditions and whether the pitch was a fast ball or curve, whether it was high or low, inside or outside.

What kind of a hitter was Ted Williams? Well, in 1939, when he was twenty years old, he broke in with the Red Sox by batting .327 and driving in 147 runs.

Eighteen years and two wars later, at the age of thirty-eight, he batted .388 and had 38 home runs.

In between, there were many highlights, many dramatic moments, and, of course, much controversy. The saga of Ted Williams was not confined to runs, hits, and errors.

Williams grew up in San Diego, a scrawny, string-beany kid whose mother worked with the Salvation Army and sent notes to school saying, "This boy is underweight; his tonsils should be checked."

But the scrawny kid loved to hit a baseball and would do so as long as anyone would throw them to him on the playgrounds of San Diego.

"One of the great thrills of my life," he once said, "was when I was fourteen and discovered I could hit whatever my friend Wilbur Wiley threw."

Williams averaged .430 for his three seasons on the Herbert Hoover High team. Ewell Blackwell, who later was a standout with Cincinnati, pitched for a rival school, and remembered Williams as having even then the greatest eye–wrist coordination of any hitter he ever saw.

When he was seventeen, Williams signed for $150 a month with San Diego of the Pacific Coast League. The schoolboy was a pro in his home town.

In his first time at bat, he took three strikes down the middle, but he doubled the next two times up, and the career of Ted Williams, master hitter, had begun.

Williams hit .271 in 42 games. He was a boy among men, some of whom were old enough to be his father. The next season he hit 23 homers, batted .291, and was called the best prospect in the league.

Frank (Lefty) O'Doul, who once won a National League batting championship, and who now ran the San Francisco team, said, "This boy is going to make a name for himself before he's through." If O'Doul only could have known.

Eddie Collins, the general manager of the Red Sox, went to San Diego for a look and came back with the following analysis: "We have to buy him."

And so the Red Sox did. The story came out of the winter meetings in Chicago on Dec. 7, 1937, and began this way: "Ted Williams, a stringbean 19-year-old outfielder from San Diego of the Pacific Coast League, was purchased by the Boston Red Sox this afternoon for a large unannounced amount of cash."

The stormy, volatile relationship between Williams and Boston baseball had begun.

"The Kid."

Clubhouse man Johnny Orlando, one of the few in the game to really get close to Williams, was the one who first called him "The Kid," a nickname that stuck and the one he liked.

Because of floods in California, Williams had reported late to spring training in Sarasota, Florida, in 1938. It was not the last time that would happen, though never again would bad weather be the reason.

"Who are you?" Orlando wanted to know.

"I'm Ted Williams."

"The Kid has arrived," announced Orlando. "You dress over there with the rookies, Kid."

And Williams was a kid, still growing both physically and emotionally. His concentration and desire to succeed were and always would be so over-whelming that he would be forever subject to the occasional tantrum.

In an exhibition game in Atlanta that first spring, Williams misjudged a foul fly, picked up the ball, and threw it over the grandstand roof. Joe Cronin took him aside for a fatherly chat, and it wasn't long before the Kid was in the minor league training camp.

Williams spent a season with the Red Sox American Association farm club in Minneapolis, and tore the league apart. He also tore his hand up and jeopardized his career by putting his fist through a water cooler after fouling out.

In 1939, he returned to Sarasota, and this time there would be no demotion. The Red Sox were a team of sluggers, but all the fence-busters—Jimmy Foxx, Cronin, Bobby Doerr, Pinky Higgins, Jim Tabor, Ben Chapman, Joe Vosmik—were right-handed hitters. Williams was on the perfect team for him, though not in the perfect ball park.

The right-field bleachers at Fenway Park were almost 400 feet from home plate. Yankee Stadium in New York and Briggs Stadium in Detroit, with their short porches in right, were more tailored to Williams's dead-pull hitting style.

Still, he had enough power to hit 31 homers his rookie season. Ironically, a bull pen was built the next season that brought home-run territory 20 feet closer, yet Williams had 8 less homers.

Before many game had slid past in 1939, it was obvious that Williams was something special. Fans stayed to watch him bat one more time, even if the game was one-sided.

They loved the way he loped around the bases, even if he was sometimes lackadaisical in the field.

Pitcher Joe Heving described him by saying, "Williams is killing the ball at the plate and leaving it alone in the outfield."

The first time the Red Sox went into New York with Williams, the Yankees held a meeting to discuss the best way to pitch to the new phenom.

It was agreed that the proper procedure was to pitch him high and tight, then low and away.

The next day Spud Chandler, who had done the pitching was asked about the game plan.

"I'll tell you what I found out," said Chandler. "I found out that high and tight is ball one. Low and away is ball two, and then you have to throw the ball over the plate. That's when the trouble starts."

Life was a dish of ice cream in Williams's rookie season.

"I can't imagine anyone having a better, happier first year in the big leagues," he wrote. "Every day was Christmas. I always tipped my hat that year."

In 1940, however, Santa Claus left town. The impetuous Williams, disgusted after a few bad afternoons—uncommon as they might have been—said things that leaped into headlines, especially in Boston, which at that time had nine newspapers and fierce sports-writing competition.

The first big flare-up was the "To hell with baseball, I'd rather be a fireman" episode. That brought out the method actors from opposing dugouts. They rang cowbells when he came to the plate. They wore firemen's hats, they screeched sirens, and they got under Williams's sensitive skin.

Next came the pigeon-shooting caper in Fenway, when Ted gunned down about forty of the dirty birds after a game. The Humane Society chastised him for this, and so did the papers, even though owner Tom Yawkey had been a pigeon shooter for years.

Stories appeared quoting Williams as saying Boston was a lousy sports town. He said he hated the park and the fans, that his $12,000 salary was peanuts, and that he wanted to be traded.

With Babe Ruth.

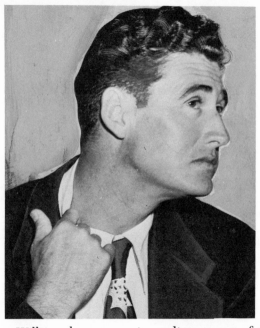

Williams became an immediate target of the left-field boobirds, and his feud with the Boston press had begun. He made peace with the fans in 1952, but the feud with the fourth estate lasted until the day he retired.

Years later, after an ear examination before going back into the Marines, Williams said, "If the doctor only knew I could hear those hecklers in the fortieth row, he'd know my ears are all right."

"Ted's idea of the perfect ball game," said Fred Corcoran, his agent, "would be one where he had 5 homers in 5 at-bats in an empty park."

But neither the feud nor the fans kept Williams from hitting a baseball better than anybody else in the game. It's possible that the controversy made him even more determined to succeed.

Williams batted .344 in 1940, and in 1941 hit the jackpot twice. On July 6, with two on and two out in the all-star game in Detroit, he smacked a game-winning home run off Claude Passeau of the Cubs.

Williams came to bat only because Billy Herman had made a wide throw to first, trying to complete a double play on Joe DiMaggio's hard ground ball.

With the count 2 and 1, Williams, whom Passeau had fanned the previous inning, slammed the ball deep into the right-field stands.

Films of that game show Williams, happy as the Kid he was, doing a little hop, skip, and jump between first and second, and clapping his hands for joy.

He was the big story in sports and, in September, made the cover of *Life*. Inside was a series of stop-action photos of Williams, in gym shorts, demonstrating his swing.

Then, on Oct. 1, in a season-ending doubleheader in Philadelphia, Williams finished with a real flourish.

He went into the day batting .3996, the first time he'd been below .400 since early May. One quick hit and he would be the first man since Bill Terry in 1923 to finish above that figure.

The night before the doubleheader, he was unusually jittery and couldn't sleep. He and clubhouse man Orlando walked the streets of Philadelphia, talking about baseball and other things.

It was Orlando who got closest to what made Ted tick in those days.

"If you're nice to him," said Orlando, "he'll give you the shirt off his back. He's terribly shy and bashful and hates to be in the limelight. The time to help him is when he goes O for 4."

That little night stroll around Philly may have been just what the doctor ordered, because the next afternoon Williams went 6 for 8 in the double-header to finish at .406.

He singled the first time up, then smashed a homer and 2 more singles. He was now well over .400 and could have sat out the second game. Legend has it that manager Joe Cronin suggested this, but that Williams refused.

Both parties agree there is a semblance of truth to the story. However, Cronin said years later than though he may have mentioned such an idea to Ted, he never seriously thought Williams would take him up on the suggestion. And Williams says that's about the way it was.

The Kid had 2 more hits in the second game, including a double off the loudspeaker horns in deep right center, to finish at .406.

Forty years and thousands of baseball players later, he remained the last one to reach .400. He had averaged .464 against the Yankees, .462 against the As, and over .400 against three other teams.

By this time Ted Williams, baseball hero, was indistinguishable from Ted Williams, controversial personality. This two-sided mirror would continue right up to his retirement.

The controversy in 1942 came early, after Williams's 1-A status in the draft was changed on the eve of his induction to 3-A. Politicians eager for a headline suggested that Williams was getting preferential treatment because he was a sports hero. Newspapers throughout the country debated the burning issue, "Is Ted Williams a draft dodger?"

The irony of all this conjecture is that Williams would eventually serve as a Marine pilot in both World War II and the Korean conflict, would be shot down, and would miss four and one-half seasons of baseball.

The draft-dodging references only further inflamed Williams's relationship with the press. He had been deferred because he was the sole support of his mother, and said: "If I didn't think I was doing right . . . I wouldn't face this thing, because I know I'm in for a lot of abuse."

However, so great was his charisma—though nobody used that word in those days—that when he showed up at Sarasota for spring training in 1942, he was applauded by the snowbirds down for the Florida sun.

Williams had a great 1942 season, and won the triple crown: he led the league in batting (.356), home runs (36), and runs batted in (137). He also led in runs scored (141), walks (.145), and slugging percentage (.698).

In May, Williams enlisted in the Navy's V-5 program, effective at season's end.

"Slugging Teddy Enlists" screamed the *Boston Globe*'s page one headline.

During the year, Williams took naval aviation courses at Mechanic Arts

High School in Boston, and, when the season was over, he, shortstop Johnny Pesky, Braves catcher Buddy Gremp, and pitcher Johnny Sain were called into service.

In midseason, though, there had been another temper tantrum.

Heckled by the fans one day in July, he was taken out of the game by Cronin for "loafing" and was fined $250.

The next day, the mercurial Williams was properly remorseful.

"I deserve to be put out of the park. I was too damn lackadaisical. I was all set to take three strikes down the groove just to show them [the fans] 'what the hell.' Then I thought I'd drive some fouls into the left field stands and knock some teeth out."

The Kid was a little older but still the Kid.

Williams and Pesky went through preliminary training at Amherst College. Ted reported a day late, hiring a cab from Boston to take him the hundred miles to the western Massachusetts town for $25. He roomed with Philadelphia pitcher Joe Coleman from Natick, except for two months spent recovering from a hernia received doing push-ups.

Then it was on to Chapel Hill, North Carolina, and Kokomo, Indiana, for flight training.

Williams took to flying the way he had to hitting and fishing, his other great passions. They were all challenges—the pitcher, the fish, and the airplane.

"Here we are, Ted, beat us if you can."

Williams was commissioned a second lieutenant in 1944 in Pensacola, Florida. He served as a pilot instructor during the war, and in 1946, along with dozens of others whose careers had been interrupted by war, returned to baseball.

He was now twenty-seven years old. Had the three seasons away from the sport dimmed his batting eye or dampened his enthusiasm for the game?

You could, as they say, look it up. In 1946 Williams batted .342, was named the most valuable player in the American League, and played in his first and only World Series.

That season the Red Sox, with Williams, Pesky, Higgins, Doerr, Rudy York, and Dom DiMaggio, won 104 games and drew 1,416,944 fans to Fenway Park. It was the first time in history that attendance had passed the million mark.

At chummy Fenway, this wrecking crew won 61 and lost only 16. They had winning streaks of 15 and 12 games, and clinched the pennant with Williams's inside-the-park home run (the only one of his career) in Cleveland.

It was also in 1946 that Cleveland playing manager Lou Boudreau pulled his famous shift on Williams. Ted so rarely hit to left field that once, as a joke in an exhibition game in Dallas, everybody on the opposition except the pitcher and catcher left his position and sat in the right-field bleachers.

Boudreau didn't go that far, but, for its time, the shift he devised was a radical one. Williams had had 3 homers against the Indians in the first game of a doubleheader July 14. The first came with the bases loaded and the Red

Sox behind, 5–0. The next came with two on to tie the game. The third came in the ninth, to win, 11–10.

Boudreau in that game had had a homer and 4 doubles and his team had still lost.

The first time up in the second game, Williams cleared the loaded bases with a double. He now had had 11 runs batted in, and there were still eight innings to go. Boudreau had seen enough.

When Williams came to the plate again, the Cleveland defense began moving. Third-baseman Ken Keltner went behind the second-base bag. Boudreau, the shortstop, moved to the right of second. Pat Seerey, the center fielder, shifted to right, the right fielder went to the foul line, the second baseman moved closer to first and onto the grass in short right, and the first baseman guarded the line.

The only man to the left of second base was left-fielder George Case, who was 30 feet beyond the skin part of the diamond.

Williams in later seasons tried to hit to left against the shift, with indifferent success. But even so, the Boudreau shift was strictly a gimmick that never seriously detracted from his prowess as a hitter.

Finally, it was also in 1946 that Williams had 4 hits, including 2 home runs, in the all-star game played in Boston. The last was off the so-called Eephus

All-Star homer.

pitch of Truett (Rip) Sewell of the Pirates, a high-trajectory, slow-pitch softball type of delivery that Ted deposited into the right-field bull pen.

The year was such a great one for Williams that his failure in the World Series against the Cardinals stands out in contrast. It wasn't that he did anything bad, but he didn't do much of anything.

Williams had only 5 singles, 1 a bunt, in twenty-five at-bats, and only 1 RBI.

In an exhibition game against a team of American League all-stars, played before the series to keep the Red Sox active, Washington pitcher Mickey Heafner had plunked Williams on the elbow with a pitch.

Though Williams did not use this as an excuse for his poor showing in the series, there is little doubt that the injury affected his swing.

He pointed out that he wasn't the first one to have a good season and a bad series. However, he was unhappy with the Red Sox loss and disappointed in his own performance, and gave his World Series check to Johnny Orlando.

The failure of Williams to hit against the Cardinals was voted the second biggest flop of 1946 in a wire service poll, running just behind Billy Conn's fold-up against Joe Louis in a heavyweight title bout.

"The Boston fans were swell to me, even though I was a flop," he was to say later. "I wanted to lift my cap to their applause, but for some reason, I couldn't do it."

This tipping of the cap business was to surface often, down through the years.

The next season, when it was written that he'd tipped his cap in an exhibition game, Williams denied it. "I did not. My brow was sweaty and I was just brushing away the sweat."

Williams told sportswriter Clif Keane of the *Globe* that he realized tipping a cap in appreciation was a reasonable gesture, but early in his career he'd been criticized so much, "It riled me to a point where I said, 'I'll never tip my hat again', and, so help me, I never have."

The years flew past and the baseballs flew out of the park, and so did the dual role of Ted Williams as slugger and disturber of the peace.

He signed a $75,000 contract in 1947 and was called the greatest player in the world by Eddie Collins. He won the triple crown again that season, but lost the most valuable player award to Joe D. by one vote.

He won the batting title again in 1948 and 1949, when he was also named the most valuable player after 159 RBIs and 43 homers, both career highs.

However, the Red Sox as a team were doomed to bitter disappointment. They lost a play-off to the Indians for the pennant in 1948 and were beaten out by the Yankees in '49, finishing one game behind, after losing in New York on the final two days of the season.

Williams described the five-hour train ride back to Boston as "like a funeral."

And always, there was the feudin', fussin', and fightin', the headlines and the denials. Decades later, these controversies seem tempests in a very small teapot, but the competitiveness of the sporting press of the time must be kept in mind. No deviation from the norm was too trivial to be chased into a forty-eight-point headline.

In January of 1948, Doris Soule Williams and Theodore S. Williams became parents of Barbara, a baby girl. Time for joy, for celebration, for congratulations, except that when Mrs. Williams checked into a Boston hospital, Ted was in Florida.

He was quoted as saying he didn't know if he'd come to Boston.

"What'll I do there?" he asked.

Well. Talk about your insults to motherhood, your desecration to the American way.

"Ted Fishing When Baby Arrives," screamed the headlines.

Barbara was born January 28 and Ted reached Boston on February 2. He said he had had trouble getting plane connections and added, "To heck with public opinion. It's my baby and my life."

The episode did not put him in the running for Father of the Year, nor did it put the Boston press on Williams's Pulitzer Prize list.

In spring training of 1948, Williams had an appendicitis scare during an exhibition game in New Orleans, and was sent home. Though an operation was unnecessary, it was another in a series of ailments and injuries that would chew at him during his career.

He missed 14 games because of tonsillitis in 1939, chipped an ankle in 1941, was hit on that elbow before the 1946 series, lost 18 games in 1948 when he ripped a muscle in his side banging into the Yankee Stadium wall, was out for 10 games in 1950 because of a wrist injury, jammed his foot in a 1956 shower accident, and suffered from sinus and inner-ear problems that led to his discharge from the Marines during the Korean War.

And there were the two big injuries—a left elbow fractured while catching Ralph Kiner's drive against the wall in the 1950 all-star game, and a collarbone broken during spring training in 1954.

Williams continued to be an intriguing mixture of charm and petulance. In 1949 he threw his bat high in the air after being called out on strikes. In 1949 he also sent roses to an ailing scoreboard boy.

A handwriting expert diagnosed his signature this way: "He's assertive, has a good sense of humor, and likes the limelight. You can't push him around. He's stubborn. Loyalty is indicated in the loop he makes in the 'W' that begins his last name."

Williams became the first Boston player to make $100,000 in a season when he signed for that amount in 1950.

In May, after he had dropped a fly ball in the first game and fumbled a ground-ball base hit in the second, he made obscene gestures to the booing fans and spit in their direction.

After the game he castigated the fans and said, "You can quote me in all the papers," which the newsmen were happy to do.

The Rev. John Kennedy, writing in a Hartford, Connecticut, diocesan paper, commented: "What Williams did was disgusting. It was completely out of place in an adult. But in their way, the fans were quite as disgusting as Williams. They were like a pack of animals—howling, bellowing, screeching, yelping, yowling in a way not even remotely human. They behaved like denizens of a zoo which have not been fed or watered for a week."

The next day, after a severe reprimand by Yawkey, Williams issued a formal apology. There was, however, no promise that he wouldn't do it again.

Doctors took thirteen bone chips out of Williams's left elbow after that all-star crash in Comiskey Park in 1950. Diagrams of the injured elbow and photos of the X-rays were on the front pages of the Boston newspapers.

"I'm the guy who said they'd never catch me running into a fence," he said.

Williams was out of the lineup for sixty-six days. On his first game back, he had 3 singles and a 3-run homer against the St. Louis Browns.

But the elbow still pained him. To strengthen it, he went fishing every day during the off season, poling a boat across the flats in Key West.

Though he played in only 89 games in 1950 and batted only .317, his lowest in nine major league seasons, he made the cover of *Time*.

Manager Steve O'Neill, not a Williams favorite, made the Kid play most of the exhibition games in spring training of 1951, which rankled the slugger.

Fans booed him in Tampa when he failed to run out a ground ball. He turned and spat in their direction. In the fifth, he homered, and spat again. In the seventh, during a Red Sox rally, Williams struck out twice. The second time, he spun around and made a motion as if to throw the bat against the screen. The fans responded with boos and catcalls.

"I'm sick and tired of these exhibition games," he told O'Neill.

"Ted will play tomorrow," O'Neill told the press.

In 1951, Williams said, "The fans are still jerks, but I'm not going to give them the satisfaction of getting under my skin any more. They can shout as much as they want and I'll just give them a big smile. What I say under my breath is another thing."

For Williams, every day was no longer Christmas. There was much talk that winter of trading him. Said Williams: "If the time has come for me to leave Boston, then the time has come for me to leave baseball."

And he did leave the game, for the better part of two seasons, not through a trade or retirement, but because at the age of thirty-three he was called up for a second tour of flying duty.

He was out almost all of the '52 season and four-fifths of '53, and never dismissed the bitterness that came from being called up twice.

On April 30, in his last at-bat before rejoining the Marines, he hit a 2-run homer off Dizzy Trout to beat Detroit. His flair for the dramatic never left him.

This was the day his love–hate relationship with the Boston fans returned to its original state. They gave him a day that afternoon, these same people who had burned his ears off for years. They presented him with a Cadillac and a memory book with five hundred thousand autographs, and they told him how much they appreciated the way he hit a baseball.

And Williams responded.

"This is the greatest day of my life," he said to the fans, "and I'll always remember it."

He also said that his baseball career was over, that he'd be too old to return to the game when he got out of the service.

So off he went, this thirty-three-year-old athlete who had flown fifteen hundred hours in World War II, but who had been in a cockpit only once since becoming a civilian.

Williams was assigned to the third Marine wing in Korea, with the 223d Squadron. One of his mates was John Glenn, later the first American to make a manned space flight.

There is a photo of Williams's ditched Pantherjet in the *Boston Globe* files. It looks like a charred hot-dog roll. This was the plane he landed in Korea after it was hit by enemy small-arms fire late in 1952.

As Williams describes the episode in *My Turn at Bat*, the plane started to shake and the stick stiffened up. He thought he'd have to bail out and was worried about breaking his kneecaps when he was ejected from the cockpit.

So he stayed with the ship and as it got back over an American air base, there was an explosion in the plane. The wheel door blew off, and fire and smoke billowed out.

Williams came in at 225 miles per hour, twice as fast as normal. Only one wheel came down and the plane skidded for a mile, ripping up the runway. The skid marks were 2000 feet long. Williams was unhurt.

Williams flew thirty-nine missions, contracted pneumonia, was sent to Japan for treatment of an inner-ear infection, and finally was mustered out in July, 1953.

At first, he said that he probably wouldn't play for the rest of the season, but after throwing out the first ball at the all-star game in Cincinnati, he changed his mind.

"Tell the Boston fans to get their lungs warmed up," he said. "It looks like I'll be back."

On Aug. 6, 1953, he made his first appearance in a game since his April farewell of a season before and popped up as a pinch hitter.

Four days later, before a Sunday crowd of twenty-seven thousand, it was different. In the seventh, he pinch hit against Mike Garcia of Cleveland, and, on a 3-and-1 pitch, smashed the ball into the right-field stands, three rows behind the Red Sox bull pen.

For the rest of that season, the thirty-four-year-old Williams, who had been scrunched up in the cockpit of a jet for a year and a half, batted .407 in 91 at-bats. Of his 37 hits, 13 were homers. In 37 games he had 34 runs batted in and a slugging average of .901.

"The ball," he said, "looked as big as a grapefruit."

The Red Sox of the early '50s, however, stumbled around in the middle of the American League pack. Without Williams in 1952, they finished sixth, and fourth the next season. Attendance went steadily downhill and after eight post-war years of better than a million, slipped in 1954 to 931,127.

The prospect of an even bigger decrease in interest loomed when Williams announced that 1954 would be his last season.

The rumor had first worked its way to the surface during the winter, when Williams admitted he was thinking of quitting.

But it wasn't made official until April, in a three-part *Saturday Evening Post* piece under Williams's byline, as told to New York sportswriters Joe Reichler and Joe Trimble.

By giving the story to the New Yorkers, Williams, of course, had slipped a curve ball past his private demons, the Boston writers who had covered him since 1939.

The article, entitled "This Is My Last Year," was prefaced by the following introduction:

"Here, in his own words, is the inside story of Ted Williams' tempestuous baseball career. The Kid tells why he dislikes most sports writers and some fans, and reveals that even before his recent injury he had made up his mind to call it quits after this season."

The "recent injury" alluded to was the broken collarbone. On March 1, 1954, Williams left Key West at six in the morning to drive the 280 miles to Sarasota for the start of spring training.

He got out of his car, put on a uniform, and, ten minutes later, was writhing on the outfield in pain.

Williams had been standing with Jimmy Piersall in the outfield when a fly ball was hit in his direction. He started after it, realized the ball was falling in front of him, and stumbled, landing heavily on his left shoulder.

"I heard something pop when I fell," he said. "I knew I had a broken shoulder."

Williams went to Boston, where a stainless-steel pin, 4 inches long, was put in his collarbone in an operation that took an hour and twenty minutes. The pin is still there.

The retirement story hit the magazine racks just before opening day. In it, Williams said he admired Joe DiMaggio for getting out when he did.

"Like Joe, I won't wait around for the last gasp . . . The minute I find I can't go at top speed . . . I'll know it's time to quit. That time will come next fall."

He listed some goals for what was expected to be his last season. They included batting .330, 30 homers, 100 runs, and 100 runs batted in, plus his fifth batting championship.

Williams exceeded the batting average goal, hitting .345, and certainly would have surpassed his other expectations except for the broken collarbone, which cut his season to only 117 games.

He had 29 homers, 89 RBIs, and 93 runs scored, and though his .345 average was the highest in the league, he lost out on the batting championship because his 386 at-bats was 14 shy of the number needed to qualify.

After missing the first 18 games of the season, Williams broke into the Red Sox lineup May 16 in Detroit and went 8 for 9 in a doubleheader—2 homers, a double, and 5 singles, plus 9 runs batted in.

Later that season, he was out for 20 more games because of a flare-up of the pneumonia he'd contracted in the service.

In September Williams hit his 362d career homer to pass DiMaggio, and then, in what he said would be his final game, he—what else?—hit a home run, his 366th and supposedly his last.

However, in December, with baseball reconciled to Williams's retirement, he ordered a supply of bats from Hillerich–Bradsby, the Louisville Slugger people.

"He's still on our roster," commented Thomas Austin Yawkey.

What was going on here? What about the retirement? Well, what was going on was an impending divorce from Doris Soule Williams, a divorce that would cost Williams a fistful of dollars and would be the driving force that would keep him playing baseball for six more seasons.

In January, Williams was still "retired" and talking about fishing in Chile. In March, the Number 9 uniform was hung in his Sarasota locker, but he did not attend spring training.

Then, in early May, his wife won her divorce suit. She was awarded $50,000 outright, plus $125 a week. There was no longer doubt as to whether Ted Williams would return.

He came to Boston a few days later, said he missed the game more than he had thought he would, and signed a $98,000 contract. He worked out for ten days and, on May 24, his first day in the lineup, hit—of course—a home run.

For the second straight season, Williams led the league in batting (.356), but once again didn't win the championship because he didn't have enough at-bats.

The volcanic Williams temper, dormant for a while, erupted again in the next few seasons.

In July of 1956, he spat toward the press box after his 400th career homer beat Kansas City, 1–0. This was a prelude to the silly symphony that occurred against the Yankees on Aug. 7, "Joe Cronin night," with 36,350 jammed into the old ball yard.

Early in the game, Williams had dropped a pop fly in short left field, and when the fans booed, he spat both toward the right and left field. Later, he leaned out of the dugout and repeated the performance.

Then, in the eleventh inning of a scoreless game, Williams walked with the bases loaded to force in the winning run, then heaved his bat 30 feet in the air in apparent disgust at not getting a pitch to hit.

Yawkey was out of town, but heard the game on radio, and announced that he was fining Williams $5000, a huge amount for that time.

Politicians and fans leaped to Ted's defense. A bill was filed in the Massachusetts House to protect players from profane, obscene, and impure language, and from slanderous statements directed at a participant in a sports event.

In Northampton, Massachusetts, a coin box was set out at Lizotte's Cigar Store to help pay Williams's fine.

"I feel the outburst was emotional, not malicious or spiteful," mused Charles Collatos, Massachusetts labor relations commissioner.

Letters to the editor tended to criticize the bad-mouthed fans and poison-pen writers rather than Williams.

Boston Globe columnist Harold Kaese was amused by this display of support for Boston's tempestuous sports hero.

"Throughout his career," wrote Kaese, "he has been able to emerge from the swamps of embarrassment covered all over with medals."

Apart from this incident—Yawkey never made Williams pay the fine—Ted had another good year, hitting .345 with 24 homers and 82 runs batted in. George Kell beat him out by a point for the batting title.

Would this man with the X-ray eyes ever grow old? Would he ever start going downhill as a hitter? Sure, but it wouldn't be in 1957, when Williams had perhaps the most remarkable season of a remarkable career.

At the age of thirty-eight, he batted .388, with 38 home runs. He was 7 base hits away from a .400 average at an age when most ball players are seven dollars away from opening a bowling alley in their hometown.

Williams, who hit .453 over the last half of the season, was the oldest player ever to win a batting championship. In September, after being tucked away in the Somerset Hotel for seventeen days with a heavy cold, Williams returned to the lineup and had 25 hits in his next 44 at-bats.

Included in that was a record string of reaching base 16 straight times at bat, and hitting home runs in 4 straight times at bat.

The Fenway attendance that year for a third-place team was 1,187,087, and to quote Harold Kaese again "The Red Sox drew 187,087 and Ted Williams drew the other million."

Naturally, the aging Kid made some off-the-field headlines. They came early, during the exhibition season, when Williams called Senator Robert Taft a phony, blasted President Harry Truman, criticized the Marines, and knocked the Internal Revenue Service for continually hounding Joe Louis.

He later apologized to the Marines.

The outburst was a reaction to the country's draft policies and Williams's belief that the United States hadn't tried very hard to win the Korean War.

Williams naturally didn't expect any of this to make the papers, but just as naturally it did, touching off another round of journalistic gunfire.

"You must agree with Ted Williams or he describes you as an enemy," commented New York columnist Jimmy Cannon.

Williams was named male athlete of 1957 and signed a two-year contract at $125,000 a year, but the dark side of his personality undoubtedly cost him the most valuable player award that season.

Two members of the Baseball Writers Association, the group that votes on the award, listed him ninth and tenth on their ballots, a spiteful and small-spirited gesture that will always stand as a shameful blot on the record of the association.

Williams beat out teammate Pete Runnels on the last day of the 1958 season to win the batting title again, this time with a .328 average. Injuries that year included an ankle problem in the spring and food poisoning that caused him to miss opening day.

Controversies? Two of them. He spat once more in Kansas City and was fined $250 by the league. And he hit Joe Cronin's housekeeper with a bat.

It was an accident, of course. Williams had struck out and let the bat fly, as he often did. But his time it sailed into the stands, where it struck Gladys Heffernan, housekeeper for the Red Sox general manager.

"I felt ready to die," said a crestfallen Williams. "The stickum made the bat stick in my hands."

The fans got on Ted for this and the league fined him $50 more. But Mrs. Heffernan, who escaped serious injury, said from her hospital bed that she forgave Williams, and added, "Why did they boo Ted?"

Ted with Tom Yawkey.

Once again, he'd emerged from those swamps of embarrassment covered with medals.

There would be no medals for Williams in 1959. It was his worst year in baseball. He began it with his neck in traction, the eleventh major physical ailment of his career. One account of his return for treatment to Boston in April began this way: "The Town's most publicized pain in the neck arrived here today . . ."

And when the season was over, Williams, now forty-one, had an average of only .254, the only time in his career he'd hit less than .316.

He didn't play until May 13, and in mid-June, with his average an anemic .175, he was benched for not hitting, for the first and only time in his career.

In August, he told players on the White Sox: "I've had it. I'm finished."

But the tiger still growled within Ted Williams. The flame still burned. He didn't want to go out on a sour note. He wanted to leave with the trumpets blaring and the people screaming, "One more time, Ted, one more time!"

Yawkey tried to persuade Williams to retire, to prevent further embarrassment to a marvelous career.

In his book, Williams lists Yawkey's attitude at this point as one of three mistakes the Red Sox made with him. The two others, he wrote, were when the club tried to keep him from going to spring training in 1942 during his draft board battle, and when he was asked to manage the club in 1955 when he felt he wasn't ready.

Williams persevered with Yawkey and won his argument, voluntarily taking a $35,000 pay cut, so that his salary for his last season was $90,000.

The Red Sox that season were a miserable club, racked with dissension that later resulted in the early firing of manager Billy Jurges. The team finished seventh, 32 games behind the first-place Yankees.

Williams, though he'd persuaded the boss to let him play one more season, still had doubts. Before the season, he said, "I keep thinking, 'Williams, you're dying hard.' I keep saying to myself, 'Your ankle hurts, your neck hurts, your back hurts, and you're dying so damn hard.' "

If he felt that way, why bother?

"I can certainly use the money," he said, "but mostly I'd like to redeem myself for last year, and I'd like to reach 500 homers."

He got off to a good start on opening day by smashing one of the longest home runs of his career, off Camilo Pascual in Washington.

Williams hit 29 homers that final season, with the 500th coming in Cleveland.

Before the night game, he told manager Mike Higgins he was stiff all over and didn't think he was up to playing. The manager asked him to give it a try, and promised him the next game off.

So Williams played, and his homer, in the sixth inning, off right-hander Wynn Hawkins, broke a 1–1 tie and won the game.

Williams finished at age forty-two, not only with a .316 average but with the dramatic flourish that had been his trademark for twenty-one seasons—a home run in his very last at-bat.

The Red Sox wound up their home schedule in 1960 with Baltimore, then would travel to New York to end the season. Williams, however, had already said he wouldn't go to New York. The games against the Orioles would be his goodbye song.

And so it came down to the last game, to the Kid's farewell, on Sept. 28, 1960, a cold, raw Wednesday afternoon.

The sentimental, even maudlin, headlines that morning spelled out the city's feelings—"What Will We Do without Ted?"

There was a home-plate ceremony, with broadcaster Curt Gowdy calling Williams "the greatest hitter who ever lived," and Williams saying that "despite some of the terrible things written about me by the knights of the keyboard up there . . . my stay in Boston has been the most wonderful part of my life."

He didn't tip his hat, but did remove it while making his little talk.

Williams, who didn't take batting practice that afternoon, walked in the first inning against young Orioles left-hander Steve Barber, who was very wild and would not last out the inning.

Ted was out on an easy fly to right center the next time, but in the fifth thought he'd hit homer number 521. However, the ball died in the heavy air and right fielder Al Pilarcik caught the ball against the 380-foot sign.

"If that didn't go out, nothing will today," Williams thought as he disappeared into the dugout.

He was the second man up in the last of the eighth. The lights were on; the 10,454 in the stands were shivering, and remained only because Williams would get one more at-bat.

The Kid, forty-two years old, thought about that as he came to the plate. His last at-bat in a game he'd been playing for money since he was seventeen. His last turn to do something he'd been good at since he found out he could hit whatever Wilbur Wiley threw up there.

From John Updike's marvelous piece, "Hub Fans Bid Kid Adieu": "Have you ever heard applause in a ball park? Just applause—no calling, no whistling, just an ocean of hand-claps, minute after minute, burst after burst, crowding and running together in continuous succession like the pushes of surf at the edge of the sand . . . there was not a boo in it."

Baltimore pitcher Jack Fisher's first pitch was outside. The next was a fast ball that Williams felt he should have nailed. But he swung and missed.

Fisher noted that he'd thrown the ball past Williams. Let's do that again, he thought. But Williams was quicker this time and sent a drive soaring over Jackie Brandt's head and into the far corner of the Red Sox bull pen.

"I thought about tipping my hat, you're damn right I did," he said. "But by the time I got to second base I knew I couldn't do it."

Williams ran his home run as he always had—head down and in a hurry— and though the ecstatic fans chanted "We want Ted," he never reappeared from the dugout to acknowledge the cheers.

Mike Higgins gave the crowd one last chance to acknowledge its hero. After Williams had gone to left field to begin the ninth, Higgins sent Carroll Hardy out to replace him.

The fans saw for one last time the familiar Williams lope as he came past shortstop, over the first base line and into the dugout. His eyes never looked anywhere but at the ground.

Williams finished with a .316 average and a .344 lifetime mark, good for tenth place in baseball history.

In July 1966, he was inducted into the Hall of Fame, making it on his first year of eligibility. And even at Cooperstown, he could not avoid controversy.

It was reported that, during his acceptance speech, he'd used profanity in speaking of the late Dave Egan, vitriolic columnist of the *Boston Record*.

He denied it, tapes of the speech proved he hadn't been profane, and the *Boston Herald*, which had printed the story, had to apologize.

Though Williams spent his entire career with the Red Sox, he was never approached to manage them after his playing days, nor did he seem to want the job.

He lived in Islamorada, Florida, on the Keys, and made a comfortable living as a fish-and-game representative for Sears Roebuck, with his own line of Ted Williams products.

He surprised those who thought he would never return to baseball in an active role by accepting the job of managing the Washington Senators in

Ted took off his hat this *time at his farewell to Fenway Park.*

1969. When the franchise was moved to Arlington, Texas, and became the Texas Rangers in 1972, Williams went along for one last losing season.

The Senators/Rangers of Ted Williams were not overly endowed with talent and never seriously contended for a pennant.

For a man who never had a lot of patience with himself, Williams showed an unusual amount as a manager, especially with young players.

Oddly, one he had trouble with was pitcher Joe Coleman, whose father had been Williams's roommate in the V-5 program in Amherst. Williams had always admired the slider, a pitch that got him out more than any other, and was constantly after Coleman to throw it. Coleman, however, did not like the pitch, and resisted Williams's efforts.

Williams rejoined the Red Sox organization after he left the Rangers, and every spring would work with young hitters in Winter Haven, Florida, where the Red Sox trained.

His arrival there was always an event. Kids who think baseball began with Marvin Miller pushed and shoved for his autograph. Fans, young and old, wanted to take his picture.

In 1980, twenty years after Williams retired as a player, Joe Falls of the *Detroit News* asked a hundred people on the street in Deerfield Beach, Florida, who Ted Williams was.

A hundred people knew.

24

CHAPTER 2

"YAZ SIR, THAT'S MY BABY"

CARL YASTRZEMSKI

"If he ever gets with a pennant contender, he's gonna be one helluva ballplayer."

> —Red Sox utility man Eddie Kasko,
> speaking about Carl Yastrzemski
> in 1966.

There had never been anything like it in Boston. Oh, certainly, there'd been great baseball teams—world champions—but never a season to match 1967.

The exploits of the Boston Red Sox took over the city that long hot summer. Nobody went to the beach for the weekend without a transistor radio to keep posted on the Sox.

Stop for a traffic light and you could hear, coming from other automobiles, the voices of Ken Coleman or Ned Martin.

"Adair is up with it, over to Scott, and the ball game is over. The Red Sox have won again."

Ten thousand fans greeted the team at Logan airport when it returned from 10 straight victories in the Midwest.

The Man of La Mancha was the Broadway smash that season and its hit song was "The Impossible Dream." Somebody with a sense of history tagged the '67 Red Sox with that name. It became the year of the impossible dream, when a team of underdogs would reach for and capture the unreachable star, along with the hearts of millions of baseball fans.

The season was a summer-long hurricane, and the man in the eye of that wonderful storm was Carl Michael Yastrzemski, son of a Long Island potato farmer.

From game 1 through game 162, Carl Yastrzemski in 1967 maintained a greatness few athletes would ever know. Everything he touched turned to gold. You wanted a base hit to tie the game, Yaz would get it for you. You wanted a homer to win the game, put in your order. You wanted somebody thrown out at the plate at a crucial moment, Yaz was your obedient servant.

Yastrzemski predicted home runs for his teammates and they delivered. He predicted home runs for himself—15 times it happened—and he delivered. He hit 44 homers, more than twice as many as he'd ever hit in any one season before.

Yastrzemski led the league in batting, hits, runs scored, runs batted in, total bases, and slugging percentage, and tied for the lead in homers.

"For all-around performance, running the bases, catching flies, throwing out runners, and hitting," said Dick Williams, the rookie manager of that team, "this was the greatest by a ball player for one year that I've ever seen."

Yastrzemski literally stopped traffic. If he was at bat, drivers would not go through the Callahan Tunnel until he'd finished. It was, in baseball-mad and pennant-starved Boston, the year of the Yaz.

There would be good times and bad times before and after 1967 for this intense, volatile ball player, who came to the Red Sox to replace a legend, and became one himself.

Yastrzemski was the athletic boy wonder of Bridgehampton, New York, a town of fifteen hundred residents on Long Island, about a hundred miles east of New York City. His was the familiar story of one kid in a small town being an athlete superior to anyone else.

He was an excellent football player, led the basketball team to a championship with standout performances that once included 57 points in one half, and was a baseball star.

Yastrzemski was a pitcher in Little League and, in his first game in 1952, threw a no-hitter. He pitched and played the infield in high school, turning in such statistics as 82 hits in 162 times at bat for a .506 average, He had 11 triples, 9 homers, 21 doubles, and 79 runs batted in. As a pitcher, he struck out 18 in one game and 16 in another.

Yaz also was batboy for and later played on the Bridgehampton White Eagles, a semipro team that included his father, uncles Chet, Ray, and Stanley, and cousins Mike and Jerry Skonieczny, Leo and Walter Jasinsky, Roger Tiska, Stan Emilita, Ted Scretch, Skeet Pierzynski, Joe Musnick, and Alec Borkowski.

The White Eagles were not a typesetter's paradise.

In those days there was no baseball draft. A good baseball scout, one who could not only ferret out the talent but also get close to the youngster's parents, was worth his weight in gold to a major league team.

Frank (Bots) Nekola, a Holy Cross pitcher in the late '20s and now a Red Sox scout, was precisely that sort of man. He had a gentle, nonpushy way that the Yastrzemski family appreciated. Nekola, who also signed second baseman

Chuck Schilling and shortstop/third baseman Rico Petrocelli for the Red
Sox, first saw Yaz play when he was a high school junior.

Nekola arranged to have Yaz and Schilling, who came from a nearby town,
play with a semipro team on the island. They hadn't signed yet, but Nekola
figured he had the inside track.

But when he went to watch his two proteges in action, Nekola was shocked
to find in the stands scouts from just about every major league team. He no
longer had an exclusive on his prospects.

Yaz wound up being courted by fourteen of the sixteen major league
teams. Only Washington and Cleveland stayed clear of the bidding.

He worked out in several big league parks, including Yankee Stadium. The
Yankees offered him $40,000, nice money in the late '50s, but they neglected
a couple of the amenities.

The young prospect had always admired Mickey Mantle and Bill Skowron,
so hoped to be introduced to them, as well as the rest of the team. But not
only didn't he get to meet them, he was forced to dress in batboy quarters,
away from the team. By such small slights are career directions changed, and
sometimes championships lost.

Several teams offered Yastrzemski big money, the Phils, Cubs, and Reds
among them. The Reds wanted to sign Yaz to a contract and have him in
Cincinnati uniform by that night.

The negotiating slimmed down to the Phils of Bob Carpenter and the Red
Sox of Tom Yawkey, and Yawkey won out.

Yaz had met the Red Sox owner and liked him, and that was the final push
that landed him in Boston. But the family always felt that Nekola's attitude
made the difference.

"He always said and did the right things," said Yastrzemski's father.

Yastrzemski became a Red Sox farmhand in 1959, after a year at the
University of Notre Dame. Right away, the Red Sox saw that they had
something special. He hit .377 for Raleigh his first season to lead the Carolina
state league.

On Sept. 11, 1959, he came up to Fenway and worked out, and stories in
the paper the next day referred to "Yastro, the coming superstar of the Red
Sox." The nickname didn't stick.

Yaz spent the rest of that season with Minneapolis of the American
Association and after much analysis of the rule book and shouts that he was
ineligible, played for Minneapolis in the play-offs.

It was obvious in his first professional season that though he would be a
major league hitter, he would never be a major league shortstop. He had a
strong arm, but it was too erratic for an infielder, and he had trouble making
the pivot on double plays. At Raleigh, Yaz had a league-leading 45 errors at
short.

So he was shifted to the outfield in 1960 at Minneapolis, where he hit .339,
missing the batting championship by a point. He was not a slugger, having
only 7 homers, but more of a line-drive hitter, and that's what he was known
as when he arrived at spring training in Scottsdale, Arizona, in 1961.

Ted Williams, the mighty Ted, had retired the previous September with his usual grand flourish—a home run his last time at bat. He had left behind two decades of greatness, and a great big void.

"Grab your glove, kid," the Red Sox told the twenty-one-year-old Yastrzemski, "you're in there for Williams."

By its very nature, replacing a legend, is never easy. Mickey Mantle took over for Joe DiMaggio and didn't miss a beat, but Bobby Murcer suffered in comparison with Mantle. George Selkirk was a good player but no Babe Ruth, and Babe Dahlgren was a tad shy of a Hall of Famer as a replacement for the stricken Lou Gehrig.

Who remembers Willie Mays's successor, or Stan Musial's or Hank Aaron's? Adjusting to the major leagues is tough enough for a rookie without asking him to also fill the shoes of a departed idol.

From the time spring training began in March 1961, Yastrzemski was the center of media attention.

"I don't think I ever relaxed that spring, or during the early weeks of the schedule," he told reporters.

He kept telling everyone he was the first Carl Yastrzemski and not the second Ted Williams, but of course that isn't what people wanted to hear. Fans and newsmen saw the minor league statistics. They had heard and read about the potential of the new kid. They would not easily accept a maturing period.

Williams had had no problem adjusting to the majors, at least not the playing part. He had come up from Minneapolis, just as Yaz had a generation later, and hit .327, with 31 homers and 145 runs batted in.

Okay, so Yaz wasn't a big home-run hitter, but all the build-up stories had emphasized how he attacked the ball, how would he hit Musial-type line drives. He would certainly spray singles and doubles all over the place and bat well over .300, wouldn't he? Well, no, he wouldn't, at least not in his rookie season.

By July, Yaz was batting only .230. He had a terrible time with left-handed pitchers and was platooned in left field with Carroll Hardy. He was pinch-hit for many times.

Yastrzemski came on strong in the last two months to finish at .266, with 11 homers and 80 runs batted in. Not exactly a disappointment, but also a long way from being Williamsesque. He also struck out 96 times. In twenty more major league seasons he would never strike out that often again.

Yaz had joined a dismal team, managed by Mike Higgins, that finished sixth, thirty-three games behind the Yankees. All that the fans—what there were of them—had to focus on were individual performances, so Yastrzemski was always under the microscope. His .266 average, incredibly, tied him with Frank Malzone as tops on the club, a strange statistic in a park tailored for hitting.

"I'll do better," Yastrzemski said when the season was over. "Most good hitters have trouble in their first year."

And he did. He got off to a fast start in 1962, and by May was hitting .321. Higgins no longer platooned him. The team was so bad, he couldn't afford to

Yaz swings away.

bench someone with Yaz's potential. But the heat of the summer and the deadliness of losing took its toll on the intense youngster. He went from 188 pounds to 164 pounds and his average dipped to .296 by season's end.

The team finished in the cellar, and Mike Higgins was finished, period, as field manager. That winter, Johnny Pesky, one of the most popular players in Red Sox history, was named manager.

Pesky didn't fare much better than Higgins. His team wound up seventh in 1963, despite the presence of Dick Stuart and Dick Radatz, two of the most colorful players in Red Sox history. Stu, nicknamed Dr. Strangeglove for his erratic play around first base, hit 42 homers and drove in 118 runs. Radatz, a 6'5" 230-pound relief pitcher nicknamed "the Monster," won 16 and lost 9, with 24 saves.

However, Radatz and Stuart were no bigger a story at Fenway than Yastrzemski, who won his first American League batting championship. Yaz hit .321, and also led the league in doubles with 40, walks with 95, and assists for an outfielder with 18.

"For getting rid of the ball and throwing it accurately and strongly," wrote Harold Kaese of the *Boston Globe*, "Yaz today is second best only to Willy Mays."

There were, however, storm clouds on the horizon. At Fenway Park, there are always storm clouds on the horizon. Yastrzemski, a fierce competitor, had always been with a winner. Now, after three seasons with abject losers, he was having a difficult time coming to grips with that reality.

He was subject to fits of moodiness, and after the Red Sox dropped out of the pennant race—usually around the middle of June—his all-out effort slackened. He was criticized by reporters covering the team for not hustling on ground balls hit to second, for running the bases recklessly, and for lapses of concentration in the outfield.

That winter, at the Boston Baseball writers' dinner, a festive occasion when the most offhand remark can cause lasting scars, Yastrzemski opened a wound that did not heal for a decade. He had been quoted prior to the dinner as saying Pesky had made several mistakes in his rookie managerial season. At the dinner he publicly thanked Higgins, who was now general manager, for all he'd done for him, and snubbed Pesky.

The rift widened during the '64 season, when Pesky benched Yaz "for loafing," that is, not running out a ground ball in a game with the Indians, Yaz protested, saying he hadn't been feeling well, but Pesky didn't buy the excuse.

The team was hardly a dazzler on the field—newspapers had nicknamed them "The Jersey St. Jesters"—so writers leaped all over the Pesky–Yaz feud.

In September 1964, the Red Sox did what all teams do when the players are performing poorly. They fired the manager, replacing Pesky with coach Billy Herman.

Yastrzemski, who had signed for $30,000 in 1964, hit only .289, with just 67 runs batted in. General manager Higgins wanted to cut his salary, but Yaz finally signed for the same amount to play the '65 season.

He hit .312, but the Red Sox of 1965, though it may be hard to believe, were worse than the season before. They finished ninth, 40 games behind the champion Minnesota Twins. Their record was 62–100, the first time the franchise had lost 100 games since 1932.

In early May, there had been talk of a trade with the Twins, Yaz for power-hitting outfielder Bob Allison. But in the middle of the month, Yaz silenced those rumors for the moment with the best spree of his young career. In four games against the Tigers, he went 8 for 14, with 3 home runs and 9 runs batted in.

In one of the games he hit for the cycle, that is, a single, double, triple, and homer, for the first and only time in his career. Willie Horton of the Tigers, in that same series, was 10 for 17 with 2 homers and 6 RBI.

It was streaks such as the one against Detroit that led manager Herman to say, when the season was over: "Yaz hasn't even come close to reaching his potential. Someday he's going to be one of the great ones in the game."

Herman was a year early with his prediction. The season of 1966 was more of the same, both for Yaz and the Sox. He was once more the best player on a bad team that again finished ninth. And the trade rumors resurfaced—Yaz for Tom Tresh of the Yankees, Yaz for Tommy Agee of the White Sox.

But certain signs on this team indicated that a corner had been turned. Instead of worn-out retreads and young mediocrities, there were promising kids such as Joe Foy, George Scott, Rico Petrocelli, Reggie Smith, Tony Conigliaro, Mike Andrews, and Jim Lonborg.

The Red Sox played better than .500 after the all-star break, and in late September Herman called a press conference in Kansas City to outline his plans and hopes for 1967. The plans, as it turned out, would not include Herman. He got the Pesky treatment two days after the press conference. The Red Sox fired him and named coach Pete Runnels to finish out the season.

Runnels, however, was an interim appointment. The man who got the job for 1967 was Dick Williams, a spare part on several major league teams for a decade. Williams, managing in the Red Sox system at Toronto, was known as a sarcastic, play-no-favorites disciplinarian, a type foreign to the Red Sox locker room, which had long been known as the country club of baseball.

Yastrzemski had been named team captain in 1966, the first time the Red Sox had ever had one. Williams took the captaincy away, saying there was room for only one man at the top and guess who it would be?

Yaz was delighted.

"Happy is not the word. I'm relieved. I'm just twenty-seven years old and that's not old enough to be burdened with other people's problems. When I read Dick Williams wasn't going to have a captain, the first thing I thought was that now I can go back to just being the Red Sox left fielder."

Yastrzemski would say many times in his career that he was not a rah-rah type, and that any leading he would do would come from his performance on the field.

In a way, Yastrzemski's career can be broken into the four seasons of a year. The first part was his troubled spring, a time of struggle and unrealized potential. Then came the brief but glorious summer, when he was the best-known athlete in America. This was followed by a long and tempestuous autumn, when fans expected a repeat of 1967, only to be both disappointed and angry when Yaz fell short of continued immortality.

And finally, after the marvelous Indian summer of 1975, came the winter of his career, when Boston fans realized that for two decades they'd been watching a special baseball player.

The kid from the potato fields of Long Island didn't know it when the 1967 season began, but the troubled spring of Carl Yastrzemski was over.

He'd spent the winter in a vigorous conditioning program in Lynnfield, under the direction of physical culturist Gene Berde. Yaz lifted weights, he ran, he strained, he huffed and puffed, and never was he in better shape for the start of a season.

Harold Kaese wrote, after Yaz hit 2 homers and saved a spring training game in St. Petersburg against the Cards with a great catch, "For his six seasons with the Sox, Carl Yastrzemski has a lifetime average of .293, absurdly ordinary for a hitter so adept at laying the wood on the ball. His RBIs are also hard to fathom. He has never batted in 100 runs a season. He is a better hitter than that and this should be the year Yastrzemski proves it."

Prophetic words, but even Yaz had his doubts as to how good he could be.

"I could never do what Frank Robinson has done in Baltimore," he said. Robinson had won the triple crown in 1966 with 49 homers, 122 runs batted in, and an average of .316. Little did Yaz know that his numbers when the '67 season ended would be very close to Robinson's figures of the year before.

"I don't have the capability to hit a lot of home runs," Yaz said. "I have limitations. Personally, I think I'm the type of player who can blend in with other players and help win a pennant."

Dick Williams, asked in spring training to assess his team, stared with those cold eyes of his at the questioner, and replied; "We'll win more than we lose."

A modest prediction? Not when you consider that the Red Sox franchise hadn't won more than it lost in any season in the last decade.

An indication that 1967 might be both different and interesting came almost immediately. Soft-throwing left-hander Billy Rohr, who had never seen Yankee Stadium, let alone pitch there, started the road opener.

For eight innings, he had a no-hitter. Then Tom Tresh, leading off the ninth, hit a 3-and-2 pitch to deep left center, into the stadium's "death valley." Yaz, who reacted to the crack of the bat as quickly as any outfielder in the majors, broke back and to his left and made a tumbling, over-the-head catch to keep the no-hitter alive. Two batters later, Elston Howard, who would join the Red Sox in May and be a vital cog in the pennant drive, broke the no-hitter up with a single to right.

But the tone of the season was set. Game after game was won in some dramatic way. Comebacks became the expected rather than the unusual. Ordinary players became one-day heroes. Players such as Dalton Jones, Bill Landis, Jerry Adair, Gary Waslewski, George Thomas, Jose Tartabull, Russ Gibson, Darrell Brandon, and John Wyatt had their moments in the sun and shortly afterward, faded from the major leagues.

Towering over them all was the majestic—yes, even heroic—figure of Yastrzemski. He is not a big man, only 5'10" and 185 pounds, but in 1967 he seemed 10 feet tall.

In his previous five seasons the Red Sox had finished sixth, eighth, seventh, ninth, and ninth again. Even so, defeat had never become acceptable to Yastrzemski. In 1967, he got to see the other side of the coin, and teammates saw another side of Yastrzemski.

"God he was aggressive," said Thomas, a free-spirited utility man of whom Williams once remarked, "He's as funny on the field as he is off it."

Thomas said that in 1967, Yaz "wasn't as self-centered. He was a help to the other ballplayers. He'd be yelling all the time and getting the other guys on the bench to help."

Thomas cited a game in August as a case in point. Tony Conigliaro had hit a 2-out, 2-run homer in the bottom of the tenth to win a game in the most dramatic of ways.

"Yaz was the first man on the top step to shake hands," said Thomas. "Everybody saw this and thought that if he really cared about Tony winning a game, everybody should care. We started playing baseball instead of being individuals."

At the all-star break, Yastrzemski was hitting .336, with 18 homers, only 2 less than he'd previously hit in an entire season. Said third base coach Eddie Popowski:

"Except for the long ball, this is the same player I had when I managed Minneapolis."

But the long ball made so much difference. Until 1967, Yaz had been a left-center field line drive hitter, and many of his homers had landed in the friendly Fenway nets. But with the added strength from the off-season conditioning program, he decided to change his stance and become a dead pull hitter.

"That took a lot of guts, changing what had always worked pretty well for him," said Gentleman Jim Lonborg, a tall right-hander who would win 22 games and the Cy Young award that season.

Though he'd made three other all-star teams, Yaz had never started one until 1967. As left fielder for the American League, he had a double and 2 singles in that game.

In June, just before a series in Chicago, White Sox manager Eddie Stanky called Yastrzemski "an all-star from the neck down." When the season was over and Yaz had won every award in sight, Stanky was asked again about his remark.

"The quote was true,." he replied. "Carl had the reputation of being a moody ball player. I imagine what I said hurt him a little bit, but in a way it was a compliment, and maybe it spurred him on to being a complete ballplayer."

As the long season approached an exciting climax, the daily progress of the Red Sox was the most important item in Boston.

When the team fell into a swoon and lost 4 straight to the Angels in Anaheim, the whole city suffered. Williams benched George Scott for being overweight and the city debated the act as though it were a rise in taxes.

There was a shooting in a Boston parking lot, and when a policeman asked a witness as to the time of the crime, the witness replied: "The best I can say is there was one out in the last of the tenth."

Toward the end of August, Yaz ran into a dry spell at a bad time—a 4-game series at Yankee Stadium. He had had no hits in his last 16 at-bats, including twenty-nine innings of a twilight doubleheader.

"You need a rest," Williams said. "You won't play tomorrow against lefty Al Downing."

"I'll be ready if you need me in the late innings," replied Yaz.

He entered the game in the eighth inning the next night as a defensive replacement, and in the eleventh, slammed a home run into the second deck in right field to win the game.

In Detroit, the Red Sox were trailing the Tigers by a run with two out and nobody on in the ninth and Yaz homered off Fred Lasher to tie the game. Dalton Jones, not a long ball hitter, then won it with another homer.

Yastrzemski became a celebrity, somebody recognized away from the ball park.

"Before 1967," he said, "I could come and go as I pleased and no one ever bothered me. I could go to a store or a movie and no one would recognize me. Now it's different."

Driving back to Boston from New York with his son Mike, he stopped at a gas station along the Connecticut Turnpike to buy some candy bars.

"I came out of the station and there was a crowd of people around the car. I signed autographs for twenty-five minutes."

He changed his telephone number three times that season. He rented a cottage at Humarock Beach in Marshfield, only to find that kids would gather and stare at the house where the famous ball player lived.

After the tragic beaning of Conigliaro in mid-August, Yaz went for the long ball even more.

"You know you're not supposed to swing for homers," he said, "but with Tony out, we've lost a lot of our power."

He finished with 44 homers, breaking Williams's Red Sox record of 43 for a left-handed hitter and tying with Harmon Killebrew of the Twins for the American League lead.

"At the all-star break, I felt I'd be doing well to end up with 30," he said. "I was afraid I'd get weaker physically in the second half, like the other years. But it never happened. I was strong all along."

However, the impossible dream seemed to have ended when the Red Sox lost two games (one to Luis Tiant) to Cleveland in late September to fall behind the White Sox.

Then the Whites lost a doubleheader to the lowly Kansas City As, with Williams listening to the games on the car radio, and the Red Sox were back in the race.

They had to beat the Twins at Fenway on Saturday and Sunday, and hope that the Tigers, also in contention, would do no better than a split in their 4 games with the Angels.

The Red Sox won on Saturday, 6–4, getting a break when ace Minnesota left-hander Jim Kaat pulled a muscle in his pitching arm while leading, 1–0, in the third inning. Yaz had 3 for 4 with 4 runs batted in, 3 coming on a game-winning homer in the seventh inning.

On Sunday, the Red Sox fell behind Dean Chance, 2–0, with Yaz's error in left field contributing to one of the runs. Then Boston scored 5 times in the sixth, with Yaz driving in the first 2. He had 4 for 4 that final afternoon, but none of the hits was any more vital than a play in the eighth, when the Twins put on one last charge.

With two out and none on, Killebrew and Tony Oliva singled, and Bob Allison, the man Yaz might have been traded for a couple of seasons earlier, looped a ball into the left-field corner.

It seemed a sure double, but Yastrzemski backhanded the ball on one bounce and threw Allison out with plenty to spare at second base. Instead of having a run in and the tying run at second, the inning was over.

"When I saw Allison go I said to myself 'Wonderful,'" gloated Williams. "Yaz will throw one of his eight hundred strikes to the base."

Yastrzemski in the two games had gone 7 for 8, and driven in six runs. In the final two pressure-packed weeks, he had 23 hits in 44 at-bats for an average of .523.

He hit safely in 11 of the 12 games, drove in 16 runs, scored 14, and hit 5 homers.

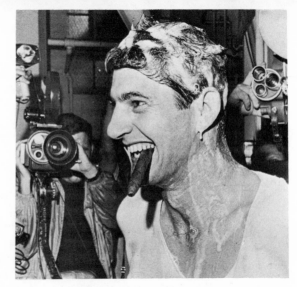

Pennant celebration in 1967.

"If any player in baseball history—Babe Ruth, Roger Hornsby, Ty Cobb, Lou Gehrig—ever had a two-week clutch production to equal Yastrzemski's," wrote the perceptive Kaese, "let the historians bring him forth."

The pennant was not won yet. The Tigers had to lose to the Angels, or there would be a play-off in Detroit with the Red Sox the next day, with Lee Stange pitching for Boston.

So the Red Sox players, most of them still in their sweaty uniforms, sat around the clubhouse and listened to Tiger broadcaster Ernie Harwell's play-by-play description of that Detroit–California game.

The Angels took an 8–5 lead into the ninth, but Bill Freehan doubled to open that inning for the Tigers. Don Wert walked and Yastrzemski, in his undershirt, began to pace the locker room.

Lennie Green pinch hit. The Angels changed pitchers, bringing in veteran left-hander George Brunet. The Tigers switched pinch hitters, sending up Jim Price to bat for Green. Price flied to center field.

The dangerous Dick McAuliffe came to the plate. "Get him out," yelled Yaz, as if Brunet could hear through the radio loudspeaker, "and we'll send you a case of champagne."

McAuliffe hit into a double play. The game and the season were over and the impossible dream was a reality. The Red Sox were champions of the American League for the first time since 1946.

Yastrzemski, the man who had led them there, was emotionally exhausted. Tears of joy filled his eyes as he embraced Williams and then Yawkey, the millionaire owner who had become a close friend.

Clubhouse man Donny Fitzpatrick, also a good friend of Yaz's was asked for his thoughts on such a joyous occasion. Fitzpatrick had been a batboy and clubhouse assistant in 1946, the last pennant season.

"I thought I knew what excitement was." Fitzpatrick replied, "but nothing came closer to this year or that guy." And he pointed to Number 8, who had shaving cream in his hair, a cigar in his mouth, and happiness all over his face.

Perhaps the World Series against the St. Louis Cardinals could have been nothing but an anticlimax after such a season. Still it was exciting, with Yastrzemski continuing to play a dominant role.

In game two, after Bob Gibson had beaten the Red Sox in the opener, Yaz homered off Dick Hughes in the fourth to open the scoring. In the seventh, with Boston clinging to a 2–0 lead, Yaz slugged a 3-run homer off left-handed reliever Joel Hoerner to put the game on ice for Lonborg, who had a no-hitter for seven and two-thirds innings.

Cards starter Nelson Briles plunked Yastrzemski with a pitch in the first inning of game three, precipitating a mild uprising. Both clubs charged onto the field, and manager Williams claimed that Briles had thrown at his star.

Yastrzemski homered again in game six, which the Red Sox won to knot the Series at 3 victories each. But he and the rest of the Sox were stymied once more by the awesome Gibson in game seven, and the Cardinals were the champions. They had beaten the Red Sox, 4 games to 3, just as they had in 1946.

Yastrzemski batted .400 in the '67 series, with 2 doubles and 3 homers among his 10 hits. It was a fitting finish to an unforgettable season.

He got nineteen of twenty first-place votes for most valuable player in the American League. A Minneapolis writer selected Cesar Tovar of the Twins, whose MVP qualities were not immediately perceived through his statistics—a batting average of .267, with 47 runs batted in and 6 homers.

Yastrzemski had been a semiregional hero before 1967. After it, his name was nationally known. He went on the Ed Sullivan show and the Merv Griffin show. At Roosevelt Raceway in New York, there was a Carl Yastrzemski night. He headlined the camping show in Boston that winter and drew record crowds. He was chairman of the drive to raise money for retarded children.

Yastrzemski was voted the number-one newsmaker in New England and nosed out Johnny Unitas of the Baltimore Colts as the Associated Press's Athlete of the Year.

Sports Illustrated named him Sportsman of the Year.

The Portland Printing Company of Boston put him on their staff, and when the firm placed a small classified ad asking for a secretary for Yaz, it got five hundred responses.

"When he was seven or eight years old," Yaz's father told *Globe* writer Roger Birtwell, "he would get a basket and go all over the farm picking up rocks. Then he'd take the rocks and a sawed-off bat and spend hours trying to knock the rocks over a tree. He'd say to himself, 'Now I'm Ted Williams,' or, 'Now I'm Stan Musial.' Now here he is, famous, and other kids are hitting rocks and saying, 'Now I'm Carl Yastrzemski.' "

Yastrzemski went to Canada to speak at a banquet and later said, "The fifteen hundred people there knew more about the Red Sox than they did about the Montreal Canadiens."

One day that winter, Yaz watched the highlight films of the impossible dream season, and afterward remarked to a reporter, "Even after I see it, I can't believe it all happened. It'll never be the same again."

And, of course, it wasn't. Yastrzemski won the batting title in 1968 with a

.301 average, the lowest winning mark in American League history. However, his homer total fell to 23 and his RBIs to 74.

And the feisty Red Sox spirit that had carried them from the bottom to the top in one season took a nasty turn. Bickering replaced comradeship. The hard-driving Williams let up a little, and when he tried to reapply to whip, the strategy didn't work.

The Red Sox, feeding off their 1967 success, set an all-time Fenway attendance record of 1,940,788, but finished fourth, 17 games back of first-place Detroit.

The next season was worse. The Sox ended up 22 games back, and Yastrzemski, though playing all 162 games, hitting 40 homers, and driving in 111 runs, batted only .255. He had run-ins with Williams, who stole a page from history, accused Yaz of not hustling in a game in Oakland, and fined his star $500.

It wasn't all sackcloth and ashes. Yaz hit a homer in Anaheim that was measured at 539 feet, and in Yankee Stadium belted one halfway up the third deck, 405 feet away and 100 feet high when it struck the stands.

But he was twice thrown out of games for arguing, and fans at Fenway Park began to boo him.

"I don't blame them," said Yastrzemski. "They're frustrated just like I am. After you win a pennant, that's all you want again."

Then, in mid-September, Williams was fired. The impossible dream most definitely was over, and so was the golden summer of Yastrzemski's career. What followed was an excruciating autumn of discontent and grumbling, in which Yaz was the most visible symbol of the team's failure to repeat 1967.

Yastrzemski had an excellent 1970, hitting .329 with 102 runs batted in and 40 more homers, and winning the most valuable player award in the all-star game. Yaz had 4 hits, played the entire 12 innings, and became the first player on a losing team to receive the MVP award.

He lost the batting championship on the last day of the season—by less than a point—to Alex Johnson of the Angels. Johnson had 2 for 3 and then left the game in the fifth. His average figured out to .3289. Yaz had finished his season the night before at .3286.

Despite Yaz's excellent year, the Red Sox finished 21 games behind, and Yaz's critics sang the same tired tune, namely, that Yastrzemski had undermined rookie manager Eddie Kasko by running to owner Tom Yawkey with complaints.

Yaz had his worst season in 1971. His average dipped to .254, with only 15 homers and 70 runs batted in. He got into a silly spat with outfielder Billy Conigliaro, who accused the Red Sox star of getting rid of Pesky, Ken Harrelson, and brother Tony by running to the front office.

He hurt his hand and went 81 games without a home run against left-handers, and the booing reached its peak. His parents sat in sky-view seats and cringed at the cruel remarks around them.

"Some people have short memories," said his father. "He's tried a million things to get going. Maybe he's tried too many."

Even his peers wondered whether Yastrzemski was at the crossroads.

"I've never seen him like this before," said Tigers manager Billy Martin after Yaz had 1 scratch hit in a 4-game series with Martin's team. "I think he's a little depressed."

As 1972 began, the most asked question in spring training was whether Yastrzemski could come back. It was pointed out that Babe Ruth hit .372 after a .290 season and that Tris Speaker bounced back from a .296 year to average .378.

But in Yaz's case, the average he was trying to recover from was a sickly .254. In Winter Haven, a fan yelled, "You're too rich to run," after Yaz loafed on a ground ball. The trade talk began again, Yastrzemski for Joe Torre being the most persistent rumor.

As May began he was batting .143, with 6 meager singles his only hits. On May 11 he hurt a shoulder in a collision with Angels catcher Art Kushyner and missed 26 games. The Year of the Yaz seemed an eternity ago.

The rest may have been just what Yastrzemski needed. In the first 12 games after his return he boosted his average 125 points. On July 23 he hit his first home run since the previous September.

The fans were still booing him lustily, but he was subtly providing the drive for a team on its way into a pennant race. The Red Sox took over first place in September. On the 30th, Yastrzemski's homer in the tenth beat Jim Palmer of Baltimore, and the Sox went to Detroit needing 2 wins in 3 games for the Eastern Division championship.

They didn't get those victories, with a fluke in the first game contributing mightily to the failure. With the Red Sox leading, 1–0, and Lui Aparicio on first base, Yastrzemski lashed a drive to left center field off Mickey Lolich. It seemed a sure triple, but Aparicio slipped rounding third and was trapped, ending the inning. The Red Sox never scored again, and lost the championship the next night.

That winter Yastrzemski investigated the possibility of playing in Japan. "The idea intrigued me," he said. A $300,000 one-year contract offer undoubtedly was part of the fascination. But he stayed in Boston, had a decent season (.296, 25 homers, 95 RBIs) and continued to be booed. Once he returned from an 8-game trip in which he'd hit .552 and the boos were as thunderous as ever.

Yastrzemski had become, in the words of *Boston Globe* columnist Leigh Montville, "an every summer debate." He was named captain again in 1974, batted .301, was team MVP, made the all-star team once more, and hit his 300th homer. And was booed.

He didn't know it, but when the 1974 season ended, so did the agonizing autumn of his career. Rookies Fred Lynn and Jim Rice joined the Red Sox for the last month of 1974, and you did not need to be overly perceptive to see that they would bring a new dimension to the Red Sox.

Before the 1975 season began, Yastrzemski, who had never been a rah-rah man, gave a locker-room pep talk. He told his teammates that they had the worst attitude he'd ever seen in spring training, and that if this kept up the Red Sox would finish in last place. He said each player should be aware of the little things that go into winning games, instead of moaning and complaining.

Yaz playing first—safe by a fingertip.

This, coming from a man who had so often been accused of me-firstism, was extraordinary, and, what's more, it worked.

"Every time somebody scratched himself," said utility infielder Bob Heise, "he got a pat on the back."

With Rice, Lynn, and Carlton Fisk to share the pressure, Yastrzemski became more relaxed. Until September, perhaps the incident he'll be most remembered for in that remarkable season was piling dirt on home plate after being called out on strikes by Lou DiMuro.

But down the stretch, playing with a bad shoulder, he was a vital force, and in the play-offs, was the Yaz of '67.

He batted .455 in the 3 games against Oakland and played sensationally in left field, even though he hadn't played out there all season. In the game-three clincher he threw out Reggie Jackson trying to stretch a single, and then in the eighth, cut off a Jackson line drive up the alley, holding what seemed a sure triple to a single and stifling an As rally.

"Those two plays were killers," lamented Jackson. "Yastrzemski carried that team through these three games." Yastrzemski himself categorized the cut-off on the Jackson hit as the most important single play he'd ever made.

In the World Series with the Reds, Yaz had 9 singles in 29 at-bats for a .310 average, and drove in 4 runs. But it would be his fate to make the final out of game seven after Joe Morgan had put Cincinnati ahead in the top half of the ninth with a single off Jim Burton.

*Carl's 3,000th hit
in Sox-Yanks game.*

Three years later, Yastrzemski again would make the final out of a long and, for the Red Sox fans, heartbreaking season, popping up to Graig Nettles with two on and two out in the ninth of the play-off game with the Yankees at Fenway Park. That moment was perhaps the low point of his career and he wept in the locker room afterward.

By that time, Yastrzemski was no longer booed. On his 37th birthday in 1976 he went 4 for 5 and threw a runner out at the plate and got a standing ovation from the twenty-seven thousand fans. That same year he said, "I used to think that talent was everything, that if you had it you could win. Now I realize it's talent plus attitude."

By 1978, Yastrzemski was firmly entrenched as "the grand old man." In 1979, he hit his 400th career homer off Oakland's Mike Morgan, who had been born the year Yaz broke in with Raleigh.

And then, in September of that year, came the Yaz Watch, as thousands waited patiently for Yastrzemski to reach 3000 hits, something only fourteen others in major league history had accomplished. His first hit had come on April 11, 1961, off Ray Herbert of the old Kansas City As.

He got number 3000 on Sept. 12, 1979, after three nonproductive games. The hit came off Jim Beattie of the Yankees, in the eighth inning of a 9–2 Red Sox victory. Jackson, playing right field, picked up the ball after it had eluded the glove of second baseman Willie Randolph, and carried it to the infield to give to Yastrzemski.

A full house of 34,337 saw the historic hit. Yastrzemski thus became the first American Leaguer and only the fourth in major league history to amass both 400 homers and 3000 hits.

The competitive fires that burned in Yaz at twenty were still glowing at forty-two when Number 8 finished his twenty-first season as a member of the Red Sox.

He had been taken for granted through much of his career, more appreciated in enemy ball parks than at Fenway. But he made sixteen all-star teams and won a triple crown and three batting championships.

Carl Michael Yastrzemski had many great seasons and a couple of bad seasons, but never a dull one. If you wanted a line that would describe his career, it might be this: Nobody wanted to win more than he did.

PART II

═BASKETBALL═

Professional basketball was hardly an instant success in Boston. For a long time the game itself, although originating only a hundred miles down the road in Springfield, ran a poor second to hockey during the winter in Greater Boston.

Kids had their pick of frozen ponds, and for every youngster who dribbled a basketball in a stuffy gymnasium, there were ten—no, fifty—strapping on skates for a game of shinny.

Into this indifferent atmosphere in 1946 came Walter Brown, founder of a team in a new league, the Basketball Association of America.

"Boston is full of Irishmen," Brown said to team publicist J. Howard McHugh. "We'll put them (the players) in green uniforms and call them the Boston Celtics."

Ah, the Boston Celtics. The community was slow to accept this team, and even into the '60s, when the Celtics were building a dynasty unequalled in sports with Red Auerbach as coach, they got only lukewarm local attention.

They opened at home against the Chicago Stags on Nov. 5, 1941, before a crowd of 4239 at the Boston arena. During the warm-up, Keven (Chuck) Connors, who would go on to greater fame in a television series portraying "the rifleman," shattered the glass backboard with a set shot.

Connors was a better actor than he was ballplayer, but as the pro game caught on around the country, Celtics players became household names to basketball fans, who appreciated the style of play that won championship after championship.

The four chapters that follow deal with **Bob Cousy, Bill Russell, John Havlicek,** and **Dave Cowens,** the best and brightest stars in the Celtics firmament.

But the list of memorable Celtics also includes Bob Brannum from

41

A toast by Cooz: Walter Brown, Bob Cousy, Bill Russell, Red Auerbach.

Michigan State, the team's first enforcer; Long-Armed Don Chaney, who had no peer as a defensive specialist; Chuck Cooper from Duquesne, the first Black to play in the NBA; Gene Conley, a terrific back-up for Bill Russell; Hank Finkel, 7 feet tall, who performed the same function for Dave Cowens; Larry Siegfried, a back-court tiger; Jack Nichols, a left-handed dentist who averaged 9 points a game in the middle '50s; Charlie Scott, a high-scoring guard who was a Celtic only two years, and Paul Silas, a Celtic only four years, but a terrific rebounder who was part of two championship teams.

And, of course, these names, indelibly etched in Boston basketball history:

BILL SHARMAN—Played from 1951 to 1961...6'1", 190 pounds, out of Southern Cal...Averaged 17.8 points per game as deadly shooting guard ... One of the best free-throw shooters ever ... In basketball Hall of Fame.

EASY ED MACAULEY—Averaged 19 points per game as first high-scoring Celtic ... Played in Boston from 1950 to 1956.

SAM JONES—Outstanding shooter ... Averaged 17.6 per game from 1957 to 1969 ... 6'4" forward from little North Carolina College ... Best year was 1964, when he averaged 26 points a game ... Great at bankshots and deadly in clutch.

TOM HEINSOHN—Machine-Gun Tommy from Holy Cross ... 6'7" and very aggressive ... Averaged 18.6 from 1956 through 1965 ... Scored 31 points in game that won first Celtics championship ... Rookie of year in 1956–57 ... Coached two Celtics championship teams.

FRANK RAMSEY—Created six-man role ... Played from 1954 to 1964 and came off bench for instant offense ... Was college star at University of Kentucky ... Expert at drawing fouls.

K. C. JONES—Teammate of Bill Russell at San Francisco ... Great defensive player and sure passer ... Played from 1958 through 1967 ... Later coached Washington and was assistant with Celtics.

JIM LOSCUTOFF—Nicknamed "Jungle Jim" ... Policeman of team from 1955 to 1964 ... Not big scorer (6.2 average) but that was not his main job ... Played college ball at Oregon.

TOM SANDERS—Nicknamed "Satch" ... 6'6" forward from NYU who always played opponent's high-scoring forward ... Tenacious shadow on defense ... Always cool, impossible to rattle ... Averaged 10 points a game from 1960 to 1973 ... Coached Celtics briefly.

DON NELSON—Picked up as free agent after being released by Lakers ... Averaged 11 points per game from 1965 to 1976 ... 6'6" forward who went to Iowa ... Slow, but excellent shooter and tough offensive rebounder ... Later coached Milwaukee Bucks.

BAILEY HOWELL—One of few trades Celtics ever made, and probably the best ... Came to team from Detroit in exchange for Mel Counts ... Averaged 19 points from 1966 through 1970.

PAUL SILAS—Was a Celtic only four seasons, but was big contributor on championship teams in 1974 and 1976 ... Marvelous team player and great offensive rebounder.

JO JO WHITE—Smooth, cool guard from University of Kansas ... Had excellent line-drive jump shot ... Averaged 18 points per game over 10-year span.

CHAPTER 3

"FOLLOW THE BOUNCING BALL"

BOB COUSY

"The first time he tries that fancy Dan stuff in this league, they'll cram the ball down his throat."

—Pro scout's evaluation of Bob
Cousy prior to the 1950 draft.

The vignette will remain, for those who were at the Boston Garden that St. Patrick's Day afternoon in 1963, a moment frozen in time.

The man in short pants, wearing Boston Celtics jersey Number 14, was at center court trying to tell the 13,909 in attendance what the day meant to him. He was having trouble, fumbling for words, pausing often to brush away tears.

He tried and tried and still the words wouldn't come. And the packed house fell silent, perhaps feeling an empathy for the emotions it knew must be surging through the man.

Joe Dillon of South Boston, a thirty-two-year-old water-division worker for the Metropolitan District Commission, and also a walking sports encyclopedia, decided to break the silence. Dillon had the voice for it, a voice that could shatter glass.

"If you ever heard Joe Dillon's voice," said a friend, "you never forgot it."

Certainly nobody who was in the Garden that afternoon ever forgot it.

"We all love ya, Cooz," thundered Dillon, his words reverberating off the Garden rafters and cutting through the smoke-filled silence like a knife through butter.

The tension was broken. Cheers cascaded down from the stands then, and though Bob Cousy broke down and sobbed at least twenty-five times during a seven-minute speech that took twenty minutes, he made it through the most emotional tribute to an athlete in Boston history.

The decks were so awash with emotion that even Dolph Schayes, scoring star of the visiting Syracuse Nats, wept copiously.

"It was raining outside and pouring inside," commented Jerry Nason of the *Boston Globe.*

But then, nobody expected that this farewell to the man who had brought a new dimension to the game of basketball would be a lah-de-dah tea party. Bob Cousy played with fire and emotion. He would say goodbye the same way. He would leave them with something to remember, just as he had given them something to remember every time he had come out on a court.

Cousy dressed James Naismith's dowdy YMCA game in brand-new clothes. There were great players before Cousy's time, plenty of them, but none with his flair.

The object of the game after all, was simple. Put a round leather ball into a 10-foot-high basket whose circumference was slightly larger than the ball. Cousy introduced new, imaginative methods of reaching that objective. And along the way, he made himself the standard by which all other players would be judged.

His name became a cliché to those of lesser skills. If a kid persisted in throwing behind-the-back passes that went astray, he was sure to hear: "Who do ya think ya are, Cousy?" If a schoolboy began to draw an inordinate amount of attention for his play, someone was sure to comment: "He's good, but he ain't no Cousy."

It is no exaggeration to say that Cousy's name is synonymous with basketball, the way Babe Ruth's is with baseball. Long before Earwin Johnson came out of Michigan State and was called "Magic," Cousy worked his own magic act.

Some of that Cousy magic seems elementary now. Even 6'9" forwards dribble behind their backs, and 6'5" guards dribble through their legs, change directions seven times while bringing the ball up-court, hang in the air for what seems an eternity, and dunk the ball.

Still, there was a mystical something about Cousy that remains... well... different. Grainy, black-and-white films of the Cousy-directed Celtics may look hopelessly outdated, but Cousy's actions aren't. The amazing peripheral vision as he whipped a pass to a teammate cutting from either side, the instincts that told him when to drop a pass off to a man trailing him on a fast break, the half-court bullets that he threw, the behind-the-back stuff not for showtime but at precisely the right moment—these Cousy tricks are as fresh as tomorrow.

And yet, when Cousy first began to play basketball, on the asphalt playgrounds of St. Albans, in Long Island, New York, he wasn't considered good enough as a twelve-year-old to make the junior varsity at Andrew Jackson High School.

Until that age, he had lived on the East Side of New York, where his father drove a cab and where only French was spoken in the house for the first five years of his life.

The move to St. Albans in Queens took Cousy away from stickball and other street games. He practiced and played basketball all the time, joining outside leagues after being cut from the high school jayvees.

He even learned to dribble with his left hand, something many right-handed players never learn to do. This would come in handy when he refined his ball-handling tricks at Holy Cross College and in the pros.

Cousy was cut again his sophomore year, but when Lew Grummond, the coach, saw him playing in amateur leagues, he was impressed and restored him to the jayvees.

Cousy didn't become a regular on the Andrew Jackson varsity until the last part of his junior year. By then, word was getting around that here was a kid who could turn a basketball inside out.

He won the city scoring championship as a senior, getting 28 points in his final game to take the title by 8.

Recruiting in those days was not nearly as sophisticated or intense as it became later, when 250 colleges might have scouts sitting on the doorstep of the latest high-school phenom, who is usually 7 feet tall and often has an agent.

The romancing of a potential college athlete in the late '40s was more of a sit-in-the-kitchen-with-the-folks kind of thing. And that's what General Al McLellan, basketball coach of Boston College, did with Cousy.

He came to St. Albans and described to the Cousy family the many educational, athletic, and social benefits available at BC. Cousy visited the campus, and things began to look good for a college that had never been known for its basketball prowess.

Enter Ken Haggerty, another Andrew Jackson grad, who was then attending Holy Cross and playing on the basketball team. Haggerty spoke of Cousy in such glowing terms to Holy Cross coach Alvin (Doggie) Julian that Julian decided to see for himself.

He liked what he saw, and invited Cousy to sit on the Holy Cross bench for a game against the Merchant Marine, so the kid could get the flavor of what it might be like to play for the Crusaders.

There was also the offer of a scholarship, and so in September 1946, Cousy entered Holy Cross College, a Jesuit institution in Worcester, forty miles west of Boston. Also in his class were future teammates Andy Laska, Frank Oftring, and Bob McMullan.

Though Worcester had a basketball tradition, Boston was a dribbling desert. Its winter sport was hockey. The ponds froze, the pucks came out, and the skating began. Basketball was for skinny guys wearing knee guards, and was played in gyms with running-track balconies, so that it was almost impossible to take shots from the corners.

In fact, though a few of the immediate suburbs—Somerville, Chelsea, and Cambridge, to name three—knew the difference between a bounce pass and a hook shot, Boston itself couldn't care less. The high schools didn't even have varsity teams until after World War II.

The midwest was the hotbed of basketball. Everybody knew that. Strange stories of Hoosier high-school hoop hysteria seeped out of Indiana. Every back yard had a net. The bigtime coach was Adolph Rupp of Kentucky. The bigtime player was George Mikan, a myopic, broad-beamed, wide-shouldered hook-shooting hulk at DePaul University in Chicago.

In the East, if you wanted to make a name in the sport, you played in New York City, for NYU or CCNY or LIU or even St. John's. You played where the dream was to look good in Madison Square Garden. Star in the Garden and your name went around the country.

Holy Cross didn't even have a gym good enough for its home games. They were played in Worcester Municipal Auditorium, an ark of a dusty downtown building that was, as its name implied, not a place to play basketball, but a meeting place, with a stage at one end and a balcony at the other.

In this improbable setting, better suited to *Our Town* and high-school graduations, the Fancy Pants A.C. put on basketball shows the likes of which have not been seen since either in Worcester or, perhaps, anywhere else.

That's what the sports pages called the Holy Cross varsity of those years— the Fancy Pants A.C. The team relied more on guile than power. They passed the basketball ("whipped it" would be a more appropriate description) as though it was on fire. Each player was also adept at moving without the ball, an expression that became a tired cliché in the '70s but which was a breath of fresh air in the stand-still '40s.

As a freshman, Cousy was on the second platoon of the Holy Cross team that won the NCAA championship in 1946–47. The starters were George Kaftan, Dermie O'Connell, Haggerty, Bobby Curran, and Joe Mullaney.

Big games were moved out of the auditorium and into Boston Garden. Through the Cousy years, into the Togo Palazzi years and ending with the Tom Heinsohn years, the city that cared only about ice hockey during the winter flocked to the building on Causeway Street to see some of the best college basketball in America.

Cousy became a sometime starter in his sophomore season, but ran into early difficulties with coach Julian. Early in the season, communication between the two was at a minimum. Cousy thought he wasn't playing enough and Julian thought Cousy was too much of a free lance and a showboat when he did play.

"I was 90 percent wrong," Cousy would say years later. But at the time, he thought he was 100 percent right, and so wrote to Joe Lapchick, the coach at St. John's, saying he wanted to get out of Holy Cross and asking for a transfer. Lapchick advised Cousy to stick it out.

The breakthrough came after Julian benched Cousy for a game against Chicago Loyola at the Garden. With five minutes to go and Holy Cross trailing, the Garden crowd began chanting, "We want Cousy, we want Cousy," and Julian sent him into the game. Cousy scored 11 points, including the winning basket at the buzzer.

He was the star in his junior and senior seasons. Buster Sheary had replaced Julian as coach, and he and his fancy play-maker hit it off from the start. However, though Holy Cross was rated one of the best teams in the nation—in 1949–50 it had a 26-game winning streak—it couldn't win the National Invitational Tournament in New York either season.

However, by his senior year Cousy was the best-known collegian in the country, and there were some good ones. He was named to an all-America team that included Sherman White of LIU, Dick Schnittker of Ohio State, Paul Unruh of Bradley, Kevin O'Shea of Notre Dame, Whitey Skoog of Minnesota, Dick Dickey and Sammy Ranzino of North Carolina, Clyde Lovellette of Kansas, Don Lofgran of San Francisco, and a guard he later teamed up with for many seasons on the Celtics, Bill Sharman of Southern Cal.

Cousy didn't captivate every fan. Some basketball purists were offended by what they considered an overly flamboyant style. They didn't like the sudden passes that could handcuff a teammate, or the keep-away dribbling that made him a one-man show, or the look-one-way, pass-another flashiness that occasionally resulted in a pass into the third row.

The purists were looking at the forest, but seeing only the trees. They were looking at the final score and overlooking the fun that led to that final score. A basket counts only 2 points, they insisted, so what difference does it make how the baskets are come by? On an excitement scale, merely all the difference in the world.

Cousy brought basketball into the twentieth century and made it a bigtime spectator sport.

"There are a lot of great players," said Lapchick, an original Celtic and a respected coach for many years, "but no one does it the way he does, and that's what they come to see. And that's what they talk about when they go home."

Pro basketball was barely out of the dusty barn stage when Cousy graduated from Holy Cross. The NBA had been in operation only four seasons, and at various times included such teams as the Providence Steamrollers, the Pittsburgh Ironmen, the Toronto Huskies, the Sheboygan Redskins, the Anderson Packers, the Cleveland Rebels, the Waterloo Hawks, and the Detroit Falcons.

The dominant team as the 1950 draft approached was Minneapolis, featuring guard Slater Martin, forward Jim Pollard, and same 6'9" George Mikan who had been a college star at DePaul. The Lakers had won the championship the last two seasons.

The Celtics, on the other hand, were a miserable lot. John (Honey) Russell had coached them their first two years, finishing last and next to last. When Julian took over, the results were no better. The Celtics were next to last in '48 and on the bottom again in '49. They were not what you'd call the most exciting act in town.

Into this mess rode Arnold (Red) Auerbach. Auerbach had coached the Washington Capitals for three seasons with considerable success and had been hired by Celtics owner Walter Brown to bring a semblance of order to a depressing and depressed situation.

The Celtics, as a reward for finishing last, got to draft first, and Auerbach did not score a public relations coup when he bypassed Cousy and instead selected Chuck Share, a 6'11" bear out of Bowling Green.

Yikes!! It was as though the new coach had spit on Bunker Hill Monument, as though he'd called Paul Revere a communist. Cousy had taken it for granted he'd be selected by Boston. So had the Celtics fans, what few of them were hanging around.

The press landed on Auerbach with every typing finger. They questioned his expertise and demanded an explanation. Auerbach gave them one that angered them even more.

"We need a big man. Little men are a dime a dozen. I'm supposed to win, not go after local yokels."

The local yokel had finally been picked by Ben Kerner, operator of the Tri-Cities franchise. Tri-Cities was a team that represented Moline and Rock Island, both in Illionois, and Davenport, Iowa. The NBA was not exactly big-city glitter and show biz in those formative days.

On June 6, 1950, a small story appeared on the news wire, to the effect that Bob Cousy had signed to play with the Tri-Cities Hawks for an estimated $9000 a season. Here, fate and luck, an unbeatable combination, took over the game.

Cousy never wore a Hawks uniform, because Kerner traded him to the Chicago Stags. Cousy never wore a Stags uniform, either, because the Chicago team folded and their players were put into a pool, to be distributed to the surviving teams in the struggling league.

The Stags had two established stars—Max Zaslofsky, who could score, and Andy Phillip, a play-maker. After much wrangling, the names of Zaslofsky, Phillip, and Cousy, the spectacular but by now somewhat bewildered collegian, were put into a hat.

Representatives of the New York, Philadelphia, and Boston teams were asked to select one name each from the hat. None of the three wanted Cousy.

For a reason Celtics owner Walter Brown could never satisfactorily explain to his dying day, he gave Ned Irish of the Knicks the first choice. Irish said thanks and came out with Zaslofsky, the player the Knicks wanted most.

Then it was Brown's turn and he did not hide his disappointment when the slip of paper read, "Bob Cousy."

"When I drew Cousy I could have fallen through the floor. I didn't have any secret feeling that maybe it would all turn out for the best in the long run."

Several championships later, Auerbach would say: "We got stuck with the greatest player in the league when we drew his name out of a hat."

However, at the time, the man who would someday be voted the best professional basketball coach in history said about the out-of-the-hat pick, "Cousy will have to make the team." Auerbach, of course, was needling the New England press and fans a bit with that remark. There was little doubt Cousy would make the team.

Auerbach was not a lover of razzle-dazzle. He was never one for making the game complicated. Even Cousy, in his book, *The Killer Instinct*, said that Auerbach's coaching philosophy was, " 'Keep it simple and execute properly.' I don't think we used more than six plays in my thirteen years as a Celtic."

So it would be interesting to see if the "Keep it simple" coach and the "Play it flashy" rookie could work together.

Cousy averaged 15.6 points a game his first season and finished second to hat partner Andy Phillip in assists. He was named rookie of the year, and the back court Celtics jumped from last place to second.

The Ed Leedes and Sonny Hertzbergs of Cousy's first season were gradually phased out, and in their places came the people who would be the foundation for the Celtics dynasty—Sharman, Sam and K. C. Jones, Frank Ramsey, Jim Loscutoff, Tommy Heinsohn, Satch Sanders, John Havlicek, and William Felton Russell.

Before Russell arrived, the Celtics won admiration and applause and nothing else. However, they were exciting, with a good fast break, and Cousy was the motor that made that break go.

The Celtics were wiped out in 2 straight in the play-offs in Cousy's rookie season, and were shot down by the Knicks in the first round the next year. But the crowds were coming and the shaky Celtics franchise, while still not exactly a gold mine, struggled along.

Early in his career, Cousy received some front-office backlash. In 1952, driving in to a game from Worcester, he was late because of a flat tire. The Celtics lost the game and Brown was furious.

"It was just the most important game of the season. There is no excuse for his being late. Cousy is getting a fortune ($14,000) to play for us. The next year Cousy will live in Boston."

The next year, and for all the remaining years, Cousy continued to live in Worcester, but Brown and Auerbach still had moments of doubt.

"Cousy can make the club or he can kill it," said Auerbach. "Lately he's been trying too much of that behind-the-back stuff. The other clubs are wise to us and are jamming the middle. I've got to temper Cousy. He's back where he was three years ago. He makes a spectacular play but we lose the ball."

Brown criticized Cousy for not shooting enough. At a weekly luncheon, Auerbach rapped him for not passing enough. Cousy was caught in the middle. He was confused and felt unappreciated and thought about asking to be traded.

A few days later, Brown admitted he'd made a mistake in knocking his star.

"We are definitely not going to trade him," Brown told newsmen, "and I am through popping off."

A decade later, at Cousy's emotional Garden retirement party, Brown said: "The Celtics wouldn't be here without him. He made basketball in this town. I don't know but what he made basketball, period. If he had played in New York he would have been the biggest thing since Babe Ruth. I think he is anyway."

There would be many big moments and exciting games before that final tribute. One of the biggest was on March 21, 1953. The Celtics had never advanced beyond the first round of the play-offs, but this night they had a chance.

They'd beaten Syracuse in the first of a best-in-3 series, and were taking on Dolph Schayes and Paul Seymour and the rest of the Nationals in the Garden.

Cousy, playing on a bad leg, had scored only 7 points in the first half, and it wasn't because he was passing well, since he had just 1 assist. He made 18 points in the second half, but when he missed a teammate who was open under the basket with less than a minute left, it appeared the Nats would win by a point and square the series, with the deciding game back in Syracuse's snakepit.

However, Cousy tied the score at 77 with a free throw in the last seconds, setting the stage for the most incredible game and performance—along with Wilt Chamberlain's 100 points in Hershey, Pennsylvania—in the history of the NBA.

The game went four overtimes before the Celtics pulled it out, 111–105. In the first overtime, Cousy scored 6 of Boston's 9 points, including another game-tying foul shot in the dying seconds.

He scored all 4 points the Celts made in overtime number two and made 8 more in the third, including a 25-footer with three seconds left to tie the game once again, 99–99.

By this time five Syracuse players had fouled out. So had four Celtics. In addition, Schayes and the Celtics' Bob Brannum had been ejected for fighting way back in the second period.

Then Syracuse's Seymour sprained an ankle. If he left the game, the Nats would be down to four men, and would be forced to use a player who had already fouled out, thus creating a technical foul every time a personal was called. So Seymour stayed in the game, planted under the basket and all but useless on defense.

Chuck Cooper of Boston drew his final foul in the fourth overtime, but had to stay in because the Celtics had no extra players. Playing-coach Al Cervi made the extra free throw resulting from the Cooper personal and technical, and Syracuse led, 104–99.

However, Cousy made 5 straight points to tie the game, and scored 9 of the 12 the Celts would make in those five minutes. He finished with 50 points, including 30 of 32 free throws.

Referees Arnie Heft and Charlie Eckman called 107 personals in the game, and the Celtics made 57 of 65 free throws.

Walter Brown walked out at the end of the second overtime, saying, "This is too much for me." He came back, however, for the final minutes. Publicity director Howie McHugh was seized by severe headaches that grew worse as the game pounded along.

The game lasted three hours and eleven minutes and was the final straw that later led to the adoption of the twenty-four-second clock. In close games, Cousy could control the ball for minutes at a time with his keep-away dribbling tactics. The maneuver could be interrupted only by fouling him, so the final moments of Celtics games often turned into a foul-shooting contest.

East stars: Bob Cousy, Bill Sharman, and Ed Macauley.

The rule that makes it mandatory for a team to shoot within twenty-four seconds after gaining possession of the ball ended that, and though it was fun for Celtics fans to watch Cousy outwit five opponents trying to steal the ball, the twenty-four-second clock saved the NBA.

In 1954, before a crowd of 16,487 at Madison Square Garden—one of his favorite arenas—Cousy won the most valuable player award in an all-star game that still rates as one of his best performances.

Lapchick, coaching the East stars, had sent Cousy in to dribble out the clock in the last minute, the twenty-four-second rule still being a few months away. But Bob Davies, whose hands were just about as quick as Cousy's, and who had been razzle-dazzle king of the league until Cooz came along, stole the ball and scored to send the game into overtime.

Jim Pollard of the Lakers had already been voted MVP of the game. But now in overtime, Cousy scored 9 points, so the ballots were tossed out and new ones distributed. This time, Cousy won the award.

From 1950 through the '56 season, Cousy was always first or second in assists and in the top five in scoring, but a team other than the Celts— Syracuse, Philadelphia, Minneapolis—was always the champion.

Then along came Russell, and also Heinsohn. Cousy had somebody to get him the ball so he could work the fast break. The dynasty was born.

Through his career, Cousy kept trying new things. He became proficient at the length-of-the-court slingshot pass, something that in lesser hands might have gone into the second balcony. Cousy's hands were slender and tapered, and, like his long arms, out of proportion to his 6'1" frame. He was able to dribble higher than most guards and could still control the ball.

Midway through his career, he began to shoot occasionally off his right foot, which is terribly awkward looking and against all accepted standards for right-handed shooters. Though it was never his best offensive weapon, it was another useful one.

Cousy played on his first NBA championship team in 1956–57, seven seasons out of Holy Cross. The Celtics won the Eastern Division with a 44–28 record, and knocked off Syracuse to reach the finals. These finals, against Bob Pettit and the St. Louis Hawks, were among the most memorable in NBA history.

It went the full seven games, and got off to a bad start for the Celtics when the Hawks beat them in an overtime opener in Boston, 125–123. The Celtics retrieved that one by beating the Hawks in game four at St. Louis.

Six days later, in the showdown at the Garden, the Celtics became NBA champions for the first time, beating the Hawks 125–123 in double overtime. Cousy was not the star of the game. In fact, he scored only 6 points. Heinsohn made 17 baskets in 33 attempts, and Russell swatted away some shots that would have won the game for the Hawks.

Still, after seven years as an also-ran, nobody felt better about sipping the victory champagne and nobody deserved it more than Cousy.

Titles came almost as regularly as sunrises after that. Of his last six seasons, it was only in 1957–58, when Russell was sidelined in the finals with a bad ankle, that the Celtics were denied the NBA championship.

In 1959, Cousy signed the biggest contract in the NBA, more even than the giant Chamberlain, whom he once characterized as "the biggest complainer to hit the NBA. I'm 6 feet 1 and it's difficult to feel sorry for a man 7 feet tall."

In 1960 Lapchick, then head coach of the Knicks, called Cousy the best player in the history of basketball. Cousy described his outlook and his method of playing the game as follows: "What I do amounts to thinking before the shot and playing with good players. If I played with hackers, some of the things I do could look awful bad."

He always disagreed with those who felt that sometimes his passes were too sudden and too tricky for his teammates.

"It seems to me," he told writer Ed Linn, "that other players have the responsibility of being ready to receive a pass any time they break into the open. After a man has played with me a few weeks, there is no excuse for his being fooled."

Bill Sharman, noting how quick Cousy was at responding to suddden situations, said that Cousy never fooled him because he was always looking for the pass. And if Sharman was open, Cousy invariably got him the ball. "It's the percentages," he said. "Bill's push shot is surer than my lay-up."

In 1961 and again in 1962, Cousy talked of retiring. The competitive juices, even in a man as fiercely motivated as Cousy, were not flowing as freely as they once were. He could get up for a battle against Guy Rodgers of Philadelphia or Oscar Robertson of Cincinnati, but for your run-of-the-mill NBA game, the motor was slowing down.

He was still among the leaders in assists, but no longer in the top twenty in scoring, turning that department over to Sam Jones, Heinsohn, and Russell. At the end of the 1962 season, a year in which the Celtics won 60 games and lost only 20, and then had beaten both Philly and Los Angeles in exciting 7-games series to capture the championship once more, Cousy sat down with Brown and Auerbach to discuss his future.

That was the year the Celtics had edged the Lakers in overtime, 110–107, in the seventh game at the Garden, surviving only because Frank Selvy of the Lakers had missed a short jumper that would have won for Los Angeles in regulation.

Cousy averaged 15.8 points that season, almost exactly what he'd made in his rookie year. He'd finished third in assists, behind Robertson and Rodgers. He was far from washed up, but the NBA years were eating at him. He talked with Auerbach for half an hour and with Brown for almost an hour.

And when the talks were over, Cousy decided, at the age of thirty-three, to give it one more season.

That season and his career would end in triumph. He would go out, not with a T. S. Eliot whimper, but with a bang.

Most of the dynasty was still with him. Sharman was gone, but Russell, Ramsey, Heinsohn, the Jones boys, Loscutoff, Sanders, and a crew-cut rookie named Havlicek from Ohio State were there to make sure the championship banner hung from the Garden rafters.

Though he played less minutes than ever before and his scoring average dipped to 13.2, Cousy remained third in the league in assists. They had his big retirement ceremony on March 17, and a Syracuse player said, "I knew we were in trouble when I noticed that even the referees were crying."

There were still games to play before Cousy officially retired, however, and it all came down to one last hurrah—the championship clincher with the Lakers on April 24, 1963.

The Celtics led the series, 3 games to 2, as the teams took the floor in L.A., but the emotional edge was with the Lakers. They'd kept the series alive by beating the Celts three days previously in Boston, in a game Cousy characterized as "the lousiest game I'd played in years." He'd fouled out, and the performance had done little for his peace of mind.

When Cousy arrived in L.A. for game six he walked into his hotel room and for thirty-six hours did not leave except to practice. His meals were sent up. He did not answer the phone. He was getting ready for game six. More, he was psyching himself up so there wouldn't be a repeat of his sorry game-five performance. He wanted a blue ribbon for his final appearance.

He and the rest of the Celtics played well, and when the fourth quarter began they were ahead by 14 points. Cousy got a rest, and slowly the Lakers bit into the score. Cousy returned and fourteen seconds later sprained his left ankle. The pain was so bad that he had to roll to his right side to take the weight off the injured ankle.

He was helped to the bench and as soon as he sat down, the pain eased. Trainer buddy Leroux (who later would be co-owner of the Boston Red Sox) strapped the ankle and Cousy stood, gingerly putting some pressure on it.

The Lakers were now a point behind with almost three minutes remaining. It was, as they say, still anybody's game. Cousy wanted it to be his.

Auerbach asked him how he felt.

"I think I can go," Cousy responded.

"Go in for Havlicek," said Auerbach.

Cousy didn't score for the rest of the game and every time he cut on the ankle he could feel a stab of pain. It is impossible, of course, to measure the emotional lift his return gave the Celtics, but the fact is that when Cousy came back the team steadied, and beat the Lakers 112–107.

With three seconds to go and the game tucked away, Sam Jones passes the ball to Cousy. The basketball was in his hands for the last time as a Celtic. But not for long. The jubilant Cousy threw one final slingshot pass, not down-court this time, but into the rafters as the final buzzer went off. He had gone out a champion.

In thirteen seasons, Cousy had scored 16,955 points for an 18.5 average, and dished out 6949 assists, 5.4 a game. In 109 play-off games, he'd also averaged 18.5 points. He'd played in 13 straight all-star games and was twice named MVP in that game. And when anybody sat down to pick an all-time NBA team, Bob Cousy's name was sure to be on it.

After his retirement from the Celtics, Cousy coached for six seasons at Boston College, the school he had almost attended eighteen years previously. His teams performed extremely well, twice going to the NCAA regional tournament and in 1969 losing to Temple in the finals of the NIT in New York City. His top players at BC were Terry Driscoll, who later played in the NBA, all-time school scoring leader John Austin, Jimmy O'Brien, who played in the ABA, and play-maker Billy Evans.

Cousy's record with the Eagles was 117–38, with four seasons of 20 victories or more. However, the recruiting game—promise them anything but get them to your school—gnawed at Cousy, and in 1968, he resigned from Boston College. For the first time in twenty-five years, he would be away from the game that had been so much of his life.

Not for long. The competitive spirit that raged within him wouldn't stay quiet. The pros came calling, and after turning down a job to coach the New York Nets of the ABA, he took one, at more than $100,000 a year, to coach the Cincinnati Royals of the NBA.

The Royals, despite the presence of Oscar Robertson, Jerry Lucas, and Tom Van Arsdale, and later, of Tiny Archibald, were not a solid team, and no amount of coaching could make them one.

But if the Royals couldn't attract people to the old barn in Cincinnati that was their home, owner Max Jacobs thought that the name Bob Cousy might. To entice fans further, it was widely publicized that Cousy would return to active status. At forty-one, he would be a player, oldest in the history of the league.

The hitch in this was that technically Cousy was still the property of the Celtics, and there would be several go-rounds with the stubborn Red Auerbach before Cousy could be activated.

Meanwhile, the name of perhaps the greatest player in basketball history did not seem to be turning on the fans of Cincinnati. The Royals had averaged six thousand per game the previous season, and that's about what they got for Cousy's opener against the Knicks, which the Royals lost.

However, the team then flew to Boston, and in Cousy's first joust back home against the Celtics, the Royals prevailed, 110–108.

Cousy the coach didn't become Cousy the player until December of 1969, and in order to activate him, the Royals had to make a trade with the Celtics.

"Cousy is still our property," Auerbach insisted. "If you want him, you'll have to deal with us."

Said Cousy: "I think this has kind of chipped away at a friendship established twenty years ago." But if there was animosity, it didn't last long. The bond of twenty years was too strong for that.

The coach, wearing Number 19 because Robertson wore Number 14, played in only 7 games for a total of thirty-four minutes, and was a factor in only 1, a 106–105 loss to the Knicks.

After three seasons in Cincinnati the Royals moved to Kansas City, and Cousy, who had thought seriously of resigning, instead moved with them.

The K.C.–Omaha Royals, with Archibald leading the league in scoring (30 points per game) and assists (11 a game), were an improvement over the Cincinnati version, but still finished under .500, at 36–46.

The summer after his first season in Kansas City, Cousy was named coach of an AAU team that would play a 6-game series against the Soviets' 1972 Olympic champions. He had an exceptional bunch of kids, including future pros Bill Walton, Sven Nater, Ernie DeGregorio, Tommy Henderson, Ron Behagen, Fred Saunders, and Bobby Jones.

Walton was injured early in the first game of the series and did not play again. The American stars won the series, 4 games to 2, with the nation watching on television a marvelous victory for the United States in game five from Madison Square Garden.

However, Cousy the professional coach was facing what the pop psychiatrists call a midlife crisis. His family had grown up without his really noticing. The common, everyday things that affected most husbands and fathers had almost passed him by.

After training camp in the fall of '73, he told the Royals' general manager Joe Axelson he wanted to resign. Axelson persuaded him to stay the season.

But Cousy didn't make the entire season. Archibald injured his foot early and was out for the year, and without him, the Royals were lost.

On the night before Thanksgiving, the Sixers walloped the Royals, 103–90. It was Cousy's last game as coach. He resigned. The flame had finally gone out, or at least had been smothered.

Cousy remained on the fringe of basketball afterward, of course. You don't stop eating after you give up pizza. He became the TV analyst for college games in the Worcester area, and later for Celtics games, and drew high praise for his candid comments.

The pro game was truly bigtime by 1980. The average salary was $97,000 a year, with the stars of the game making seven or eight times that. The league had expanded to 23 teams by 1980 and the play-offs ran almost to June.

And it would be well to remember that the man who lit the fire to the modern era was the one nobody wanted, the French-American from Long Island whose name was picked out of a hat in a Chicago hotel in 1950.

"Hey kid, who d'ya think ya are, Bob Cousy?"

CHAPTER 4

"THE MAN WHO CHANGED BASKETBALL"

BILL RUSSELL

"Before Russell leaves this town, the Boston Celtics will dominate basketball as no team, not even the Lakers with Mikan, ever dominated it."
— *Boston Globe* editor Jerry Nason,
after Bill Russell's rookie season

He was not your Dick-and-Jane storybook hero. You'd never find him between the covers of *Frank Merriwell Stars for the Home Five*.

Bill Russell was outspoken, impatient, irreverent. He marched to a different drummer. No, more than that. He *was* a different drummer.

He was also, when he joined the Boston Celtics in 1956, young, gifted, and, hardly least of all, Black. Before he flicked a last enemy shot away from the basket, he would have led the Celtics to 11 championships in 13 years and be known as the best defensive center ever to play the game.

More, he would be known as the man who revolutionized basketball, changed it as much as did the elimination of the double dribble or the adoption of the twenty-four-second rule.

Until Russell came along, a pro basketball center had two physical characteristics, bigness and slowness. These characteristics made him a center. If you were bigger than anyone else on the floor, it logically followed that you would have a better chance of scoring more points than anyone else. And because you were slow, you weren't asked to play much defense.

Big men and offense were synonymous. The big man got rebounds and sometimes scored off them. He took hook shots. He played the pivot and handed off so others could make lay-ups.

Guards played defense. Why else, after all, would they be called guards?

Russell brought a new style to the pros. He was as tall as most centers, but had better agility and quicker reflexes. And he played a thinking man's game. No goonball for William Fenton Russell. He got inside the opposition's mind, figured out their moves and how best to counteract them. Not just the man he was guarding, but any offensive-minded opponent.

He had an instinct and an awareness of everything happening around him, and could leave his own man to deflect what appeared to be a sure lay-up by another opponent.

"The eagle with the beard," poet–player Tom Meschery called Russell, and the description fit perfectly.

Russell's blocking of shots not only prevented an almost certain basket, it often started a sequence of events that led to a Celtics basket. Until he came into the league, most blocked shots wound up in the second row of the stands. It was enough that the basket was prevented. Possession of the ball was never a factor.

Russell carried that particular defensive maneuver a giant step further. He didn't block the shot so much as deflect it. He flicked the basketball away, not out of bounds, but back into the field of play, where, more often than not, a Celtic teammate would gain possession.

And since the opponent, suddenly called upon to make the transition to defense, was still in an offensive frame of mind, the Celtics were quicker at making the switch to the other end of the court. Thus, the transition fast-break basket was born.

Equally important was the intimidation factor. Once Russell had blocked a few shots, the specter was always present. The shooter never drove for a lay-up without the thought in the back of his mind that Russell might be swooping down out of nowhere. The result was that the man often changed his shot—arched it more, to keep it away from Russell's magic fingers.

After a few blocks, the magic fingers didn't even have to be there. The thought was enough to spoil the shot.

Nothing in the growing-up years of Bill Russell gave any indication that he would be a force in such a uniquely American sport. Born on Lincoln's birthday in 1934 in Monroe, Louisiana, he moved with his family to Oakland at the age of nine. His mother died when he was twelve and she was only thirty-two.

Russell was gangly and awkward and not much of an athlete in his subteens, in contrast to older brother Charlie, who became a basketball star at Oakland Tech. Bill tried out for football at McClymonds High but was cut. He tried out for basketball as a sophomore and didn't make that team either.

Enter junior varsity coach George Powles. Perhaps it is giving Powles too much credit to say that he looked beyond the tangled feet and ungainly body and saw raw talent, unlimited potential, and great desire. Perhaps what he saw was only a kid who desperately wanted to be part of a team.

Whatever, Powles issued Russell a jayvee uniform. To say that a star was born would be grossly overstating the case, although by his senior year, Russell was 6'5'' tall and the first string center.

He was not, however, somebody who brought the college scouts to the McClymonds High gym in droves. The most he ever scored was 14 points, and that in his final high school game.

A University of San Francisco scout was at that game, to look at a player on the other team. He came away impressed, not with Russell's scoring but with his rebounding and shot blocking. It was that game that first cracked open the door that led to an athletic scholarship, and eventually to stardom with the Boston Celtics.

Russell graduated from high school in midyear, and toured the Pacific Northwest with a group of California schoolboy all-stars.

In his entertaining and controversial book, *Second Wind*, Russell says it was on this trip that he really started to learn the game, and more importantly, the unique role he would play in it.

Russell watched the moves of offensive players and mapped out in his mind how he would defend against them. When the move came up in a game, he put his plan to work. He didn't imitate others, he created his own defensive reactions to offensive situations.

Russell, who calls jumping "one of the purest pleasures I know," first exhibited his leaping ability on that tour. When he returned to Oakland, he was a different, far more accomplished, player.

While he was gone, Hal DeJulio, the scout from USF, had come calling at Russell's house, asking Bill's father if Bill was still interested in attending college.

But the thoughts of continuing his education still seemed only a faraway dream, so Russell went to work in the San Francisco shipyard. DeJulio returned and arranged for Russell to work out in front of San Franciso coach Phil Woolpert, a workout that did little to enhance the nervous Russell's chances.

Afterward, he continued to work in the shipyard during the day, play basketball at night, and wait for the call he didn't really think would come.

It did, however, in the form of a letter saying he'd been granted a scholarship. Bill Russell, the skinny kid who only a few short years ago couldn't make the high school varsity, was on his way.

Two men were influential in helping Russell make the transition from McClymonds High senior to University of San Francisco freshman. One was freshman coach Ross Guidice, a former USF player, who spent long hours helping Russell improve his game.

The other was K. C. Jones, who would become a lifelong friend. The silent K.C. was Russell's roommate as a freshman, and spoke only when the subject was basketball. When it was, Jones would speak for as long as Russell was interested, which was long indeed.

"K.C. and I created a little basketball world of our own," Russell wrote in *Second Wind*. "Other players were lost in our conversation because we used so much shorthand that no one could follow what we were saying. Most of the players weren't interested in strategy, anyway. Basketball talk was mostly an ego exercise."

Russell, above everything else, was a winner. His high school team lost only 3 games. His USF freshman team went 19–4. And after a mediocre and dissension-riddled sophomore year of 14–7, Russell and winning became synonymous. San Francisco, in Russell's junior and senior seasons, had a remarkable 57–1 record and won consecutive NCAA championships. Then he played on the 1956 Olympic team that went unbeaten and won the gold medal in Melbourne.

And the Celtics of the Russell era made the finals in twelve of his thirteen years, winning the championship 11 times. If ever the phrase "sports dynasty" had any meaning, it was the Russell-led Celtics from 1956 through 1969.

Russell once said he always looked for the perfect game. He never got it, of course, knowing better than anyone the little things that went wrong on any given night. His personal best, he said, was a 65 rating on a scale of 100 for a game in 1964 in which he had more than 30 rebounds, blocked a dozen shots, and scored well. What more could he have done? Well, his report card, filled in by himself, showed some missed passes and missed free throws. Nobody's perfect. Ever.

Russell was not exactly an unknown when he got out of the University of San Francisco. The lanky, leaping center was the biggest Cinderella story on a Cinderella team. The pros were quite aware of his talents. Still, he was not the highly coveted superstar that a Jerry Lucas or Lew Alcindor or Larry Bird would be.

Red Auerbach had been tipped off to Russell long before San Francisco started its rush to NCAA glory. Bill Reinhart, who had been Auerbach's coach at George Washington University, had seen Russell as a sophomore when USF beat GW in a tournament at Oklahoma City.

Russell was "only" 6'7" then, and still not very coordinated, but Reinhart told Auerbach that the young man had great potential and to keep tabs on him. Auerbach appreciated his old coach's advice and respected his opinion, but didn't get to see Russell play until a holiday festival tournament in Madison Square Garden in Russell's senior year.

Auerbach's theory was that there was no sense scouting players you weren't likely to get, and if Russell turned out to be the gem Reinhart thought he would, the Celtics would not have a chance at him in the draft.

The Celtics' coach was at that holiday festival in 1955 not to look at Russell, but to check out a brash, offensive-minded forward from Holy Cross named Tommy Heinsohn.

In those days, each NBA franchise had what was called a territorial pick, meaning a collegian who had played within fifty miles of that particular franchise. Wilt Chamberlain began his career with Philadelphia as a territorial pick, even though he'd played college basketball at Kansas, a thousand miles from Philly. Eddie Gottleib, who ran the Warriors—some say he also ran the league—finessed the NBA into okaying Wilt as a territorial pick because the big man had played schoolboy ball at Overbrook High in Philly.

San Francisco met Holy Cross in the tournament semifinals, and Heinsohn did not have a particularly good night. Russell had read all week about the sensational local boy from northern New Jersey, and was determined to stop him.

The final statistics showed Russell with 24 points and 22 rebounds. Heinsohn managed just 12 points, only 2 in the second half, and USF won, 67–51.

For Auerbach, the game did not diminish Heinsohn's NBA potential. He knew the aggressive, crew-cut youngster had the right stuff to be a great pro, especially if he lost about 15 of the 235 pounds he was carrying. But Russell's performance opened Auerbach's eyes to what a unique talent he was, and it also made a believer out of Heinsohn.

After Russell was drafted by the Celtics, but while he was still an Olympian, there was considerable doubt as to how much input a defensive expert would have with Bob Cousy's fast-break team. Heinsohn helped soften the cynicism by touting Russell to the Boston press at every opportunity.

Auerbach actually got a double bonus out of that holiday festival game. He saw in K. C. Jones the perfect leader of the Celtic's full-court press, a hound of a player who would make the opposition earn every basket.

Jones was not a highly coveted collegian, so Auerbach figured to have little trouble drafting him. Russell, however, was another matter.

Auerbach had been impressed enough by Russell's performance against Holy Cross to do some further checking, an attribute that always kept Auerbach a half-step ahead of everyone else in the NBA.

He called Woolpert, the USF coach, who told Red that because Russell had been a track man, he'd have no trouble adjusting to the Celtics fast break. Pete Newell at the University of California reassured Auerbach that Russell would not be a liability as a shooter. Don Barksdale, who had played for Auerbach with the Celts, said that though Russell was skinny, he wouldn't be pushed around by the bulkier centers in the NBA.

Then came the clincher, from Fat Freddie Scolari, who had also played for Auerbach. Scolari said Russell was a terrible shooter, but then added, "He's also the greatest basketball player I ever saw." Scolari added that if Auerbach wanted somebody who could get the ball better than anyone in basketball history, Russell was the man.

These thoughts from basketball people whose opinions he respected were enough for the Celtics' coach. Now he had to work at having a chance to draft Russell. The Celts would pick seventh, and if the draft went along normal lines Russell would be certain to be gone by that time. However, Rochester, which was drafting first, figured that the Harlem Globetrotters would be offering Russell big money, and Rochester owner Les Harrison didn't want to compete with that.

When Harrison talked with Russell, he found the asking price was a $25,000 contract, very heavy cash in 1956, and too much for Harrison. He told Auerbach he'd draft Sihugo Green of Duquesne.

With Rochester out of the way, Auerbach now had to work on St. Louis, next in the draft. He offered the Hawks Easy Ed Macauley for their first draft choice. Macauley had been an all-America center at St. Louis University before becoming a Celtics star. In addition, he had a youngster in St. Louis who needed continual medical care, and so would welcome a trade.

St. Louis owner Ben Kerner made the deal, but also insisted on the addition of the talented Cliff Hagan of Kentucky, who was coming out of the army to join the Celtics. It was a deal, as they say, that helped both teams, but history shows that it helped the Celtics much more than it did the Hawks.

The worry about Russell joining the Globetrotters, incidentally, was groundless. Russell had no thought of letting his talent play second fiddle to clowning.

Auerbach didn't see his prize prospect play again until the 1956 Olympic squad took on an all-star team at College Park, Maryland. Russell's performance was so inept Auerbach wondered if he'd been a sucker to trade such obvious talent as Macauley and Hagan for a promise that might never be realized. Still, too many basketball-wise people had touted him, so Auerbach wrote off the bad performance as a severe case of nervousness.

The Celtics began the 1956–57 season without Russell, who didn't join them until after the Melbourne Olympics. He signed a one-year contract for $19,500 on Dec. 19, 1956, had his first pro practice at the Northeastern Universty gym, and on Saturday, Dec. 22, made his debut as a professional.

Russell came into the game midway through the first period and by halftime had picked up 3 personal fouls. In all, he played twenty-one minutes, took 11 shots and made 3, and missed all 4 of his free throw chances.

He would never be known as an exceptional shooter.

"Bill Sharman used to tell me he aimed at the front of the back rim before he shot," Russell once said. "I could never do that. When I shoot the ball, I just shoot it."

The highlights of his first game, however, would be a microcosm of his career. He had 16 rebounds in twenty-one minutes, and late in the game, blocked 3 straight shots by Bob Pettit of the Hawks.

The team Russell joined in 1956—he was the only Black on it—was a crowd-pleasing mixture of kids and veterans that had won plenty of applause but no championships.

There was Cousy, of course, and Sharman, his eagle-eye back-court mate. The rookie Heinsohn and rugged Jim Loscutoff were the forwards and veteran Arnie Risen the center until Russell came along. For relief, Auerbach had heady Andy Phillip, Jack Nichols, the left-handed dentist, Lou Tsiropoulos, Dickie Hemric, and Frank Ramsey, an all-purpose player from Kentucky who would, for the next few years, be known as the "best sixth man in basketball."

The team had averaged 106 points per game the season before to lead the NBA, yet had given up 105 points each game. They'd finished 6 games behind Philadelphia and had lost to Syracuse in the Eastern finals.

Obviously something was missing, and that something was Russell. Cousy now had somebody to start the devastating fast break. The Celtics could now cheat on defense because they knew Russell was in the middle to drop off his man and swat away seemingly sure baskets. The Celtics had found the missing piece to the puzzle. The dynasty was born.

Boston won 44 and lost only 28 in Russell's rookie season to finish first, 6 games ahead of Syracuse. They beat the Nationals 3 straight for the Eastern title and then faced the Hawks for the championship the first time a Celtics team had ever made it that far.

NBA final series are often among the most exciting events in American professional sport. Forgotten are the dreary, go-through-the-motion games of mid-January, as the two finalists go at each other like saber-toothed tigers.

The championship round that April of 1957 came down, as it often does, to one unforgettable seventh game. St. Louis had stayed alive with a 2-point victory in game six and came to Boston for the dramatic finish on Sunday afternoon, April 13.

The Celtics led by 7 going into the last quarter, the Hawks went ahead by 4 with two minutes left, and the Celtics jumped back on top by a point, only to have Pettit tie the game with five seconds remaining.

In the first overtime, Jack Coleman of St. Louis tied the game with nine seconds left. Sharman, deadliest shooter in basketball, had a chance to win it, but his jumper at the buzzer rimmed the hoop. Score, 113–113.

Heinsohn, who had scored 37 points, fouled out early in the second overtime. Still, the Celtics hung on and Ramsey put them ahead by one.

Then came two remarkable plays.

Remarkable play number one: The Celtics missed a shot and the Hawks began a fast break, with Russell seemingly caught under his own backboard. But as Jack Coleman went up with what seemed to be a cinch lay-up, Russell loped down-court and, seemingly from out of nowhere, batted the ball away.

Remarkable play number two: With one second left and Boston ahead, 125–123, St. Louis playing coach Alex Hannum took the ball out under his own basket and flung it the length of the court. The ball caromed off the far glass and into the hands of the remarkable Mr. Pettit, who was standing inside the foul line, perhaps 8 feet from the basket.

This was a shot Pettit could make ninety-nine times out of a hundred. This was the hundredth time. He had to rush the shot and missed it, and the Celtics were champions of professional basketball for the first time. It would hardly be the last.

Not everyone fell in love with the new NBA defensive force right away. After Russell had blocked several of Harry (the Horse) Gallatin's shots, the Knick forward, never one of Russell's favorite people, said, "Give him four or five years up here, and then I'll have an opinion. I've seen too many flunk out after a year or two."

And Gottlieb down in Philadelphia complained that Russell wasn't so much a great defensive player as he was an illegal goaltender. Gottlieb accused Russell of playing an illegal one-man zone. Russell denied the charge, and Auerbach, naturally, called it ridiculous. Supervisor of officials

Jocko Conlan agreed, saying that Russell was circumventing no rules with his shot blocking and defensive genius.

When Russell shut down scoring champion Neil Johnston of the Warriors, Johnston commented: "I just had a bad night. I don't think Russell did anything special to bother me."

In his fourth game as a pro, Russell grabbed 34 rebounds, only 5 off the record at that time. And he did it against a tall Philadelphia team, despite fouling out with eight minutes to go.

The Russell style hit the NBA like a bombshell, and capacity crowds turned out to see the new curiosity. In his first five games, he played before fifty-four thousand fans in an era when the average arena seated only twelve thousand and the average attendance was much less than that.

The early Bill Russell was not a wave maker. He signed autographs, and if he had thoughts about being a Black man in a white man's world—and he must have—he did not make them public. If he wondered about the merits of grown men making a living by running around in their underwear chasing a round leather ball, he kept it to himself.

But Russell's perceptiveness was not confined to a basketball court. He could see, feel, and hear the inequities, and just to make sure he knew, these inequities were sometimes painfully hammered home.

In November of 1958 the Celtics scheduled a regular season game with the Lakers in Charlotte, North Carolina. When the team arrived Russell was told he couldn't stay at the same hotel as the white players, and was stuck in what he called "the worst goddam fleabag I have ever been in."

He contacted Auerbach, who said he was sure there'd been a mistake and that it would be straightened out. But meanwhile, there was a game to be played.

Russell responded by saying that he didn't care about the game, he cared about segregation, and he did not want to play in Charlotte. Auerbach pointed out that he, being Jewish, knew a little something about discriminatory treatment of minorities.

"I know you're Jewish," Russell replied, "but your face is white."

Russell played that night, however, as did the rest of the Blacks—Sam and K. C. Jones and Ben Swain of the Celtics, and Elgin Baylor, Ed Fleming, and Bo Ellis of the Lakers.

But the incident was one more racial log on the fire that would flame ever hotter and brighter in Russell's soul. Ironically, the slur in Charlotte had come at a time when the U.S. State Department had just requested Russell to join other players on a foreign tour as a goodwill ambassador from a country that too often treated Blacks as second-class citizens, if it noticed them at all.

There was other organized nastiness. Name calling from the stands was the least of it.

In 1961, the team played an exhibition in Marion, Indiana, and the players were given the keys to the city. After the game, several players, Russell included, went into a half-empty cocktail lounge for a drink. They were told

they couldn't sit at a table without reservations, so headed for bar stools. The bartender told them the stools were reserved.

"Okay," said Carl Braun, a white player, "we'll have some beers standing up."

"Sorry, buddy, I can't serve you," the bartender replied.

One thing led to another, and the next morning Russell and party were in the mayor's office, demanding redress.

The owner of the lounge was there and was read a statute that said it was illegal to practice discrimination in a public place. That was that. No apology No fine.

"They gave us the key to the city," said Sam Jones, "but it didn't open any doors."

A week later the team played an exhibition against the Hawks in Lexington, Kentucky, where Ramsey and Hagan had gone to college. Sam Jones and Satch Sanders were refused service in a hotel coffee shop, and when Russell heard about it he was on the phone, checking planes out of Lexington. No amount of persuasion from Auerbach would change the players' minds, and the game was conducted without Sam, K.C., Satch, and Russell.

But the indignities that Russell suffered because of the color of his skin did not appear to detract from his performance on a basketball court. Indeed, they may have spurred him on.

Ed Macauley, the man Auerbach traded to get the draft rights to Russell, may have explained the Celtics center's influence better than anybody. Macauley told Joe Fitzgerald, who ghosted Auerbach's autobiography: "To be a great shooter, you must be able to concentrate. There can be only one thing on your mind when you go up for a shot: the hoop. This is where Russell changed things. Now you had two things to concentrate on: the hoop and 'Where is he?'"

Russell's second season was almost a carbon copy of his first, with one glaring exception. The Celtics did not win the championship.

They had a 49–23 record, capturing the Eastern Division easily. Russell, who led the league in rebounds with 22.4 per game, scored 30 points in the contest that clinched the regular-season title.

Boston took Philly 5 games in the Eastern play-offs. In the middle 3 games, Russell had 25, 28, and 40 rebounds.

Then, in the third game of the championship round against the Hawks, Russell blocked a Pettit shot, fell awkwardly to the floor, and badly twisted his left ankle. Though the Celts prolonged the series to 6 games, the team was not the same without the big man to get them the ball. The Hawks wrapped it up with a 119–110 victory in a game in which Pettit scored 50 points.

It would be a long time before the Celtics came away empty again.

Russell had some new teammates in 1958–59. Phillip, Nichols, and Risen had retired. K. C. Jones came out of the army and 6'8" Gene Conley of the Milwaukee Braves came out of the World Series to be Russell's competent back-up center.

Bill Russell driving to the basket.

The Celtics record improved to 52–20. Russell averaged 23 rebounds per game, 7 better than league runner-up Dolph Schayes. Seventeen times he had 30 or more rebounds in a game.

Still, the Celtics almost didn't make it to the finals, as Syracuse had them tied in games at 3 each and were 16 ahead of Boston in the second period.

However, the Celtics chipped away at the lead, and even though Russell fouled out halfway through the last quarter, Boston prevailed. They then swept through the Lakers in 4 straight, the first time in NBA history that a championship had been decided that way.

Said Lakers coach Jim Kundla: "It's going to be a long, long time before anybody beats that crew over there."

Russell was still signing autographs then, mostly because everyone else did. But the practice seemed strange and demeaning to him. What did they do with those pieces of paper? Why was he under an obligation to sign them? Did the ones who asked for the autographs really care at all about Russell the human being, and vice versa?

In 1964, he quit signing, and overnight became, in the minds of many, the great but rude player who hated kids. That was okay with Russell. He was saying and doing other things by then that rocked the establishment boat.

"I very rarely answer my critics," he said. "I don't have to. I only answer to myself. I've set the standards I live by."

In 1960, though, the rebel in Russell was merely smoldering. He had a new basketball adversary that season, a mountain of a man whose name would be coupled with Russell's as long as the two were in the NBA together.

Wilt Chamberlain, 7'2" and 275 pounds, came off a year of barnstorming with the Globetrotters to join the Philadelphia Warriors. Chamberlain combined massive strength with agility. Get him the ball inside and he was virtually unstoppable.

There will be no attempt here to downgrade Chamberlain's abilities. He was a marvelous amalgam of power and coordination. He put together numbers that are likely to last as long as Dr. Naismith's game is played.

In his rookie season, Chamberlain averaged 37.6 points per game. In 1961–62, his third season, he averaged an incredible 50.4. Think about that. Fifty points every time he took the floor—the first and only point-a-minute man in the NBA.

Chamberlain scored 100 points against the Knicks in one game. He had individual games of 78, 73, 72, and 71. When he retired in 1973, he owned fifteen of the sixteen highest single-game totals in NBA history. Elgin Baylor's 71-point performance in 1960 was the only interruption.

Lifetime, Chamberlain averaged 31 points and 22 rebounds. On Christmas Eve, 1960, against the Celtics, he pulled down 55 rebounds, a record not likely to be broken. And in 1045 NBA games, Wilt Chamberlain never fouled out.

Those numbers are down in black and white in the Official NBA Register. But there are other statistics in there, significant ones. The cold print shows that in Chamberlain's fourteen seasons as a pro, the teams he played with won only 2 championships. Russell's won 11.

An argument can be made that Russell's surrounding cast was better, that Cousy, Sharman, the Joneses, Havlicek, Heinsohn, Ramsey, Loscutoff, Sanders et al., stack up better than those who aided and abetted Wilt. Perhaps, but not by a whole lot. Hal Greer, Luke Jackson, Chet Walker, Billy Cunningham, Wali Jones, Paul Arizin, Tom Gola, Larry Costello, Tom Meschery, Elgin Baylor, Jerry West, and Gail Goodrich were not exactly bums.

The real question is, would the Celtics have won so many championships if the situation had been reversed, that is, if Wilt had played for Boston and Russell for Philly, San Francisco, Philly again, and finally Los Angeles?

This is a little like debating whether Dempsey would have beaten Louis, or vice versa. You can argue either position with success. And yet, having seen the styles of the two players, a feeling exists that Chamberlain would not have made the Celtics the force Russell did.

Russell was the ultimate team center. Chamberlain quite simply was not, and when he did try to channel his enormous talents into a team style, he was not nearly so successful. Wilt could rebound, he could hand off, he could

Chet Walker, Bill Russell, and Wilt Chamberlin in action.

block shots, and he most certainly could score. But he lacked something—
call it a sense of purpose or of knowing what it took—that Russell possessed.

The first time Chamberlain and Russell met, in Boston, both came away
with impressive statistics. Chamberlain had 32 points to Russ's 22, but Wilt
took 21 more shots. Russell had 35 rebounds, Chamberlain 28. Who won? It
wasn't Philadelphia.

In Paul Sann's biography of Auerbach, *Winning the Hard Way*, Red says:
"I'm not taking anything away from Chamberlain's one-man offense. It was
something to behold. The question is, can you win with it? Can you use the
rest of your stars as nothing more than a bunch of highly paid errand
boys? . . . Maybe you can, but the records tell you what happens in the
process."

Auerbach always insisted there wasn't a player in the league that would not
rather have Russell than Chamberlain for a teammate.

The Celtics game plan for dealing with Wilt was not exactly revolutionary
or complex. They did not double or triple team him. They let him earn his
points off Russell, and the rest of the Celtics played their men one-on-one.

The Russell–Chamberlain duels of the '60s were marvelous to watch—
strength against agility, power against quickness, offense against defense.
And despite the intensity of the rivalry, Wilt and Russell were good friends,
at least until an incident in 1969.

The media made the rivalry a good-guy-vs-bad-guy sort of thing, with
Chamberlain the villain and Russell the one-for-all musketeer who would be
the first to rescue a basketball from a burning building.

But the fact is, the two respected each other's ability, socialized frequently,
and laughed at the wrestling-match headlines.

Then came the 1969 finals, Celtics vs. Lakers, teams tied at 3 wins each
and playing for the championship in the Los Angeles Forum. It was Russell's
goodbye game. He'd decided in midseason that it would be his last year.

The Celtics were ahead of the Lakers by 13 points with five minutes left
when Chamberlain hurt his leg and asked out of the game. Without him, the
Lakers cut the lead to almost nothing. Then Chamberlain asked coach Bill
Van Breda Kolff to get him back into the action. But the coach, incensed
because Wilt had taken himself out, refused. The game ended and the
championship drifted away as the two argued on the Lakers' bench.

Russell, who didn't feel Wilt was hurt that badly, had wanted him in there
so that the final victory would not have an asterisk on it.

"Wilt's leaving was like a misspelled word at the end of a cherished book,"
Russell wrote. "My anger at him that night caused great friction between us
later."

Chamberlain's version of the incident differed somewhat. He said that
after he'd been out of the game for about a minute the pain went away,
helped a great deal by the spraying on of a local anesthetic. Wilt said he
signalled Van Breda Kolff that he was ready to go back in, but the coach
ignored him. Twice more, Wilt said, he told the coach he was ready, and
finally Van Breda Kolff said "We don't need you."

Speaking in Wisconsin, that summer, Russell said, "Any injury short of a broken leg or a broken back isn't good enough. When he took himself out of that final game, well, I wouldn't have put him back in . . . either."

Chamberlain was stung deeply by Russell's criticism. At first he thought that perhaps Russell had knocked him on the spur of the moment, and that he might apologize when he thought the situation over.

But no apology was forthcoming, and the friendship between the two great centers ended the same day as Russell's playing career.

However, that falling out was far in the future in 1960, when Russell once again led the Celtics to a championship. Boston, helped by an 11–1 start and a 17-game winning streak, finished with a 59–16 record, best in NBA history to that time.

The Celtics beat Philadelphia and its awesome rookie in 6 games to take the Eastern finals, then went the limit against St. Louis before gaining the championship. Russell had 22 points and 35 rebounds in the final game.

"Bill Russell is a fantastic basketball player," said the Hawks' Pettit, who had battled him for four seasons.

Russell's all-time single-game rebound high, 51, came that season against Syracuse.

The next year the Celtics won 57 and lost 22, and beat Syracuse in the Eastern finals, with Russell scoring 25 points, pulling down 33 rebounds and blocking 6 shots in the clincher. Once again the Hawks were victims in the finals, this time in 5 games.

"He's in another world," said Alex Hannum. "There's nobody else like him."

Sharman retired and Sam Jones took over his starting spot. Bob Cousy retired and John Havlicek came along. Players arrived and left but always in the middle was the Force, and always at the end of a long season, another championship.

However, Russell was beginning to have doubts about his role in life, doubts that would nag at him the rest of his career.

"Up to today, my life has been a waste," he told Milt Gross of the *New York Post* in December of 1962. "I feel that playing basketball is just marking time."

In a talk to students at St. Mark's Social Center in Roxbury in June of 1963, Russell said: "I'm twenty-nine years old and haven't had a job yet."

Asked why he walked to center court when introduced, instead of dashing out as other players did, he replied: "Why run when you're going to run for forty-eight minutes? Besides, it irritates some people."

Russell irritated a lot of people with an interview published in the *Saturday Evening Post* in 1965. In it, he talked about the alleged quota system the NBA had for Blacks, saying, "Blacks have to be better players than whites to make the team. We [Blacks] have got to make the white population uncomfortable and keep it uncomfortable because that is the only way to get their attention."

He also lashed out at the be-nice-to-the-public image athletes were supposed to project.

"What I'm resentful of," he said, "is when they say you owe the public this and you owe the public that. You owe the public the same thing it owes you. Nothing. Since I owe them nothing, I'll pay them nothing. I'm not going to smile if I don't feel like smiling, and bow my head, because it's not my nature.

"I'd say I'm like most people in this type of life. I have an enlarged ego. I refuse to misrepresent myself. I refuse to smile and be nice to the kiddies. I don't think it's incumbent upon me to set a good example to anybody's kids but my own."

Well, sir. Talk about trampling on the American flag or spitting at Betsy Ross.

The love affair between Boston fans and Russell was considerably cooled. Russell was upset over the furor his statements caused, saying that he wasn't treated fairly in certain segments of the press.

"When I wrote that magazine article that I didn't like to give autographs, I meant to everyone, not young, white children in particular. I believe I owe Boston fans or any fans just my two hours in a game. If I choose to be noncommunicative it is to all people, not just white people."

But the damage was done, except that Russell did not consider it damage. He had spoken his mind. He would not be a hypocrite, talking out of both sides of his beard. He had said what he felt in his heart, and let the chips fall where they might.

"In the future," he said, "I'll never fail to speak my piece when I believe I'm right. In the past, I haven't been able to sleep after games because I couldn't get unwound."

Again, the off-court controversy did not appear to affect his play. The championships continued to come—five, six, seven in a row.

Then it was 1966 and Red Auerbach announced before the season began that it would be his final year as coach. He let everyone know in advance so they wouldn't think he was leaving on top. The challengers would have one last shot at him.

None of the shots would be a direct hit. The Celtics won their eighth straight championship, beating the Lakers in a dramatic seventh game. Russell averaged 23 points a game in the championship round, making an astounding (for him) 51 of 57 free throws.

After the first game against the Lakers, Auerbach sprang a real surprise. The coach for next season, he announced, would be William Felton Russell. He would be the first Black coach in an American professional sport.

At the emotion-packed Celtics break-up dinner that spring, the new coach posed for photos with the old one, and cracked, pointing to Auerbach: "This is what I'll look like twenty years from now."

In his talk, the new coach told his team: "I love you guys and I don't like very many people. I don't even like me most of the time. This championship has meant so much to me. It was for Red and for the memory of Walter Brown."

Russell also revealed his vulnerability, even while on top.

"One time this season," he said, " I didn't think I was going to make it. I get scared. I get lonesome. I get worried. I get scared of losing, and I get scared of winning."

Russell would not have a champion in 1967, his first season of coaching. The Celtics, though still formidable, were getting old, and though they had a commendable 60–21 record, Philly blitzed through with a 68–13 mark, the best ever.

And that April, Convention Hall in Philadelphia rang with the cries of "Boston is dead, Boston is dead." The Sixers, with Chamberlain, Greer, Walker, Jones, Costello, Cunningham, and Jackson leading the way, beat the Celtics in 5 games for the Eastern championship, then went on to whip San Francisco in the finals.

It was Chamberlain's moment in the sun in his rivalry with Russell. But even in victory, Russell's shadow haunted the big man. In Chamberlain's biography he wrote:

"When Boston was winning, it was always Russell who was responsible, Russell who made the Celtics a great team, Russell who beat me. But they wouldn't give me the same credit for our victory."

Fans were wondering if the thirty-four-year-old Russell had come to the end of the playing road. Chamberlain said, "The stupidest thing he ever did was to coach. He ought to quit and go back to being just a player."

But Russell had no such intentions. In September of 1967 he signed a two-year contract worth $400,000. And when the 1967–68 season was over, he had won his first championship as a coach.

The team finished second to the Sixers during the regular season and looked to be ready for the dustbin when Philly beat them in Boston, 110–105, to take a 3-to-1 edge in the Eastern finals. But in a comeback that was one of the most satisfying episodes of Russell's career, the Celtics won 3 straight—2 in Philadelphia, to eliminate the Sixers.

Then they took the Lakers, 4 games to 2, for championship number ten in the dynasty.

Russell, met by Coach Auerbach just prior to another win.

There would be one more banner hoisted to the rafters in the Russell era. His last team, the 1968–69 bunch, was not a great one. It was a curious mixture of old-timers such as Bailey Howell and Russell and Sam Jones, castoffs such as Emmett Bryant and Bad News Barnes, rookies Rich Johnson, Mal Graham, and Don Chaney, a nucleus of players in their prime, Havlicek, Sanders, Larry Seigfried, and Don Nelson.

This hodge-podge outfit limped home fourth, behind Baltimore, Philadelphia, and New York, and appeared to have little hope of lasting in the play-offs. However, some magic was still left.

The Celtics stunned Philadelphia in a 5-game blowout, and then surprised the Knicks on their home court in game one of the Eastern finals. That advantage held on throughout the series, and the Celtics advanced to the championship round against a Laker team that had won 55 and lost 27 during the regular season.

Los Angeles won the first 2 games, but lost the next 2 in Boston, the fourth one by a point. The teams traded home victories and the Lakers were a 5-point favorite in the seventh game at the Forum.

Jack Kent Cooke had loaded the Forum ceiling with balloons, to be loosed as part of the victory celebration. The celebration was never to be. The game ended with the balloons still tied to the ceiling, Chamberlain arguing with Van Breda Kolff, and the Celtics the winners, 108–106.

Russell had been named sportsman of the year that season by *Sports Illustrated*, and said, "This is the first trophy I will discuss with my children. A trophy of this kind is for being a person. It says to me, 'You've been a man. I respect you.'"

The season had been a strain, however, both physically and emotionally. He missed ten days in February after injuring a knee, and a trainer Joe de-Lauri said, "I've never seen him in pain like that."

In July of 1969, Russell decided to retire.

"If I continued to play I'd become a mercenary, because I'm not involved any more. I've played basketball for twenty-five years and that's enough for anybody."

Russell always had a sense of the ridiculous, and when he retired he said, "There I am, seminude before ten thousand, thirty-five years old, talking about who should take the shot to win a basketball game."

In February, Russell was voted professional basketball player of the decade, an easy winner. In 1974, he was named to the basketball Hall of Fame, and true to his code, did not show up for the ceremony.

The '60s had some great athletes—Sandy Koufax, Hank Aaron, Rod Laver, Cassius Clay/Muhammad Ali, Arnold Palmer, Bobby Hull, and Bobby Orr among them.

An argument, a very good argument, could be made that William Fenton Russell was the very best of the lot.

CHAPTER 5

"WHAT MADE JOHNNY RUN?"

JOHN HAVLICEK

"I'll be honest, He turned out better than I thought he would."
—Red Auerbach, midway through
John Havlicek's career

The first eight choices in the NBA draft of 1962 were big men, huge men, front-court people. None was smaller than 6'7'' and most were 6'9'' or better.

The selections went like this: Billy McGill to Chicago; Zelmo Beatty, St. Louis; Paul Hogue, New York Knicks; Chet Walker, Syracuse; Jerry Lucas, Cincinnati; Dave DeBusschere, Detroit; Wayne Hightower, San Francisco; and Leroy Ellis, Los Angeles.

Then it was the turn of the Boston Celtics. They were the champions, as usual, and their needs did not appear great. They had K.C. and Sam Jones and Bob Cousy, getting older but still the magician, at guard. Bill Russell, who made all the difference, was at center. They had Tom Heinsohn, Satch Sanders, and Jim Loscutoff at forward, and for instant offense, there was Frank Ramsey, the best sixth man in basketball. How could you improve on that cast?

"The Celtics take John Havlicek of Ohio State?" boomed Arnold (Red) Auerbach, cigar smoker, lover of Chinese food, and keeper of the dynasty.

Havlicek? John Havlicek? Oh, yeah, the kid that played with Lucas. Hatchet man, wasn't he? Why would the Celtics draft a hatchet man with Loscutoff on the club? Besides, Havlicek was only 6'5''—too big for a guard and not big enough for a forward. Where could he possibly fit in on this team?

Those who wondered didn't know about the perpetual motion part. They didn't realize that once Havlicek started running he wouldn't stop for sixteen seasons and would be regarded as the very soul of that most worn-out of sports expressions: "He came to play."

John Havlicek always came to play. Packed house or empty arena, crucial game or merely finishing out the season, April play-off or January yawner, Havlicek gave you a hundred cents on the dollar.

And in the process, he became one of the most admired of athletes in an America growing more cynical by the week, as big money and no-cut contracts removed the word "incentive" from the vocabulary of many professionals. It is not an exaggeration to say that Havlicek became the standard by which other basketball players of his time were measured.

There was, of course, more than 100 percent effort on Havlicek's part. Mere hustle would have brought pats on the back but little else. Hustle would have cloaked him with the mantle of greatness. There was production, leadership, and a performance under pressure that was always steady and often brilliant.

Havlicek became the one you looked to for the tying basket at the buzzer, for the dramatic steal of a pass, for the play that would ignite a comeback.

He was the first rookie in Auerbach's coaching career to be equally adept at playing both the front court and back court. Rather than being too small for a forward and too big for a guard, he was too quick for forwards assigned to play him and too big for guards given the job of staying with him. His so-called liabilities became his assets.

Said Bill Russell, in his book, *Second Wind*: "Havlicek is so good and durable in this role [playing either guard or forward] that if I were playing an imaginary pickup game among all the players I've ever seen, he's the first one I would choose for myself."

Havlicek's appearance changed over the years. He went from crew-cut to long sideburns to styled hair, from Ohio country clothes to big-city fashion. But the inner Havlicek didn't change. When he retired in 1978, he was still the same organized, tireless, patient, disciplined, self-motivated person he'd been growing up in Lansing, Ohio, where his father Frank ran a grocery store.

Lansing was a town—just a few blocks, really—on Route 40, about 150 miles out of Cleveland. The big deal in Lansing, if you were a sports fan, was listening to Indians games on the radio in the summer and rooting for the Browns in the fall and winter.

And, of course, playing games. Havlicek's childhood sounds like that of much of middle-America in the '50s—go to school, eat, sleep, and play the sport in season.

At the age of five, young John was shooting baskets underhanded at the playground. As he grew up, he and the Niekro boys—Joe and Phil—from across the street were always heading for some ball field or playground or gymnasium. Dreams of being a nationally known sports star never danced like sugar plums in his head.

"You didn't yearn for anything more than to repeat tomorrow the things you did today," he told Bob Ryan in *Hondo*, Havlicek's biography.

Those boyhood years sculpted the man Havlicek would become. Because both his parents worked, young John would often be home alone. He made the beds, he washed the dishes, he became . . . well . . . tidy and neat and organized.

And always, he ran. He ran to school, he ran State Route 40, from mile marker to mile marker. He had it all figured out. So much time to get home from school, so much time to eat, so much time to play ball during lunch break.

"He'd come home late sometimes," said Mrs. Mandy Havlicek, "and I'd ask him where he'd been. He'd say he'd been down at the schoolyard playing. I'd say, 'Who with?' and he'd say, 'Oh, nobody, just by myself.'"

There wasn't a background of sports in the family. His father, who had been born in Czechoslovakia, liked European sports—gymnastics, soccer, weight lifting. His brother was more of a cowboys-and-Indians kid.

"I don't know how John got interested in sports," his mother told Leigh Montville of the *Boston Globe*. "I just know he was always coming into the room, going to bed, throwing his balled-up underwear in the air and catching it, like it was some kind of game."

Havlicek's first coach was Al Blatnik, whose brother John had been an outfielder with the Phils. At nearby Bridgeport High ("I always made the teams I tried out for") Havlicek quickly became a three-sport star. He hit .480 and .450 his last two seasons on the baseball team. He could throw a football a mile and, as the quarterback, scored 3 touchdowns as Bridgeport beat Martin's Ferry, where Lou and Alex Groza played, for the first time in thirty years.

There was a parade in town and a day off from school as a reward for that accomplishment.

Though basketball was not as big as football in the scheme of things at Bridgeport High, Havlicek was the main man on that team, too. He went from 5'11" as a sophomore to 6'3" as a senior and led his unbeaten team into the state play-offs, averaging 30 points and 20 rebounds a game.

But in the first round of those play-offs, Havlicek and three other starters had the flu and Bridgeport went down. His last high school game was spent on the bench in civilian clothes.

The realization that perhaps he could cope in a basketball world outside Bridgeport hit Havlicek after he'd played on an Ohio all-star team that practiced in Middletown. Middletown was the home of Jerry Lucas, the most publicized schoolboy player in the country. Havlicek traveled through Kentucky, Indiana, and West Virginia with his all-star mates and more than held his own.

Four of these players—Lucas, Havlicek, Mel Nowell, and Gary Gearhart—accepted scholarships to Ohio State and became the nucleus of a team that in two years would win the national championship. Another young player, not part of the all-star group, would also be a decent player at Ohio State and would go on to much greater fame as a college coach at Indiana. His name was Bobby Knight.

With such a collection of talent, the Ohio State freshman games were better attended than the varsity's.

In Havlicek's sophomore season, Ohio State beat NYU and Satch Sanders in the NCAA semifinals, and then whipped California to win the championship. The Buckeyes went undefeated the next regular season, when Larry Siegfried was a senior, but lost in overtime to Cincinnati, 70–65, as Havlicek scored only 4 points.

Ohio State lost only 1 game in Havlicek's senior year, and again reached the finals of the NCAA, once more against Cincinnati. However, Lucas injured his knee in the semifinals against Wake Forest, and Cincinnati repeated its triumph over OSU, this time by 11.

In three college seasons, Havlicek had lost only 6 games, and in his senior year, made many all-American squads. Even so, he wasn't chosen for the Olympic team in 1960, a disappointment he classifies as his biggest in sports.

"I will never get over it," he said, "because you get only one chance. I knew I should have been there and I wasn't."

When Havlicek signed with Boston in July of 1962, he talked about how thrilled he was, and said: "I consider the Celtics the New York Yankees of basketball."

Still, there were early doubts. Havlicek had come to Boston while attending Ohio State, for a talk with Auerbach and Celtics owner Walter Brown. The neighborhood around the Garden did not exactly enchant a kid who'd come from an Ohio town of six hundred people.

"I arrived late one night," Havlicek said, "and there were winos in the doorways and no decent places to eat."

Before he signed with the Celts, Havlicek had had a try-out with the Cleveland Browns as a wide receiver, and that experience was also a contrast to his first impression of the area around Causeway Street in Boston.

The Celtics were as disorganized as Cleveland coach Paul Brown was organized. The place the Celtics played in was old, and the neighborhood was seedy, with screeching railroad cars, drunks, small bars, and constant traffic jams. The Celtics had a small office staff and seemingly ran their business out of a battered hat. And Auerbach, the boss man, seemed surly and short-tempered.

The atmosphere was just the opposite of everything Havlicek had known growing up. So even though he compared the Celtics favorably to the Yankees, Havlicek approached his new life with some trepidation.

He had almost caught on with the Browns, even though he hadn't played football in college. He'd decided to give pro football a try because the season was shorter and because he didn't think football was as strenuous as basketball.

"If those football coaches had been smart enough to make him a defensive back when he tried out with the Browns," said Auerbach, "we'd never have gotten him. Woody Hayes told me that if he'd been able to persuade John to play football at Ohio State the kid would have been an all-time quarterback."

Havlicek always felt that he could have made it in pro football. It would have been interesting if Brown had said to the rawboned kid with the big hands and 4.6 speed, "Young man, we think you can help us. Sign right here."

Brown didn't, however, and so we'll never know about the road not taken. Certainly it couldn't have turned out better than the path Havlicek did follow.

Fred Taylor, his coach at Ohio State, said about Havlicek: "I've never seen a boy practice so hard. From the moment he steps on the floor until I call a halt, he goes at top speed."

The Celtics would put that endurance to a test immediately, with interesting results. Jim Loscutoff, the team's enforcer, guarded Havlicek in one of Auerbach's no-holds-barred preseason scrimmages.

Up and down the court the two went, with Havlicek relying on hustle and Loscutoff on muscle. Eventually the exhausted Loscy and the bruised and battered Hondo effected a compromise.

"I'll stop running," offered Havlicek, "if you stop beating me up."

Havlicek and Bob Cousy worked well together. John never stopped moving without the ball and Cousy, who usually had it, would eventually hit his teammate with a pass at precisely the right time.

Cousy also ran a little test on the rookie in that preseason camp. He operated on the theory that every man has his breaking point, and so, in an intrasquad game in which the two were on the same team, the Celtics backcourt star decided to make the rookie work.

"I'm going to run him and run him and run him," said Cooz. And he was right. Every man does have his breaking point. Cousy ran himself into exhaustion while Havlicek, seemingly fresh as a mountain flower, waited for the next fast break.

Havlicek's endurance qualities were legendary by the time he retired.

"I try not to let myself think about being tired," he said after one of his forty-eight minute marathons. "If I do feel a little tired, I tell myself the other guy must feel the same way, too. You have to push yourself."

It became commonplace, toward the end of a game, to contrast Russell—sweat dripping off his beard, eyes hollowed with the strain of the action—with Havlicek,—looking as though he'd just come in from a walk on the beach.

But Siegfried, his teammate at Ohio State, never bought the "tireless Havlicek" business.

"Look at his nostrils after a game," said Siggy. "You could fit a half dollar in each one."

Havlicek spent much of his rookie season adjusting to Boston and to the way the Celtics did things. The team practiced at Babson College in suburban Wellesley. How you got there was your own business, but you'd better be there on time. Havlicek had purchased a car in Boston, but after watching the madhouse way the locals drove, he sent the car to Ohio.

The Celtics were a team coming off its fourth straight NBA championship,

"Hondo is always diving for a ball ... or ... or"—Jerry Lucas.

with some of the all-time greats on its roster. Yet there was no playbook. Auerbach would introduce a play, and Havlicek would write it down and memorize it.

Though the Celtics were in the middle of creating a dynasty, the Garden was less than half filled for most games. This was a culture shock to someone accustomed to playing before a full house in college.

Havlicek survived. He didn't play much at the beginning of the 1962–63 season, being primarily an aggressive defensive replacement.

Jerry Lucas says that the first picture that comes to mind when Havlicek's name is mentioned, "is Hondo diving for a ball, flying into the stands, or even hopping over the scorer's table to get at it."

Other teams would drop off him, daring him to shoot.

"Don't let them insult you," Auerbach told the rookie. "When you've got the shot, let it go."

"He was so unselfish in the first part of his rookie season," said Russell, "that he would always pass the ball, even when he was wide open. Everybody urged him to shoot more, and so one night, he did what they told him. He went out and put up 42 shots."

Havlicek, who always paid attention because he felt he could learn something, listened to his elders and his peers and did shoot more. He played a lot in the second half of that rookie season and finished with a 14 points per game average.

However, he was nosed out by Chicago's Terry Dischinger in the rookie-of-the-year balloting, a vote that so incensed Celtics owner Walter Brown that he matched the $200 prize given Dischinger by the league.

Late that season Russell was asked to assess Havlicek.

"He's another Frank Ramsey," said the Celtics center. "He has great ambition, he hustles, and is a wonderful competitor. I'm not saying he's going to be a great player."

Ten seasons later, Russell, now a telecaster, did a game in which Havlicek played forty-eight minutes against the Knicks, getting 25 points and 9 assists.

Again he was asked for an appraisal of his former teammate.

"He's crazy," cackled Russell. "One of these days he's going to find out he can't do that any more."

Teammates kidded Havlicek about his tidiness, his desire to have everything just so.

Tommy Heinsohn, first his roommate and then his coach, said, "He's the only guy I know who, when he unpacks, puts his socks on hangers."

When Havlicek eats a steak, he does so systematically, first slicing every bit of fat from the meat and pushing it to one side. When the procedure was mentioned to him, he replied, "You'd eat that stuff?"

He analyzed everything. Teammate Steve Kuberski said, "I'll be watching a football game and say, 'Hey, that was a great catch' and let it go at that. John will say, 'Oh, the defensive man didn't read his key right and the receiver ran a Z out and was wide open.' "

This detached, analytical approach enabled Havlicek to remain cool when all about him pandemonium reigned. He could take everything into account—how much time, the score, who had the ball, what the opposition might do, who the officials were—and at the same time, scrape away the nonessentials, just as he did the fat from a T-bone.

Cousy retired after the 1963 season, and Jerry Nason of the *Globe* wrote in his farewell to the Cooz: "They'll be having a day for John Havlicek before he's through."

There would be many a big moment before that time arrived.

Havlicek, though still not a starter, led the Celtics in scoring in 1963–64 with a 19.8 average. In the play-offs, Boston beat Cincinnati and San Francisco, losing only 1 game in each series, to clinch its sixth straight championship. Havlicek averaged 15.7 points in those play-offs.

Frank Ramsey retired in 1964, and Havlicek, who had been sixth man without portfolio during Frank's last season, now officially took over the job. He rarely started but was in the game early and, almost always, in at the finish.

The Celtics won again in Havlicek's third season, but wouldn't have except for the play that broadcaster Johnny Most made famous—the "Havlicek Stole the Ball" screech that ended the semifinal series with Philadelphia.

The teams were tied at three victories apiece, with the deciding game at Boston Garden. The Celtics had blown an 18-point lead, but had recovered to lead by a point with five seconds remaining. They apparently were home free, since they had the ball out of bounds.

However, Russell, throwing the inbound pass, hit a guy wire that supported the basket, a circumstance that led the Celtics center to say afterward: "I brought the game right down to the wire, didn't I?"

The situation wasn't quite so funny at the time. Philly now had possession of the ball out of bounds at their end of the court with the same five seconds left and Wilt Chamberlain camped under the hoop.

In the time-out huddle preceding the final play, Russell said, "Somebody bail me out. I blew it."

Here is the way Havlicek remembers those final five seconds: "It was pretty routine, historic only because of the timing and circumstances. In a situation like that, when a team puts certain people in, you expect certain things to happen. They had Luke Jackson, Red Kerr, Hal Greer, Chet Walker, and Wilt in there, so we expected a lob to Wilt, with Jackson going for the rebound."

But what Philadelphia planned to do was inbound from Greer to Walker. Kerr would then set a pick for Greer, who would get a pass and shoot.

"The official handed the ball to Greer," continued Havlicek, "and I started counting in my head. One thousand one, one thousand two, one thousand three. Greer still hadn't passed, so I knew something was happening behind me. Guys were getting pressured so that Greer couldn't get the ball to anyone.

"When that happens, you try to take advantage. I leaped, and when Greer did throw the ball, I deflected it back to Sam, who dribbled out the clock."

Most, high above courtside, began screaming into the microphone: "It's over. It's all over. Johnny Havlicek has stolen the ball. Havlicek stole the ball. He stole the ball."

Years later, when Most was honored, someone mentioned that the broadcaster had made Havlicek famous.

"Wrong," said Havlicek. "I made Johnny Most famous."

Was the play a gamble? If he'd missed the deflection, would Philly have had an easy basket? Havlicek doesn't think so.

"I had at least a foot between me and Walker. I was between him and the basket. If I played it right I was safe, but I'll admit that when I dropped it my heart stopped for a moment."

The Celtics took advantage of the escape and went on to beat the Lakers in 5 games for their seventh straight championship.

Heinsohn followed Cousy and Ramsey into retirement after the 1965 season. Now Havlicek was no longer the rookie, the smalltown kid from Ohio confused by the big city and the strange accents of the natives. By the 1965–66 season, though he still wore the sixth-man Superman cape, Havlicek was a veteran and a team leader.

In one way Havlicek was no different from anyone else who played for any length of time in the grueling NBA. He was susceptible to injury. Ironically, his first serious problem didn't come from a pro game. He tore a cartilage in his left knee while giving a clinic for the U.S. State Department after the 1964 season.

He was operated on that July, but, in a preseason practice, collided with

Havlicek is double teamed but gets off the shot.

Siegfried, and the knee puffed up again. During the season he had it drained fifteen times, but after rest in the off-season, he came back strong the following year.

Havlicek was relatively free of other injuries until much later in his career. Then they came in droves. At various times he had a cranky right wrist, tendonitis in the right knee, a bone spur, a bad right foot, and a damaged right shoulder that cost the Celtics a good chance to win the 1973 play-offs.

Havlicek hurt his shoulder when he ran into a Dave DeBusschere pick in the third game of the semifinal series with the Knicks in Boston.

The Celtics lost that game and were behind, 2–1, going back to Madison Square Garden. Havlicek, after a day in the hospital, went to New York with his right arm in a sling. When he walked across the floor to the bench of the hated Celtics, the Madison Square Garden fans gave him a standing ovation, a rare tribute to a visiting athlete.

Havlicek was touched by the reception.

"They showed they respected me as a player," he said. "They are the most knowledgeable fans in the league. They appreciated my style and what I had done."

Knicks coach Red Holzman, in his book, *A View from the Bench*, wrote: "It isn't often that a Havlicek comes along and touches the lives of sports people. He was the prototype of the perfect player and attitude. He was twenty-two when he entered the NBA and thirty-five when he left, and I never heard one harsh word about him or the way he played."

The Celtics, despite jumping off to a big lead, lost that fifth game in a controversial finish, and—without Havlicek—appeared done for. But when the teams took the floor in Boston for game six, Havlicek was in uniform. His right arm, packed in heat pads for five days, might not have been ready to play, but the rest of him was.

Coach Tom Heinsohn started Don Chaney and didn't put Havlicek in until the second quarter. He hit his first shot and his next, and though he did most of his passing and dribbling with his left hand, the Celtics hung on to win, 98–97.

In thirty minutes he scored 18 points and had 5 assists.

"He must have saints and angels following him wherever he goes," said Paul Westphal. "Out of the 8 shots he took, I think there was only one normal one."

The Celtics went back to New York and won again, with Havlicek once more playing a key role. However, the shoulder needed rest, not activity. He was able to use it less and less with each game, and by the time game seven rolled around, his right arm was virtually useless. The Knicks overplayed him, stole several of his passes, and beat the Celtics, the first and only time Boston had lost the seventh game of a play-off.

All that was in the dim future for Havlicek as the 1965–66 season began. It closed with another Celtics championship, but not before Havlicek had been shifted from his sixth-man role and made a starter, in the fourth game of a preliminary play-off with the surprising Cincinnati Royals.

The Celtics were forced to play in the prelims because they'd finished a game behind Philly in the regular season. They expected to breeze past the Royals, but after 3 games of the best-in-5 set, they were trailing, 2–1. That's when Auerbach, seeking some offensive spark, started Havlicek at forward in place of Willie Naulls.

The strategy worked. Boston beat Cincinnati 2 straight and then wiped out the Sixers, who had been lounging around for two weeks, in 5 games. The Celtics then went on to beat the perennial bridesmaid Lakers in 7 games for the championship. In 17 play-off games, Havlicek averaged 23.8 points.

When the Celtics won the seventh game, 95–93, at the Garden, Red Auerbach lit his victory cigar for the last time as a coach. He had announced his retirement early in the season, and during the Lakers' series, had appointed Russell to succeed him. One of Russell's first moves was to make Havlicek the team captain.

"As a playing coach," he said, "I figured I couldn't say much to the refs without getting a technical. John is a different personality. He could say things I couldn't."

Havlicek, playing all 81 games, averaged 21.4 points in 1966–67, the first

John with newly appointed player-coach Russell.

time he'd gone over 20. It was a good year for him and a good coaching debut for Russell, until the play-offs. Philadelphia, winning 45 of its 49 games of the regular season, was not to be denied at play-off time. For the first time in nine seasons, a team other than the Celtics was champion. For Havlicek, it was a new feeling as a professional. He'd known nothing but winning and success since he came into the league in 1962.

Havlicek was married in June of 1967, to Elizabeth Evans of Painesville, Ohio. Wedding guests at the ceremony in the First Congregational Church of Painesville included Auerbach, Russell, Bobby Knight, Jerry Lucas, Don Nelson, Tom Sanders, and K. C. Jones.

Beth Havlicek would be a familiar and pretty face in the Garden crowd for the rest of her husband's career. And when son Chris became old enough, he joined the Celtics family as a ballboy.

Champions die hard, and the Celtics—despite the Philadelphia Convention Hall "Celtics Are Dead" chant—weren't dead at all. Though the Sixers finished 8 games ahead of Boston during the 1967–68 season, they lost to the Celtics in a dramatic 7-game semifinal series. Havlicek rated that victory as one of the three best championships in his career, the others being 1969 and 1974.

He had averaged 20.7 points during the season and boosted that to 25.9 in the play-offs, but he remembers the postseason victory with such fondness because of the comeback the Celtics made.

Down 3 games to 1, with game five in Philadelphia, the Celtics' chances seemed slim at best. Russell told his team not to press, to just go out and stay loose and have some fun. And Havlicek, never really a rah-rah person but always a pragmatist, took a piece of chalk and scratched on the blackboard: "Pride might just be that little thing that can push you to get the money." Whatever pushed them, the Celtics beat the Sixers that night, and the next

and the next—the first time a team had come back from a 3–1 deficit to win a series. They then mashed good old Los Angeles in a 6-game final.

Havlicek played 291 of the 293 minutes in those 6 games with the Lakers. He fouled out of one game with a minute to play, and was taken out of the final one with thirty-eight seconds left, after scoring 40 points.

The irreverent Clif Keane of the *Boston Globe* was moved to write: "Two headlines you'll never see are 'Pope Elopes' and 'Havlicek Chokes.' "

Said Phil Elderkin of the *Christian Science Monitor* after the series: "If John Havlicek weren't real, he'd have to be invented."

Despite his brilliance, Havlicek never made the first all-star team in those seasons. His chances were hurt by playing both guard and forward. Oscar Robertson, Elgin Baylor, and Jerry West were automatic selections; the best Havlicek could do was second team.

By the start of the 1968–69 season, Havlicek was the acknowledged leader of a team growing old. K. C. had retired. Sam was thirty-six, Russell thirty-five, Bailey Howell thirty-two, and Sanders thirty, with bad knees.

Playing once more in every game (82), Havlicek averaged 21.6 points as these golden oldies struggled to finish fourth in the regular season.

Once again the Celtics tossed a surprise party, beating the Sixers in 5 games, the Knicks in 6, and the Lakers in 7, to make Russell's last year a successful one.

Volatile Bill Von Breda Kolff, the Lakers' coach, said after the series: "I see the television commercial that has the guy with the key in his back and I think of John Havlicek. I picture Havlicek asking Russell, 'What do you need tonight?' and Russell answering, 'Forty-eight minutes.' Then Russell turns the key, crank, crank, crank, and off Havlicek goes."

Havlicek was at the top of his game then—twenty-seven years old, a seasoned veteran of pro basketball, and one of the superstars of the NBA.

Enter, stage right, the American Basketball Association, a new league with a red, white, and blue basketball, a 3-point play, high hopes, and, allegedly, plenty of money. To make the venture go, the new league needed not only to acquire some graduating college hotshots, but also to persuade some of the best players in the NBA to switch over.

Havlicek, prime champion of the work ethic, would be a natural, and so the Carolina Cougars, in the summer of 1969, got busy.

Bob Woolf, Havlicek's agent, received a call from Jim Gardner, commissioner of the ABA. It should be mentioned that Woolf was not only Havlicek's agent, but also a friend and unabashed hero worshipper.

"You couldn't write a nice enough article about John Havlicek," Woolf told Leigh Montville of the *Globe*. "He is my idol. He's a perfect gentleman, humble, modest, a super athlete . . . I couldn't think of any individual who's more what an athlete should be."

Woolf was a skillful negotiator with sports management. If the ABA wanted to talk, he and Havlicek were willing to listen, even though they were negotiating a new contract with the Celtics at the time.

The Cougars sent a jet to Boston's Logan Airport to pick up Woolf, and then flew to Columbus to gather in John and Beth Havlicek. From there, the jet went to Rocky Mount, North Carolina, where all concerned registered at a motel under false names.

When Woolf was asked what would be a fair price for Havlicek's services, he answered, "Two million," figuring he might as well start off at a ridiculous figure and work downward. To his amazement, the ABA people talked a few minutes and then said they'd give John $50,000 for the next forty years, a two-million dollar package. Part would be cash and part investments.

Woolf was not happy with the investments arrangements and asked for two million cash, to be paid the way Havlicek desired. The ABA people said they would think it over.

Now Havlicek and Woolf had to return to Boston, to the lion's den. They had to tell Auerbach the news. Red had offered $105,000 a year and Havlicek was asking $125,000, so the two weren't that far apart. However, the ABA's offer had given the financial picture a new look.

The ABA kept calling Woolf, offering $400,000 for three seasons, with the added incentive that Havlicek would still get the money if the Cougars, or the entire league, folded, or if John were injured. It was a marvelous offer, $300,000 more than what the Celtics had in mind, even though their suggested contract would have been the biggest in their history.

Woolf's job had ended. He'd taken the negotiations as far as they would go. The decision was Havlicek's, whether to grab the money or take the lesser offer and stay with the establishment. Here is what Havlicek said, as described by Woolf in his book, *Behind Closed Doors.*

"Look, Bob, I've worked all my life and have always tried to do what was right. I never thought I'd earn more than $25,000. I just can't believe the money we're talking about, but to tell the truth, I love Boston. I love Red Auerbach and everything the Celtics stand for. I value my reputation. I value what I think is right, so my answer is this. Even if they offered me another two-and-a-half million, I would stay with the Celtics."

Corny? Perhaps. Idealistic? Maybe. But Havlicek's decision was a refreshing breath of air at a time when money and greed were replacing friendship and loyalty on almost every athlete's dance card. There was still a lot of Lansing, Ohio, in John Havlicek.

This is not to say that by staying with the Celts he had to immediately file for bankruptcy. His contract, from 1969 through the 1972 season, was said to be $500,000, the best in Boston at the time.

The Celtics, however, would not be the best in the NBA for a while. Heinsohn took over for retiring coach Bill Russell, but Auerbach could find nobody capable of taking over for the retiring player Bill Russell. There must have been times from 1969 to 1972 when Havlicek had second thoughts about staying with the sinking ship.

The Celtics' downhill slide, however, only made Havlicek's brilliance more noticeable. On a team that included Henry Finkel, Bad News Barnes, Artie Williams, and Steve Kuberski, Havlicek became a do-everything.

In 1969–70, the first post-Russell season, the Celtics finished sixth in the

Eastern division with a 34–48 record. However, Havlicek averaged 24.2 points in 81 games, a personal high. The thirty-year-old led the team in scoring, assists, steals, rebounds, minutes played, and free throws.

The next season, a wild-eyed, red-haired rookie named Dave Cowens made his appearance and the Celtics got back over .500, with a record of 44–38. That season Havlicek hit his all-time scoring average, 28.9 points per game.

When he went into his eleventh season, in October of 1971, the inevitable questions appeared. Reporters began asking about his basketball timetable. How much longer could he pound up and down the NBA hardwood? He replied that originally he'd planned to stay ten seasons and get on with his life, but that now he figured he could go a few more.

Still, he had averaged forty-six minutes a game the season before and thirty-five a game over nine seasons. Surely some of the moving parts were about worn out.

He admitted the game had become tougher. The big men were bigger, but more importantly, even the "smaller" men were bigger. When he came into the league there were three 6'5" guards, Oscar Robertson, Tom Gola, and Havlicek. Now there were at least twenty-five.

And a tiny bit of the motivation and game-day anticipation had also vanished.

"There are mornings now," he told reporters, "when I wish I weren't playing that night."

But then Mendy Rudolph or Earl Strom or Richie Powers would toss the ball up for the opening tap and the crowd would get into the game, and the adrenalin would start pumping again.

The Celtics, with a vastly improved Cowens, a silky-smooth Jo Jo White, and the nonstop Havlicek providing the impetus, got back into the play-offs in 1971–72, a remarkable return up the ladder from the chaos and confusion of a few seasons before. They won 56 and lost only 26, third best record in the NBA. Havlicek was still at his absolute best, averaging 27.5 points to finish third in the league, behind Kareem Abdul-Jabbar and Nate Archibald.

But the comeback wasn't complete, because, in the play-offs, after beating Atlanta, the Celts fell to the Knicks in 5 games.

The 1972–73 season was more of the same. The Celtics won 68 games and again whipped Atlanta in the first round of the play-offs. In the third game of that series, Havlicek hit an all-time personal scoring high of 54 points.

However, in the Eastern finals against the Knicks, Havlicek's shoulder collided with Dave DeBusschere's body, as mentioned some pages back, and the Celtics lost in 7 games.

Havlicek, who had been part of a championship team in six of his first seven NBA seasons, now had been on an also-ran for the last four. True, the last two Heinsohn-coached teams represented a return to the Auerbachian excellence, but when the buzzer had sounded to end the season, somebody else was wearing the winner's crown.

And Havlicek was now thirty-four years old. Bionic man? Maybe, but even the bionic man had to go in for a 50,000-mile check.

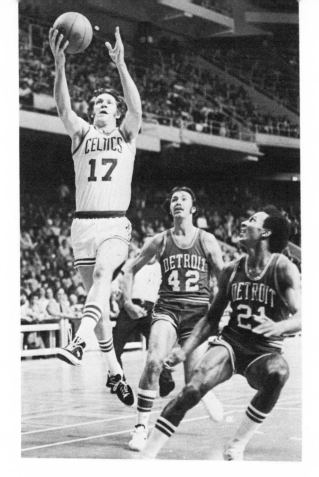

*Havlicek of the Celtics
against two Pistons.*

Havlicek proved he was far from finished in 1974 with a sensational performance as the Celtics regained the championship. They climaxed a remarkable return to the top by beating the Milwaukee Bucks of Kareem Jabbar and Oscar Robertson in a pulsating 7-game final.

Game six of that series was one of the most exciting of all time. Havlicek had sent the contest into double overtime with a rebound basket. With seven seconds remaining in the second overtime his swisher over Jabbar gave the Celtics a 1-point lead, and seemingly the victory. But the great center had the last say in this one. The Bucks got the ball to him in the corner and Kareem's sweeping 17-foot sky hook at the buzzer won it for Milwaukee.

The deciding game was played in Milwaukee, and the Celtics won by 15 points with a defense that swarmed all over the 7'4" Jabbar in the second half, holding him scoreless for an incredible seventeen minutes.

Havlicek rates that 1974 championship series, in which he was named most valuable player, as one of his top thrills in the sport.

"I can't ever remember being happier than when we won that final game," he said years later. With a couple of minutes left and the Celtics holding a big lead, Heinsohn replaced the regulars with subs, and as the final seconds ticked away, Havlicek, Cowens, Jo Jo White, and Don Chaney, players who only a few seasons before had been part of a team that was the laughingstock of the NBA, danced and hugged one another along the bench.

In the 1974 victory celebration at Boston's City Hall, Havlicek thanked the thousands who turned out and said: "There were times I worried whether Boston would ever accept us. And I wondered if I wouldn't have been better off in New York or Los Angeles, where pro basketball is really big."

He played his 1000th NBA game on Feb. 2, 1975, and received a prolonged standing ovation as he stood alone in the Garden spotlight at midcourt.

The organized, systematic Havlicek had altered his routine by now.

"I don't do a thing on the day of a game any more," he told a reporter. "I don't even wash the windows of my car, or sweep out the driveway or get involved with my kids. I'll autograph a few pictures, answer some mail, eat at 3 o'clock, take a nap, and play."

There would be one more championship season for Havlicek, in 1976, when the Celtics beat the Phoenix Suns in 6 games. The fourth game, won by the Celts in triple overtime, is the one most remembered—one of the great thrillers of NBA history.

Havlicek's big contribution to that was a one-hander with a second to go in the second overtime that seemingly wrapped up the victory, only to have Paul Westphal, now with the Suns, cleverly call a time-out.

Phoenix was assessed a technical for too many time-outs. White made the technical, but Phoenix got the ball at midcourt and Garfield Heard tossed a 22-footer that went through at the buzzer to tie the game. The Celtics, with White and sub Glenn MacDonald starring, won in the third overtime.

The year chopped Havlicek up a little more, however. He was out two weeks in March with a bad knee, coming back to get a season-high 38 points on April 12 in what he called the kind of game an athlete might have twice a season.

The last week in April he hurt his right foot and was on crutches as the opening round of the play-offs began against Buffalo. There was conjecture as to how much he could contribute, but once again Havlicek found a way. He soaked his foot in a bucket of ice on the off days, and didn't miss a game.

For his remaining seasons, Havlicek returned somewhat to the six-man status of his early days, though he played a dominant role on a team riddled with injury, doubt, and dissension. Ownership changed and the Celtics' one-for-all, all-for-one concept became shaky.

Midway through the 1977–78 season, the thirty-seven-year-old Havlicek made a decision, in the same organized, efficient way he'd played. He announced that this would be his last season, and was giving everyone advance notice so that NBA fans in the various cities could say goodbye to him, and vice versa.

And they did. They said goodbye and thanks. His last time into every arena became a John Havlicek Night, with a little gift, a standing ovation, a little speech, and a final wave.

On April 10, 1978, came the last Boston Garden hurrah, Havlicek's last game. He went out in style. He wore a tuxedo to the Garden, "because you wear special clothes for special occasions." When he came out on the court in the familiar Number 17, he trotted to the center circle and bowed low in four directions.

"It's the custom in foreign countries to bow like that," Havlicek said. "It was my own little thing."

His final game performance was also his own little thing. With the Celtics ahead of Buffalo by 7 points and 7.01 remaining, Havlicek moved from guard to forward and had his last fling as a Celtic.

He became the star at his own party. He hit from the corner, and followed with a 15-foot jumper. Then came a reverse lay-up and two more driving lay-ups. He missed a left-handed hook shot, but sank the rebound as the crowd went wild.

"The louder they cheered," said Havlicek afterward, "the more inspired I got."

With fifteen seconds left, Havlicek came out of the game, and the crowd, knowing they'd seen a special and gifted athlete in action for the last time, applauded for seven minutes.

When he retired, Havlicek had played more games than anyone else in NBA history. He was the all-time leading Celtics scorer, was second to Wilt Chamberlain in minutes played, field goals made, and field goals attempted, and third to Wilt and Oscar Robertson in points scored.

In October of 1978, his number was raised to the dusty Garden rafters to join the other illustrious uniforms.

"I'll tell you what was special about John Havlicek," said Red Auerbach. "He got the job done. Period. He didn't have a lot to say and he never made any waves, but he was someone we could always count on."

CHAPTER 6

"PLAYING WITH FIRE"

DAVE COWENS

"If David isn't aggressive almost to the point of being reckless, then he's not himself."

> —Celtics coach Tom Heinsohn in
> describing the all-out style of
> Dave Cowens

There is this stereotype of the professional basketball center. He is, first of all, Mr. Big. He is taller than a California redwood and bulkier than a refrigerator. He is King Kong, swatting away potential baskets as if they were toy airplanes swirling around the Empire State Building.

He is a heavy-legged plodder, trailing the play down-court, getting into position like a Percheron backing into its stall. He plays the game at eye level and hasn't gone to the floor in frantic, scrambling pursuit of a basketball since he was in the third grade, when he was only 6′ tall.

Into this Neanderthalic slice of the National Basketball Association in 1970 came Dave Cowens, breaker of the mold, destroyer of the stereotype. Just as Bill Russell, his predecessor with the Boston Celtics, had revolutionized the way a center played the game, so did Cowens give the position another considerable twist.

Cowens ran like a forward and hustled like a guard while retaining the basic qualities of a center. He could leap, get rebounds, block shots, score from in close, do all those things that have been a center's responsibilities since James Naismith nailed the peach basket to the wall at Springfield YMCA College.

But Cowens added some extras, bonuses that would not only help the Celtics win a couple of NBA championships, but that would also become his trademark, and, ironically, hasten his retirement.

He could either start a fast break or lead one, pounding down-court like a

92

runaway stallion—legs pumping, nostrils flaring, eyes bright as high-beam headlights.No Boston Garden floorboard escaped a Cowens knee-bone. To watch him dive after a loose ball was to see fury unleashed. Such moments, and they came often, were clinics on hustle, intensity, concentration, and all those buzz words that seldom escape the guidebooks they're imprisoned in.

No front-row patron was safe from Cowens's hurtling body, and even those in rows further back had best hang on to their hats.

Cowens, through relentless off-season practice after his rookie season, made himself into an excellent outside shooter, adding a considerable dimension to his effectiveness. Centers who had given him shooting room in his first year now had to come out and play him closely if he dropped back beyond the foul line. This opened up the area under the basket for his teammates.

Never before had the NBA had to contend with this brand of center. Players who performed as Cowens did weren't centers at all. They were forwards, which is what most critics expected Red Auerbach to change Cowens into eventually.

The redhead from Newport, Kentucky, was, after all, "only" 6'8½" tall, and, although that may be gargantuan in our workaday world, such a height was commonplace in the NBA, except at center. Center was for those 6'10" and up. Up could mean as high as 7'4".

The NBA didn't quite know how to cope with this runaway left-handed hybrid. Assign a bigger man to guard him, and by the fourth quarter the poor man would be stepping on his own tongue, while Cowens would still be going strong. However, put a smaller man on him, and the strong, rugged, 230-pound Cowens would overpower the 6'6" runt. He was Auerbach's diamond in the NBA rough.

However, when Auerbach drafted Cowens out of Florida State on the first round in 1970, nobody thought the Celts had come up with much of a gem. In the first place, Florida State was hardly what one could call a hotbed of basketball talent. In the second place, when Cowens was a junior, the Seminoles were placed on probation for two years because of recruiting violations. Consequently, few paid any attention to the basketball team—not that it had ever received much notoriety.

At the time, the Celtics were desperate for a center. In the 1969–70 season, they had played without Russell for the first time since 1956, and the absence showed. Oh, did it show. Using High Henry Finkel and Bad News Barnes as alternating centers, the Celtics finished with a 34–48 record, worst in twenty seasons. For the first time since the days of Connie Simmons, Jim Seminoff, Wyndol Gray, and Chuck (the Rifleman) Connors, the Celtics did not make the play-offs.

Plainly, what was badly needed was a Russell clone, a center who could anchor the team for the next decade or so. Cowens, a center–forward, did not seem the long-term answer, and even Auerbach admitted he had early misgivings concerning Cowens's best position.

"When I first scouted him," Auerbach said, "I didn't have any doubts about his future as a pro. But my original estimate was that he'd probably have to be a forward and fill in part time as a center."

Mal Graham, who had been a Celtics first draft choice out of NYU but whose career had ended after one season because of a blood disease, had scouted Cowens in Florida State. Graham told Auerbach and Tom Heinsohn he thought the kid could do the job as an NBA center.

The Celtics, picking fourth, might not have had a shot at Cowens except for a switch Atlanta made with San Francisco. The Hawks, who dearly coveted Pete Maravich, had exchanged draft spots with the Warriors and were selecting third.

Detroit, picking first in the draft, took Bob Lanier. The San Diego Rockets then went for Rudy Tomjanovich. It is likely that the Rockets would have taken Maravich if the Pistol's asking price hadn't been so high. When San Diego selected Tomjanovich, Maravich was left to the Hawks, and Cowens was available to Boston. Auerbach had twice maneuvered through the draft to get outstanding centers, once with Russell, and now, fifteen years later, with Cowens.

Heinsohn, still dubious despite Graham's reports, tested Cowens in some summer camp scrimmages with Don Nelson and Satch Sanders. Observed Sanders, when the elbowing was over: "We've got ourselves a horse."

Auerbach, to be doubly sure, called in the nonresident guru for a third opinion. He asked Russell for his analysis. Said Russell: "Forget Cowens's height and play him right where he wants. You won't be sorry, because nobody is going to intimidate this kid."

Cowens's first action against the people he would bump bodies with for the next decade occurred in August of 1970, in the annual Maurice Stokes Benefit Game in the Catskills. He was the most valuable player in a contest that featured some of pro basketball's biggest names, grabbing 12 rebounds and scoring 32 points.

Cowens became the number-one debate on the radio sports-talk shows during the winter of 1970–71. Some thought he was right for the job, and that his mobility and aggressiveness made up for his relative lack of height. Others, many others, looked upon him as a stopgap experiment, good only until Auerbach could come up with the real, 7', leaping McCoy in the next draft, at which time Cowens would be switched to forward.

The rookie, playing all but 1 of 82 games, averaged 17 points his first season. His aggressiveness not only made him seventh in the league in rebounding, with 15 per game (Wilt Chamberlain, Wes Unseld, Elvin Hayes, and Kareem Abdul-Jabbar were 1-2-3-4), it also earned him 15 ejections on personal fouls.

Cowens shared rookie-of-the-year honors with Geoff Petrie of Portland as the Celtics, with a 44–38 record, climbed back over .500 but for the second straight season did not make the play-offs.

Though Cowens had some fine shooting nights in his rookie season—he hit 36 points over, under, and around Jabbar in his best-scoring game—he was still unsure of himself away from the hoop.

"If there is one thing missing," said Dick McGuire of the Knicks, "it was outside shooting ... His range isn't that good."

Teams dropped off Cowens that rookie year and clogged up the Celtics' middle. Heinsohn continually harped on the weakness.

"You've got to take those shots," Heinsohn told Cowens.

"But I can't hit them," replied Cowens, who simply did not have the confidence needed to shoot from the perimeter.

"Then take 'em and miss 'em," Heinsohn said. "The more you miss now, the more you'll make later."

So Cowens spent countless hours that summer throwing one-handers from the circle. He'd go one-on-one with anybody available, and when they came up to guard against the one-hander, his quickness got him around the defense for a drive-in basket. He became adept at faking the drive and, as the defender sloughed off, stepping back and popping the left-hander. In that summer of 1971, he had added the final dimension needed to become an NBA superstar.

From the beginning, it was obvious that Dave Cowens was not your ordinary athletic hero. His life-style was more L'il Abner than it was King Farouk. He was about as far removed from the nouveau riche athletic cliché as it is possible to get. No Mercedes–Benzes or Bentleys for Cowens. No mink coats and penthouse suites with mirrors on the ceiling and assorted lovelies waiting in line.

Cowens drove a four-wheel-drive wagon. He lived in a garage apartment in Weston, wore jeans and work clothes, and his idea of a good time was sending out for a pizza.

Though he was good at analyzing a game, the young Cowens was uncomfortable with interviews. Consequently, he spent an inordinate amount of time after a game in the off-limits-to-reporters trainers' room.

Part of this shyness was because he had put so much of himself into a game that he had a difficult time coming back to earth. He also never quite came to grips with the star concept. To him, basketball was a game he enjoyed immensely, and at the same time a job he was well paid to do. He went out and played his head off for forty-eight minutes and that was that. Nobody interviewed a factory worker at the end of his day. Why should somebody who makes his living by chasing a round ball in his underwear be any different?

After he was named the league's most valuable player in 1973, Cowens was asked to comment on the award.

"It's a nice compliment on your work, I suppose," he said.

Cowens never acted like a celebrity. In June of 1970, after all the draft publicity and the interviews, but before his first season with the Celtics. Cowens played a game in the Boston Neighborhood League. The league was composed of high school stars and area collegians and games were played outdoors under lights on hot, dusty, asphalt courts.

He scored 20 points and pulled down 13 rebounds for the South Boston team in a 98–66 win over West Roxbury, and the next day in the agate-type

page of the papers the number-one draft choice of the Boston Celtics was rewarded by having his named spelled "Cowans" in the box score.

During his time with the Celtics, Cowens drove a cab, enrolled in mechanics school, attended a Christmas-tree growers' convention and bought a thirty-acre Christmas-tree farm in Kentucky, became an expert on organic gardening, covered the 1976 Olympics in Montreal for a newspaper, researched the origin of the electric chair for a Harvard professor, and hitchhiked from Boston to New Hampshire to help Larry Siegfried in his basketball camp.

Once, driving his four-wheel pickup at midnight after a home game, Cowens came upon a man named Bill Brennan, whose car had broken down. He gave Brennan, whom he didn't know from Adam's off ox, a ride home to Newton, and the next morning called to make sure the man was able to get back to his disabled vehicle.

The night following the NBA championship victory over Milwaukee in 1974, while the rest of sports-minded Boston celebrated, Cowens spent the night sleeping on a park bench in Boston Common.

He was . . . well . . . different, delightfully and refreshingly different.

He was also, in the mid-'70s, a dominant basketball player who treated every game as a crusade and played as though every game might be his last. In one play-off stretch, Cowens was in 13 games in 28 days, playing 597 of a possible 624 minutes.

"He can't play a whole career at that pace," Willis Reed of the Knicks commented. "No man can."

Reed was both wrong and right. Cowens did play his whole career at that breakneck speed, but, because he did, the career was shorter than it might have been if Cowens had paced himself.

Cowens always had a running battle with referees. He felt they never really understood the kind of game he played. The officials, on the other hand, felt he played with such intensity he didn't even realize he'd committed certain fouls.

"I make a lot of stupid fouls," he admitted, "but there are a lot called that I never really understand. I think they have to learn your game. They see me block a shot, maybe, and they think to themselves, 'He couldn't have done that without fouling,' and so they call one."

A side story of any important Celtic game in Cowens's ten seasons was how long the redhead would last in that particular game before being whistled to the sidelines.

Cowens averaged 18.8 points and 15 rebounds per game in 1971–72 as the Celtics returned to the top of the division standings with a 56–26 record. That was the year, however, that the Lakers won 33 straight, en route to a 69–13 record and eventual championship, the only one Wilt Chamberlain was ever part of.

Grabbing one of many rebounds against the Nets.

The Celtics lost in the Eastern finals to the Knicks, and Cowens, who averaged almost 5 personal fouls a game, took some criticism.

"He should block out everything people tell him and just play the game," said the Knicks' Dave DeBusschere. "He is a great player."

By the time Cowens's third season rolled around, he was an acknowledged star. His all-out style of play made him a favorite in Boston Garden and a villain to crowds everywhere else. To enemy fans, Cowens was the hit man, come to town to disable the fine upstanding athletes on the home team. Only Wilt, scowling and menacing, was more of a villain.

The score did not matter to Cowens. He played with the same intensity whether the Celtics were ahead by 30 or behind by the same amount. Red Holzman, the Knicks' coach, remembers Cowens picking up a fifth personal trying to stop a fast break when Boston was hopelessly behind late in the game.

The ferocity that burned within Cowens sometimes broke out in the wrong places. He got into a couple of off-season fights in bars, and once, when a fan came out of the stands and shoved him, he floored the intruder.

"I was pretty stupid that night," he said. "I hit him with my bad hand and made it worse."

The Celtics were merely sensational in the 1972–73 season, winning 68 and losing only 14 to finish 11 games ahead of the runner-up Knicks. Cowens was the leading vote getter for the East squad in the all-star game, and was named the game's MVP, an honor he also received for the season. He averaged 20.5 points and was third in rebounding to Chamberlain and Nate Thurmond with 16.2 per game.

However, the play-offs once again would be a bitter disappointment. After whipping Atlanta, the Celtics fell to the Knicks in 7 games, with John Havlicek's shoulder injury in game four the turning point.

Everything finally came together in the 1973–74 season. The Celtics, denied an NBA title since Russell's retirement in 1969, won the Atlantic Division with a 56–26 record. They'd been regular season champs three straight seasons, yet had not gone all the way the first two times. This spring they did, beating Buffalo in 6 games, the Knicks in 5, and the Bucks in a dramatic 7-game set.

The first play-off game with Buffalo deserves mention. Cowens had 10 points and 9 rebounds against the Braves at the end of three periods and the Celtics trailed, 81–69 on their home floor. If the Braves could negate that home-court advantage, a big upset was quite possible.

Then the volcano erupted. In the last twelve minutes, Cowens scored 9 baskets and 2 free throws for 20 points, 4 more than the entire Buffalo team. He blocked 2 shots, stole 2 passes, and grabbed 9 rebounds. He did all this despite playing the final ten minutes and twenty seconds with 5 personals. The Celtics won by 10 points.

That quarter of basketball was the quintessential Cowens, the one who operated on a different level. A bomb could have exploded next to him in those twelve minutes and he wouldn't have noticed.

Cowens averaged 19 points a game in his first championship season and was second to Elvin Hayes in rebounding with an average of 15.7.

In the championship finals, after Jabbar had tied the series for the Bucks at 3 apiece with a 20-foot skyhook in the second overtime of game six, Cowens was a key figure in game seven, played in Milwaukee.

This type of play made Cowens a "favorite" in Boston and a "villain" elsewhere.

With Cowens and a teammate constantly double-teaming and harassing Jabbar, Boston broke up a close game midway through the second half and went on to take the title, 102–87.

Cowens and the Celtics had another good season in 1974–75, winning the division once more with a 60–22 mark. Cowens, who missed the first 17 games of the season because of a broken foot, averaged 20.4 per game and was second to Wes Unseld in rebounding. But the team lost its play-off opener and home-court advantage to Washington in the Eastern Conference finals and never recovered.

The Celtics came back, though, in 1975–76, to win the last championship they would bring home in the Cowens era. They were 54–28 in the regular season and whipped through Buffalo, Cleveland, and Phoenix in the play-offs.

Cowens, who had played in 158 straight games from March 1972 to March 1974, was constantly on the go in those days, on his way to burning himself out. After winning the championship in Phoenix, he flew to Houston for some basketball camps, and followed that up with a two-week all-star tour of the Far East.

When he returned, he finished up some more basketball camps, and, when training opened, he was 10 pounds underweight. Worse, his enthusiasm for the game that had been his life seemed to be waning. Few gave it much of a thought, however, figuring that when the bell rang, the firehorse would be ready to gallop as usual.

Then, on the afternoon of Nov. 10, 1976, Cowens took an indefinite leave of absence. Just like that, out of the blue, with no warning whatsoever, he told Auerbach he no longer had the enthusiasm needed to play in the manner he was accustomed to.

Cowens made it clear that there were no problems with teammates or coaches, nor were there any physical problems.

"I just need time to work things out," he said.

He was twenty-eight years old and 8 games into his seventh NBA season.

"He's just sick of basketball. It's as simple as that," offered Don Nelson, perhaps the closest friend Cowens had on the team.

Celtics fans were mystified. Despite Cowens's denial, was it possible he was hiding a secret illness? Had he had a serious dispute with Heinsohn? Was he putting the pressure on to get more money? But the walk-out was just what Cowens said it was: he needed to get away from the game for a while.

"It came as a shock to me," wrote Red Holzman in his book, *A View from the Bench*. "Cowens was the last player I figured would walk away from the sport. I assumed he'd been having fun as the Celtics won, primarily because of him."

Cowens tried to downplay his leaving.

"I just feel like a normal person who has quit his job, that's all," he said. But of course, he wasn't a normal person, not in the sense of Joe Average who leaves a nonlimelight job. Wherever he went, he was asked if and when he would be back. He returned to the Florida State campus and played in an alumni game. He took a public relations job at New England Raceway in Foxboro, Massachusetts, "so I could see what it was like to work every day at a place you have bosses to answer to."

Several years later, he called what he had done "a selfish thing," but added, "the worst thing in the world is to be confused all the time, so I made my decision."

He said he hadn't left before the season began because even though he felt depressed during training, he thought his enthusiasm would return with the start of the season.

During this sabbatical, Cowens showed up at the Garden for a game in which the recently retired Nelson was being honored. His presence irritated some of the players, who had been losing more than winning in his absence.

"It teed me off, seeing him there," commented Jo Jo White. "Either he's one of us or he isn't."

Red Auerbach complained that people no longer said hello to him, but instead were asking, as soon as they saw the general manager, "Hey, what about Cowens?"

Then, on Jan. 12, 1977, the walk-out ended, as abruptly as it had begun.

"I thought he was coming into the office to talk about his job at the track," said Auerbach. "We talked for about half an hour and then he told me he'd decided to return. Nobody put any pressure on him."

Cowens said that it had reached a point where it was simpler to play again than to answer questions.

He made his return in typical Cowens style, riding to the game on a streetcar jammed with rush-hour workers. The game was billed as home-coming night, and 15,040 showed up to watch Cowens go against Bill Walton of Portland, not the easiest man to start a comeback against. Cowens played twenty-one minutes, and it was obvious that the lay-off had affected his reflexes and timing.

The excitement over Cowens's return was tempered for Celtics fans because that same night, guard Charley Scott slammed against the stanchion that supports the basket and broke his arm.

It was that sort of a season for the Celtics, who finished with a 44–38 mark and were eliminated by the Sixers in the play-offs. Cowens never really got back on track, averaging a career low 16.4 points per game and not finishing among the leaders in rebounds for the first time since he had come into the league.

The Celtics' slide down the hill of despair would gather momentum in the next few seasons, until in 1979 they reached the absolute bottom. Before that, however, in an incident with Mike Newlin of Houston, Cowens showed that the fires of righteousness and competitiveness were still burning.

For some time, Cowens had spoken out against what long-time Celtics broadcaster Johnny Most had called the Stanislavsky school of basketball, that is, blatant acting by players in an attempt to get officials to call personal fouls. Cowens, being rugged and not especially careful to avoid contact, was vulnerable to the Stanislavskys of the NBA.

He would brush an opponent and the player would recoil as though he'd just been hit by a truck. The more gullible officials would then call what Cowens considered a cheap, if not dishonest, foul.

One night against Houston, such a call was made, and Cowens was incensed. The breaking point had been reached. He decided that if this was the way it was going to be, those guys in the striped shirts would now see a real foul.

Newlin, the Rockets guard, was the unsuspecting victim of Cowens's intentional violence. The Rockets guard came dribbling up-court, near the scoring table, when Cowens roared alongside and flattened him with a body block. The redhead then turned to the official and said, "Now, there's a foul."

The Boston *Globe*'s Bob Ryan, though the staunchest of Cowens's admirers, did not think highly of what had happened. He took Cowens to task in a column headlined: "Shame on Cowens—His Act Indefensible."

Cowens was given equal time to reply and defended his action, saying it wasn't his intention to hurt Newlin. He said he did it to impress once and for all on referees, coaches, players, and fans that fraudulent, deceiving, and flagrant acts of pretending to be fouled when little or no contact was made is just as outrageously unsportsmanlike as knocking a player to the floor.

"I would not and never have taught youngsters to play other than by the rules, morals, and ethics of the game," he wrote.

In his well-thought-out rebuttal, Cowens listed these reasons why he disagreed with acting on a basketball court:

1. Pretending makes players think they can achieve their goal without putting in the work or effort.

2. Hostility arises among players who are being victimized by the actor's ability to make officials react instinctively to their action.

3. It distracts anyone who attends the game to study fundamental basketball skills.

4. It arouses fans who react vehemently to violent gestures or seemingly unsportsmanlike conduct.

5. If acting is allowed to continue, it will gradually become an accepted strategy and be taught to kids by their coaches.

In 1978, John Havlicek announced his retirement and Cowens was left with only the shell of a team that had won only two seasons ago. Management interference, dissension, and bad playing had forced the dismissal of Heinsohn as coach, and Satch Sanders finished up as the Celtics struggled to a 32–50 record. The euphoria of 1974 and 1976 seemed a million years in the past.

Fourteen games (a 2–12 record) into the next season, with the Celtics now owned by soon-to-be-Kentucky-governor John Y. Brown, Sanders was fired. A noon press conference was set up at the Board and Blades Club of the Garden to announce Sanders's successor.

Rumors were all over the place. Was Russell returning? Would Frank Ramsey come up from Kentucky? Would the first non-Celtic be named Coach? The answer proved to be none of the above, when the doors opened and in came Auerbach, a beaming Brown, and the new player-coach—Dave Cowens, grinning self-consciously.

Auerbach felt that by naming Cowens as coach he might restore some of the integrity the Celtics had once had.

"If they're gonna change coaches," said Cowens, "I'd rather be playing for Cowens because I know him."

The player-coach idea had brought two championships when Russell was the man. But he had championship personnel. Cowens was blessed with no such luxury. His supporting cast consisted of Marvin Barnes, Nate Archibald (recovering from serious leg surgery), Don Chaney, Curtis Rowe, rookie Cedric Maxwell, Billy Knight, Jeff Judkins, Chris Ford, and the still classy but growing older Jo Jo White.

Cowens the coach motivated Cowens the player, but the rest of the amalgam was not very successful. The season wasn't helped when Brown, without consulting Auerbach or Cowens, brought prolific scorer Bob McAdoo over from the Knicks. McAdoo was a terrific shooter but came into a bad situation and never fit into whatever mold Cowens was trying to create.

The Celtics finished last in Cowens's one season of coaching, with a 29–53 record, although at one point—just about the time the McAdoo deal was made—they gave indications they might challenge for a play-off berth.

The non-Celtic coach did arrive the next season in the person of Bill Fitch, a basketball dictator with a ready quip and an equally ready whip.

Cowens, relieved of his coaching duties, reported to camp in great shape and thus was a big factor in the dawn of the new Celtic era, the Larry Bird years. The redhead averaged 14.2 points as the Celtics won more games than anybody else in the NBA, a remarkable turnaround in one season.

The Sixers beat the Celtics in the Eastern play-offs, but would not do so in 1981, when Boston made a sensational comeback after being down 3 games to 1.

However, the 1981 accomplishments were without Cowens's help. He had reported to training camp on time and no one had any inkling that he was thinking of anything but the approaching season. Then, shortly before the opening game, he stunned Celtics fans by announcing his retirement at the age of thirty-two.

Just as Willis Reed had predicted several years before, the pace at which Cowens played the game had forced him out of it.

"The primary reason I'm retiring," Cowens said, "is that I have a highly weakened and worn-out set of feet and ankles and haven't been able to play a full season since 1976."

He said he went to training camp to give his feet a fair test and that they had flunked miserably.

"My right ankle is so weak," he said, "that I can best describe it by saying that I have a sponge for an ankle."

The abruptness of his retirement angered some fans, who had bought season tickets with the assumption that the redhead would be part of the team.

Cowens said he understood how the fans felt but that it would be more unjust to ask them to witness a deteriorated performance.

By retiring, Cowens gave up a lucrative contract that had a year to go, saying he did not want to be paid for going through the motions.

In an "obituary" column in the *Boston Herald*, Cowens outlined his reasons for quitting, and finished by stating: "I have enjoyed performing for you over the past ten years, while hopefully engraving myself into the history of the Celtics organization."

Dave Cowens did that, certainly, with an intensity, drive, and desire that few athletes in any sport ever matched.

At his retirement in 1981, Dave Cowens waves to the crowd after raising his numerals.

PART III

═HOCKEY═

The Bruins have been part of the Boston scene, and indeed the New England scene, since 1924, when a man named Charles F. Adams was awarded the franchise here, the first in the United States.

The first couple of seasons were tough going against the established teams, but in 1926, two big moves stabilized conditions.

Adams, desperately in need of strong players, bought several from the Patrick family, who ran the Western League. Among them was a defenseman named Eddie Shore. That same year, Adams pledged $500,000 to help build the Boston Garden, a building big enough to house the enthusiasts he hoped would come see his new Bruisers play.

And, over the years, they did come, so much so that the Bruins became a Boston sports institution. Through 1981 they had won four Stanley Cups and gradually established a reputation as one of the hardest-hitting teams in professional hockey.

The list of Bruins stars is an illustrious one and includes a quartet of legends: **Eddie Shore, Milt Schmidt, Phil Esposito** and **Bobby Orr**—who are chronicled in this Part.

Other extra-special Bruins include the following:

FRANK BRIMSEK—Mr. Zero...American-born goaltender who became a sensation after taking over goal in 1938...Scored 6 shutouts in 7 games...Went 231 minutes 54 seconds without giving up goal...Played through 1949.

BOBBY BAUER—Right-winger on Schmidt–Dumart Kraut line...Won two Stanley Cup champions...Retired to enter family business in 1947.

105

WOODY DUMART—Left-winger on Kraut line from Kitchener... Not flashy, but his hard shot was a perfect complement to more boisterous teammates... Held Gordie Howe to 2 goals with shadow tactics in 1953 Cup semifinals.

TINY THOMPSON—Four-time Vezina trophy winner as NHL's top goalie... Had 12 shutouts, 1.18 goal-against average in 1928–29... Voted to hockey Hall of Fame in 1959.

DIT CLAPPER—Played for Bruins twenty seasons... Was first team all-star three times... After ten years as forward, switched to defense on line with Shore... Voted to hockey Hall of Fame, 1945.

COONEY WEILAND—Scored 43 times in 44 games in 1929... After finishing with Bruins in 1939, became coach and directed team to Stanley Cup title in 1940–41... Later coached for more than twenty years at Harvard... Voted to hockey Hall of Fame in 1971.

BILL COWLEY—Perhaps smoothest play-maker ever to wear Bruins uniform... Four times NHL first all-star... A player's player... Voted to hockey Hall of Fame, 1968.

GERRY CHEEVERS—Great modern clutch goalie... Usually managed to give up one less goal than opponents... Wandered out of cage, took no back talk... Once ran up 32-game unbeaten streak... Owned string of race horses... Named Bruins coach in 1980.

JOHN BUCYK—Old dependable... Great at digging puck out of corners... Accurate, quick shot... Played twenty-one years with Bruins and chalked up 545 goals... Bruins' all-time leading scorer... Voted to hockey Hall of Fame, 1981.

Other fondly remembered names through the years include the following: Mel (Sudden Death) Hill, Herb Cain, Flash Hollett, Leo Labine, Hal Laycoe, John McKenzie, Bob Armstrong, Doug Mohns, George Owen, Bill Quackenbush, Derek Sanderson, Ed Sandford, Pat Egan, Don McKenney, Ken Hodge, Leo Boivin, Vic Stasiuk, Cliff Thompson, Eddie Westfall, Bronco Horvath, Tommy Williams, Jean Ratelle, Ferny Flaman, Eddie Johnston, Cal Gardner, Dutch Gainor, and Teddie Green.

CHAPTER 7

"GENIUS OVER ICE"

BOBBY ORR

*"People come in here with their maps and ask us to point out two places—
where did Bobby Orr grow up and where do his parents live now. We put a
couple of Xs on the map and out the people go."*
　　　　　　　　　　　　　　　—Leanne Scribner of the Parry
　　　　　　　　　　　　　　　　Sound, Ontario, Chamber of
　　　　　　　　　　　　　　　　Commerce in 1975

Boston is not a stranger to the sports superstar. It does not fall on its
weatherbeaten face every time a new phenom comes around the corner with
a scrapbook of high school clippings or a batting average of .310 in the
Eastern League.

The city has been around and has had more than its share of sports heroes,
but none has captured the hearts of its people more than Robert Gordon Orr.

Nobody—not Bob Cousy, not Bill Russell, not even Ted Williams—
received more all-out adulation and favorable press than this shy, crew-cut
youngster from Parry Sound, Ontario.

Orr played ice hockey for a living. That is like saying Picasso drew pictures
for a living. His was a style of hockey never before seen in Boston, or
anywhere else for that matter. Orr played the game with the grace of a
Bolshoi balleteer. He was Nureyev on skates. When he was into his game, the
Boston Garden was transformed into Swan Lake.

You didn't need to know a blessed thing about hockey to appreciate Bobby
Orr. You didn't have to be able to distinguish a blue line from a squall line to
understand that the moves and pivots he made on the ice were tiny works of
art. They were unique to him, his own creations.

Orr broke into the National Hockey League about the time players began
wearing helmets. The individuality that had distinguished one player from
another was now being hidden under a hat, and sometimes it was hard to tell
which one was Pierre and which one was Jacques.

Orr never wore a helmet, but even if he had—even if each player had worn bib overalls, a Lone Ranger mask, and a false nose—you'd have had no trouble singling out Bobby Orr.

Genius doesn't wear a disguise.

Orr had been in the NHL only two seasons when Bobby Hull—generally acclaimed as the best player then active—called Orr "the greatest player to come into the league since I've been here."

Veteran Ranger Harry Howell, after winning the Norris Trophy as the league's outstanding defenseman in 1966–67, Orr's rookie season, said, "I feel very good about this, especially since I may be the last guy to win it before they change the name to the Bobby Orr Trophy."

Howell knew what he was talking about. Orr won the award for the next eight seasons.

Bruins coach Harry Sinden, asked after a certain game if it had been Orr's best, replied: "How do you measure something like that? What do you call a best game for a player like this? Any time I answer 'yes', he comes right back with something better."

Orr added a dimension to the way a defenseman played the game. A few would make the occasional rush up-ice, but many more were brawny policeman types who protected their goalie and would think of offense only if there was an empty net at the other end of the ice.

An average defenseman's point totals at the end of the season might read: 4 goals, 17 assists, and 8 billion penalty minutes.

Orr's numbers were different, very different. He took his share of penalties, but his scoring totals were astronomical compared to other defensemen.

In 1969–70, for instance, he scored 120 points on 33 goals and 87 assists. The next season he was 37–102–139, and the next, 37–89–117. In 1974–75 he scored 46 goals and had 135 total points.

For many defensemen, 46 goals constituted a career.

However, Orr's genius would be flawed by the lightning that can strike both king and commoner. His career was plagued, interrupted, and finally ended by a series of knee injuries that forced him into retirement before he was thirty years old.

Athletes are considered in their prime in the 28-to-32-year age bracket. By that time, they've cast off the doubt and inexperience of youth for the maturity and confidence of midcareer. The record books are filled with statistics of athletes who had their best seasons in the 28–32-years-old range.

Yet, in 1977, after two seasons of playing hardly at all, Bobby Orr, his spirit as willing as ever but his left knee ravaged by six operations, said farewell to the game he loved to play and played so beautifully.

He was twenty-nine years old.

Orr was only twelve, a 5'2" 110-pound defenseman, when the Bruins "discovered" him in the small community of Ganonoque, Ontario. A story is always connected with the unveiling of a future legend, and the story that has come down from the mountaintop about Orr is this: Weston Adams, Milt Schmidt, Lynn Patrick, Harold Cotton, and Wren Blair of the Bruins hierarchy had gone to Ganonoque to watch the local team play a club from nearby Parry Sound. You begin scouting hockey players at an early age in Canada.

The Bruins party was there to investigate two kids named Higgins and Eaton. The group separated, sitting in various sections of the stands, and met at the end of each period to evaluate what they'd seen.

All any of them could talk about was the 110-pound Orr, who had played fifty-eight of the sixty minutes, sitting out the other two with a penalty.

"He owned the puck," said Schmidt, "even though his uniform was so big it drooped all over him."

In those days, you could squirrel away a promising youngster until he was ready for the pros. He could get experience in Canada's junior leagues and then the NHL team that owned the rights to him could sign him.

The Montreal Canadiens did not remain strong all those years because they drafted effectively. There was no draft, The Canadiens simply had a built-in appeal for every French-speaking teenaged hockey phenom in the province.

So the Bruins liked their little Parry Sound prodigy. Now, how to catch him, as it were, in their net?

As step one, the Bruins put some money into the Parry Sound team, paying for sticks, skates, and uniforms. and in 1962, Wren Blair convinced Bobby's mother to let her son play for a Junior A team the Bruins operated in Oshawa, a hundred miles away.

"Bobby wouldn't have to practice there or come to meetings," Blair promised Mrs. Orr. That pleased her, and so, on Labor Day, the Orrs signed a card with Blair, giving the Bruins exclusive rights to their son's hockey future.

The Orrs got something in return. Doug Orr received a second-hand car. The house received a new stucco job. There were reports of a $2800 bonus.

The Bruins at the time were the worst of the six teams in the NHL. If the kid was any good, it wouldn't take long for him to reach the top in that organization.

Orr had learned to skate at the age of four. There was plenty of ice in Parry Sound, where the temperature in wintertime went as low as 40 below.

When Bobby was five, he played in the minor squirts program, and even then made all-star teams a level above his age.

In his book, *Bobby Orr: My Game*, written with Mark Mulvoy, Orr tells how, as a ten-year-old, he would play all day and then after supper practice shooting against a target nailed on the garage wall. When he wanted to take longer shots, he'd open the garage doors, move back to the sidewalk, and fire away.

The pucks he shot were twice as heavy as ordinary ones because his father—a hockey player of promise as a youth who had been forced to put away his dreams after Navy service—had hollowed them out and filled them with lead.

Orr was an eighth grader when he began playing for Oshawa.

"If he'd weighed 175 pounds," said Milt Schmidt, "he could have played in the NHL even then."

Bobby Orr with Syl Apps Jr.

The drive from Parry Sound to Oshawa took three hours in decent weather and you couldn't count on decent weather in winter. Orr and his father often wouldn't get back to Parry Sound from a night game until three in the morning.

The eighth grader, now 5'6" and 135 pounds, scored 14 goals his first season. The next year, living in Oshawa and going to school there, he scored 30, and in his next, 34. Many of those he played against and with were five or six years older.

By this time, everyone in the tight little world of hockey knew about the prodigy from Parry Sound. Advertisements in the Toronto papers on the eve of the Memorial Cup tournament to decide the best Junior A team in Canada in 1966 warned, "Your last chance to see Bobby Orr play junior hockey."

The Toronto Maple Leafs reportedly offered the Bruins $1.5 million for the rights to Orr before he'd played a pro game.

But the big bad Bruins—more bad than big in those days—weren't about to deal away the future of the franchise. To sign him for the NHL, the Bruins had to dicker with Alan Eagleson, a young, aggressive lawyer who'd become Orr's agent in 1965.

Leighton (Hap) Emms will be only a footnote in Boston hockey history, but an important footnote. It was Emms, in his short term as general manager of the Bruins, who signed Orr to a contract. The historic event occurred on Emm's yacht in Barrie, Ontario, at 2:30 in the morning of Sept. 3, 1966.

The total financial package was said to be $70,000, an unheard-of amount for an NHL rookie. By tradition, rookies were supposed to be grateful for being allowed to play in the league. Money came later, and not a whole lot of that compared to other pro sports. But the money Orr received was the wedge that opened the vault for others, and in seven years the average NHL salary had shot from $15,000 to $70,000.

Orr came to Boston for the season of 1966 with more advance publicity than any athlete since Ted Williams had arrived with his bat and temper twenty-seven years before.

Orr and Williams were alike in some ways. Both were tremendously gifted, endowed with a natural flair for the dramatic, completely wrapped up in their work, and shy. Both would have played as hard before empty stands as they did a packed house. But whereas Williams smothered his shyness with outrageousness and immature demonstrations, Orr wore his shyness on his sleeve.

He was not much of an interview as a crew-cut, eighteen-year-old rookie, and though he became more polished and the crew-cut was transformed into a fashionable blow-dry style in later years, he would never be known as a conversational ball of fire.

His answers, though polite, were brief, and lacked the perception and wit reporters were after to take the interview out of the swamp of clichés and into a decent story.

However, right from the beginning, he was always good with kids. The shyness disappeared and the naturalness flowed through when dealing with innocence.

Orr was sensitive about being set above his teammates. Once, when a photographer from a national magazine asked him to go on the ice for pictures before the team started practice, he refused, saying he didn't want to upstage his teammates.

Asked in his rookie season what he thought about all the publicity, he replied, "I don't want anything more than the other players are getting."

Fat chance of that. After a decade of hockey nonentities in Boston, Orr was leaped upon by the media like a lamb chop tossed to the wolves.

He rarely criticized a teammate or opponent, and if any such stickiness was anticipated after a game, he retreated to the off-limits trainers' room.

This practice created the only controversy Orr was involved in with the Bruins, at least up to the disagreement with the Jacobs Brothers in the last messy days before he was sold to the Chicago Black Hawks.

You wanted controversy on the Bruins of those days, you went to Teddy Green or John McKenzie. You wanted humor, you went to Gerry Cheevers or Phil Esposito.

But if you were satisfied with a brand of hockey you had never seen before and weren't likely to see again, you simply kept your eyes on Bobby Orr.

Once Orr arrived, the perennially down-in-the-garbage-can Bruins became a big road attraction.

And it didn't take long for the fans or press to hop aboard the Orr-wagon. In a month they were saying he would be as great or greater than Eddie Shore, the Bruins star of the '20s and '30s, the man who had become the standard for rushing, bulldozing, fire-in-their-eye defensemen.

On opening night of the 1966–67 season, Orr got his first point, an assist on a goal by Wayne Connelly in one of only 17 games the Bruins would win that year.

Tom Fitzgerald, veteran hockey writer for the *Boston Globe*, wrote, "The high point of the occasion for the 13,909 and for the other Bruins was the calm and really major league job turned in by Orr, placed in as tough a spot as any boy ever to break into the NHL."

In the six years prior to Orr's arrival, the Bruins had finished last five times and next-to-last once. And despite his obvious brilliance, they still finished sixth, with a record of 17–43–10.

The next year, though, when the league expanded to twelve teams and two divisions, the Bruins were third in the East with a 37–27–10 record. It was the first time they'd won more than they'd lost since 1958. The good times had begun to roll.

Orr had 13 goals and 28 assists in his first season, and in the Calder Cup balloting for rookie of the year, received all but two of the votes cast.

There was trouble up the road, however, the first indication that even "immortals" are mortal.

In the summer of 1967, Orr, playing in a charity game in Winnipeg against a Canadian Nationals team, collided with Bob Leiter and stretched a ligament in his right knee.

The knee didn't require an operation, but was put in a cast, and Orr missed training camp, plus several early-season games in the autumn of 1967.

Then, in December of that season, he was hit by Toronto's Frank Mahovlich and was out three more weeks with a broken collarbone. The injuries were a prelude, a portent to what would happen to the left knee.

Orr was checked by Marcel Pronovost of the Maple Leafs in a game late in the year, and, when the season was over, had an operation to repair the damage to ligaments in his left knee.

Although Orr played in just 46 of the 81 games and scored only 11 goals, he nevertheless made the all-star team and played in the first Stanley Cup games the Bruins had been involved in since 1959.

By the time his second season was over, Orr was generally accepted as being the best player in the NHL. Harry Sinden, who had been brought up from Oklahoma City to coach the Bruins the year Orr joined them, went further than that. Said Sinden, "From the moment he came into the league, Bobby was the best player in it."

The surest sign of a player's ability is what his peers say about him. The great Gordie Howe, asked what he thought Orr's best move was, replied, "I'd say just lacing on those skates." Teammate Teddie Green said, "Hockey is a game of mistakes and Bobby doesn't make any." Said Milt Schmidt, then the general manager: "The question isn't what can Bobby Orr do, but what can't he do?"

Orr himself could not explain what he did that made him unique. His moves weren't planned, choreographed on some master sheet, and then run through on command.

"Hockey is a game of instinct," he told Mark Mulvoy. "After a game I sit in the dressing room and ask myself why I did certain things that night on the ice. Most of the time I have no answer. I had the puck at the other end of the ice and there were two players checking me pretty closely. The next thing I knew, I was all alone in front of the goaltender. I honestly do not know what I had done to get there."

Though Orr became the most prolific scoring defenseman in hockey history, it wasn't his prowess at putting the puck in the net that made him unique. Rather, it was his feel for the game, his instinct for being in the right place doing the right thing at the right time.

Bobby tangles with Toronto goalie Jacques Plante.

Carrying the puck up-ice, he was not a flyer in the manner of Montreal contemporaries Yvon Cournoyer and Guy LaFleur. It wasn't so much a feeling of, "Wow, look at him go!" as, "Here he comes and what's he gonna do?"

Orr had several speed variables and was able to shift into the appropriate one at precisely the right time. He would come across center ice at cruising speed, would be challenged by a defenseman, and would then somehow be beyond the man, still carrying the puck.

He did it by changing speeds, by faking one way and going the other, and by one of those marvelous reverse pivots that, until he came along, you saw only on a basketball floor.

Those who watched him thought he did it all by magic.

"When Orr is on the ice," wrote Chris Lydon in the *Boston Globe*, "it is his game, not because he dominates it, but because he seems to have invented it."

Pretty heady stuff for a kid not yet old enough to vote, but the best was yet to come.

In the summer following Orr's rookie season, general manager Schmidt pulled off the trade that would make the Bruins a National Hockey League force for the next decade.

In Boston, the trade would become known as the biggest heist since the Brinks job, and it would turn the Bruins into a goal-making machine.

There were other valuable additions. Derek Sanderson, a brash youngster who took no back talk from anyone, was the league's best rookie in 1967–68. Wayne Cashman, a tall, tough wingman not afraid to mix it up in the corners, came along the same season.

John Bucyk, a good player in the lean seasons, became a very good one in the fat seasons. Gerry Cheevers began to establish his reputation as a money goalie.

Hard-working, unsung Don Marcotte, feisty winger John McKenzie, steady Eddie Westfall, Dallas Smith, and Don Awrey were some of the key personnel on a team that would in the next few seasons lean heavily on the rest of the NHL.

And the spearhead of this band of hockey marauders was Bobby Orr, boy wonder. "Childe Bobby," *Boston Globe* columnist Bud Collins dubbed him, sent to lead the Bruins out of the wilderness and into the promised land.

The promised land was still a season away. In 1968–69, the Bruins finished second in the division, though they set a franchise high with 42 wins and 100 points in the expanded 76-game season.

They'd been wiped out in the Cup play-offs the previous season by the Canadiens, 4 games to 0. This season the Bruins lasted longer, hammering Toronto in 4 straight before once more falling to the unbeatable Candiens, who would go on to win the Stanley Cup for the fourth time in five years.

In April of that season, in one of those Cup play-off games against the Leafs, Orr gathered the puck along the boards and started up the ice. But inexplicably, Orr broke one of hockey's commandments. He skated with his head down, looking at the puck instead of at what was coming at him.

What was coming at him was Leaf defenseman Pat Quinn. Quinn leveled Orr with a resounding, crunching, and entirely legal body check. The Bruins star went flying through the air and landed heavily on the ice. The crowd first gasped and then, when it appeared that Orr was okay, the mood turned ugly.

"I hadn't seen so much potential for fan violence," said Schmidt, "since Rocket Richard stick-fought with Hal Laycoe in 1955."

Quinn had to have a police escort out of the Garden and though he later became a successful coach with the Philadelphia Flyers, he will always be known around the Boston Garden as the man who flattened the unflattenable.

In 1968–69 Orr scored 21 goals, had 43 assists, and got his first play-off goal, but another injury late in the season hampered his play-off performance and darkened the cloud hanging over his future.

Orr caught his skates in a rut in the ice at the Los Angeles Forum and again damaged ligaments in his left knee. The following summer, he had his second operation on the knee.

However, the physical problems would subside for the next three years, seasons in which the Bruins became the absolute scourge of the NHL.

With Esposito, Hodge, and Orr pouring in goals at a record rate, the Bruins finished second in the 1969–70 season and then won the Stanley Cup for the first time since 1941. Orr, playing in every regular-season game, scored 120 points on 33 goals and 87 assists and won the Hart Trophy as the NHL's most valuable player.

Teams did everything to try to stop him, including the ultimate compliment of using a player to shadow him throughout the game.

"I don't think putting someone on him is going to work," commented Woody Dumart, who often had the shadowing assignment when he played for the Bruins. "I wouldn't want the job, with all the moves Orr has."

He was called the equivalent of a T-formation quarterback who is a brilliant passer in the pocket and who is also extremely dangerous when forced to roll out and scramble.

The Bruins roared past the Rangers, the Black Hawks, and the St. Louis Blues in their charge to the Stanley Cup in the spring of 1970. They beat the Rangers, 4 games to 2, and then swept the next two series, winning 8 straight.

The Bruins outscored their three opponents, 65 goals to 33. Orr was routinely brilliant, with 9 goals and 11 assists, and won the Con Smythe Trophy as the play-off MVP. He climaxed the proceedings by scoring the winning goal of the deciding game against the Blues.

It was on May 10, 1970. The game, tied at 3–3, was thirty seconds into overtime when Eddie Westfall passed the puck to Derek Sanderson in the corner. Orr came roaring in from center ice, Westfall dropped back to cover the defensive spot, and Sanderson slid the puck over to Orr.

Bang, Orr pulled the trigger an instant before he was tripped by Blues defenseman Noel Picard. As the puck slithered past goalie Glenn Hall, Orr was airborne, flying across the goal mouth parallel to the ice after having let go the blast that turned the lights out for the Blues and lit up the skies for the fans of New England.

The famous game-winning shot by Bobby Orr that won the Stanley Cup for the Bruins in 1970.

"At first," recalled Westfall, "my feelings were numb. But then I just wanted to get hold of him [Orr] because it was such a dramatic goal at such a dramatic time. It meant so much to every one of us, and it was quite fitting that the guy who did more for our team than anyone all season had scored the winning goal."

The Bruins owned Boston now. Never mind that the Celtics were the greatest dynasty pro sports had ever known. The Bruins were Boston's boys of winter. If you had season tickets to their games in those days, you had a blank check to paradise.

Thousands of kids in the city and in the suburbs wore white, black, and gold sweat shirts with "Bruins" on the front, "Orr" on the back, and "4" under the name.

Because of the numerous frozen lakes and ponds, hockey had always been a popular winter sport for kids in the Boston area. Now the boom became unbelievable. Youth programs sprang up like dandelions in the suburbs. Squirt leagues, pee-wee leagues, midget leagues—nobody was too small or too young to lace on a pair of skates and wobble onto the ice.

Mothers got up at five on a Saturday morning to drive their demon defensemen to the indoor ice palace for their game. Fathers risked double pneumonia by standing in zero temperatures with a water hose in their hands, building a rink for their own Number 4s.

In the summer, the streets and playgrounds rang with the sound of sticks hitting the pavement in street-hockey games.

It was hockey overkill, the result of Bruins madness and the love affair with a young man whose scrubbed, boy-next-door image was a perfect antidote for those troubled times, when there didn't seem to be many boys next door left.

Wrote Chris Lydon, in his perceptive piece on Orr in the *Boston Globe*:

"He is above all Our Darling Boy, and he makes every spectator a protective parent. When a Detroit player was sent to the penalty box on a routine hooking call, a fan roared to the ref, 'Make that a two-and-a-half-minute penalty, two minutes for hooking and an extra thirty seconds for hooking Bobby Orr.'"

Tom Johnson took over as the Bruins coach for the 1970–71 season, Sinden having surprised everyone by resigning to enter private business.

For Orr, it was his best point-scoring year—37 goals and a record 102 assists for 139 points. The team kept pace, scoring a record 399 goals. They also gave up a team record 307.

It was a skate-and-shoot team, an "if you get 5 goals we'll get 7" offensive machine. Esposito's 78 goals and 152 assists were records that stood until further expansion in the late '70s made goals and assists as plentiful and cheap as free advice.

The Bruins had the best record in hockey, 57–14–7, losing only 4 of their 37 home games. Things looked good for another Cup in the trophy case, but it is a fact of sporting life—and perhaps of life in general—that just when the sun is brightest, the darkest cloud forms.

The Bruins had to face the Canadiens in the first round of the play-offs,

Bobby Orr—Number 4.

and though Montreal hadn't been particularly effective in the regular season, they were ready for their annual run at the Cup.

In a dramatic series highlighted by the spectacular goaltending of Ken Dryden and Gerry Cheevers, the Canadiens beat the Bruins, 4 games to 3.

Orr played every game that season and every one the next, when the Bruins climbed once more to the top of the Stanley Cup mountain. He had signed a five-year contract in August of 1971 and no one thought he would be with the Bruins for any time short of forever.

His totals for 1971–72 were 37–89–117, and for the third straight season he was named the league's MVP.

But in March of 1972, just a few days before the play-offs began, Orr took a hard hit in a game against the Red Wings, and the left knee ligaments were unstrung once more.

Orr was in 15 Cup games, getting 5 goals and 19 assists. However, he played on a knee that ached constantly and kept swelling up. In one game, Orr had to leave the bench and go to the locker room for ice-pack treatment.

In June, Dr. Carter Rowe operated on the knee, cleaning out the inside and smoothing rough edges around the cartilage area. This operation worried Orr more than the other two. The pain prior to it had been much more severe, and his play had been affected. He couldn't do the things he wanted to and this scared him. The after-effects of that third operation kept him out of the Canada–Russia series that September.

This was a highly publicized competition that matched the best in the NHL against the championship team from the Soviet Union. It also matched the NHL's hit-'em style against the passing and finesse of the Soviets. Orr would have given (if you'll pardon the expression) his left knee to be able to play.

But in Team Canada's training camp in Toronto, he found out the truth. The knee wasn't ready. It would fill with fluid and swell, and twice had to be drained. Orr fidgeted as Dr. Rowe told him time and rest were the only cures.

The Bruins' star thought he might be able to play in the 4 Soviet–Canada games scheduled for Moscow, but even that hope fell into little pieces when his knee locked during workouts in Stockholm.

So Orr concentrated instead on getting ready for the 1972–73 season, setting up a therapy routine that included skating, riding an exercise bike, heat treatments, and workouts under the supervision of Gene Berde, the well-known physical education expert who had whipped Carl Yastrzemski into shape for the 1967 impossible dream season.

Orr didn't play the first three weeks of the season. His first game back he scored a goal and didn't miss another game that year.

However, though he had a point production of 29–72–101, Orr was the first to admit he no longer skated the way he had as a teenager fresh in from Parry Sound. The injuries and subsequent operations were taking their toll.

Said Charlie Burns, of the Minnesota North Stars: "Bobby Orr is not the Orr of old. His knees won't let him be. He used to own the game, up and down the ice all night. Now he picks his spots."

Still, Orr remained the biggest sports name in New England. He was receiving a thousand letters a week, three thousand in the play-offs, and ten thousand on his birthday.

The *Globe* ran a "Letters to Bobby Orr" series. The letters were of the innocuous "Dear Bobby, I am eleven years old and want to learn how to skate backwards" type, but the series became the most popular feature in the paper.

In 1973, the World Hockey Association, which had lured away teammates Sanderson and Cheevers, made a tentative bid for Orr. The Minnesota Fighting Saints—known to some as the Fainting Saints—reportedly offered Orr twice as much as he was making with the Bruins. However, Orr was locked into that five-year pact with the Bruins, who surely would have brought the case to court if he'd broken the contract.

You could hear female hearts breaking all over New England in 1973 when, on Sept. 8, the boy wonder took himself a bride. He was married to Peggy Wood of Detroit in Parry Sound Presbyterian Church.

Said the Rev. Robert A. Crooks, who performed the ceremony: "I signed Bobby to his longest contract yet—til death do them part."

The crew-cut was gone now and so was the little-boy look. Orr's hair was styled and his face fuller. He was only twenty-five, but no longer the Childe Bobby of seven seasons ago.

The Bruins had a sensational 1974–75 season, losing only 17 games and finishing first in the Eastern Division. Orr, though nagged briefly by a bad leg that kept him out of the all-star contest, played 74 of the 78 games, getting 32 goals and 90 assists.. If he was slowing up, it wasn't apparent from his production.

The play-offs that year were climaxed with perhaps the biggest disappointment of Orr's career, except of course for the knee injuries that brought a premature end to that career.

The Bruins had breezed past the Maple Leafs in 4 straight and then whipped Chicago in a tough series, 4 games to 2. However, the old order was slowly changing, and so was the style of hockey that would win Stanley Cups. The Bruins still scored goals in clusters, but that wasn't always enough any more. A new brand of hockey had arrived, a physical style best exemplified by the Philadelphia Flyers.

In the early years of their existence, the Flyers had rolled over and played dead for the Bruins. Now they were the Broad Street Bullies and rolled over for no one, and they beat Boston in the Stanley Cup finals, 4 games to 2.

They won the deciding game, 1–0, with the only goal coming early and Bernie Parent turning back every Bruins threat.

With three minutes remaining, the Bruins threw caution in the trash can in an attempt to get the tying goal. And as they stormed the Philly net, Orr was whistled for a controversial interference penalty.

There were still two minutes, twenty-two seconds to go, but the season had ended.

Early in his career, Orr had told Harry Sinden that he didn't think he'd play past age thirty. Though he was still the greatest player in the world, that time was approaching. He would have only one more Bobby Orr type season before the bad knee took over for keeps.

In 1974–75 Orr played for his fourth coach. Don Cherry, a career minor leaguer who had carved a name for himself as coach at Rochester of the American Hockey League, succeeded Bep Guidolin. Bep, who had been at the helm for two seasons, left after firing a barrage of criticism at Sinden, who had returned as general manager.

At first, Cherry had trouble with his team of superstars and free thinkers. They had pretty much ignored Guidolin and did the same with Cherry. That would change.

Orr, playing in all 80 games, scored a career-high 46 goals and added 89 assists. But the Bruins, after finishing second in the divisions, went quickly in the play-offs, losing a 3-game mini-series to the Black Hawks.

It would be the last time Bobby Orr would play in a Stanley Cup game.

His contract was in its last year in 1975, and the World Hockey Association renewed its pursuit. Reports were that the Saints had offered Orr $5 million for ten seasons.

Bruins president Weston Adams said they couldn't afford to pay Bobby or anybody that kind of money, "even though no one loved Bobby Orr as a hockey player more than I did." Adams suggested that if the Minnesota offer were legitimate, Orr should take it.

Then, in August of 1975, the Storer Broadcasting Company sold the Bruins to the Jacobs brothers of Buffalo, who ran a sports concessions empire.

At first, everything seemed okay. Eagleson said the Jacobses offered his client $4 million for ten years, and the superstar went to training camp in Fitchburg a contented player.

The contentment wouldn't last long. Orr's knee gave out on him in camp and operation number four was performed in mid-September. Meanwhile, the Jacobs brothers had had a slight change of heart. Eagleson received a phone call saying there had been a slight misinterpretation on the contract, which had never been signed.

"I didn't misinterpret anything," said Eagleson. "He just wanted to get out of the deal and I told him if that's what he wanted, he had it. No deal."

The Jacobses reportedly had tried to insure Orr's knee with Lloyds of London, and Lloyds had turned them down.

Orr was still a Bruin, at least till the season ended. Shortly after he returned, the Bruins had a new look, thanks to Sinden's blockbuster trade that sent Esposito and defenseman Carol Vadnais to the Rangers for all-star defenseman Brad Park and smooth center Jean Ratelle.

If Orr could come back from operation number four, he would be paired with Park, the defenseman many thought would be rated number one in the NHL if Orr weren't in the league.

And for 10 games he and Park were an unsurpassed power-play team. Orr racked up 18 points in that span, but after a game at Madison Square Garden, he felt a twinge in his knee. Two days later, boarding a plane at Logan Airport, his knee locked and he couldn't straighten it. The next day he was operated on for a torn cartilage.

"Enough is enough," said Eagleson. "If he has to go through this twice a year, I'm going to recommend that Bobby call it a career."

Orr didn't agree. He got a key to the Garden, and every morning at 7:30, he'd come in for a skate. He'd lowered his weight to 180 pounds, but the knee still didn't feel right. The team, with Cherry now fully in command, was doing well, but the contract wrangle with the Jacobs brothers was tearing Orr apart.

He felt like an outsider and wanted to prove to the Jacobses that he wasn't just another player.

A new offer was presented, this one in writing. Orr would get $350,000 a year for five years. But the Jacobses would guarantee only $600,000 out of that package if something happened that ended Orr's career.

And if he did not pass his physical, he would get nothing.

Orr seethed over these conditions. He wanted more than ever to be back with the Bruins for the play-offs, and set a target data of April 6. But the day before he was scheduled to try again, he had an informal workout at the Garden and left the ice frustrated.

He called Massachusetts state treasurer Bob Crane, a close friend, and told him the knee was no good. When he tried to drive off the leg, he could get no power.

"He was in despair," said Crane. "He said he was going home, that he couldn't stand being around and not playing."

By August, Orr said his knee felt fine, and finally realized his dream of playing for the Canadian Nationals. In September of 1976, a month later, the knee would be irritated and sore, but he would still play well enough in the series against European all-star teams to be named most valuable player. When he scored against Czechoslovakia, it was his first goal since the previous Thanksgiving Day.

That series would be Bobby Orr's last hurrah.

The battle with the Jacobs brothers grew nastier. They obviously wanted to get rid of the big salary and the ravaged knees.

Eagleson took a hard shot at the Bruins' new owners. "I suppose Jacobs feels it would be crazy to give a kid a couple of million dollars when he has a questionable knee," said the lawyer. "But this kid is not a hamburger or a hot dog or a stale keg of beer. He's done everything they've ever asked him to do for the Bruins, and some people are forgetting that. He didn't get all those knee injuries playing for the Celtics. Bobby knows how he got them and he never believed anyone could treat him this way."

When Orr's contract ran out in June of 1976, he signed a lucrative contract with the Black Hawks, at $500,000 a year for six years. There were suits and countersuits, but the Bruins received no compensation for losing the best player in the game.

After ten seasons, the Orr era in Boston was over.

Jeremy Jacobs was quoted as saying he knew Orr's knee might be damaged beyond repair. He added that it had always been his philosophy that no individual was responsible for success in a team sport.

Throughout the dispute, the Jacobs brothers acted as if Orr was just another piece of damaged goods, or, as Eagleson had so aptly put it, "a stale keg of beer." Their participation was not a classic example of high-level public relations technique.

Bobby Orr played only 20 games with Chicago that year. He had three assists in his first game and was on the ice for all 6 goals the Hawks scored in their home opener.

However, the end was approaching. Dr. John Palmer of Toronto said, after an examination on Oct. 19, 1976, that Orr needed at least a week of rest.

"He's abused the knee by playing too much," said Palmer, who suggested things might work out if Orr played two games and then rested one.

On Nov. 2, Dr. Palmer said the bone had degenerated and the joint was permanently damaged.

"The knee has only a certain number of miles left on it," the doctor said, "and it's up to him to decide how he's going to use those miles."

Orr never did play another game in the Boston Garden, though he had played against the Bruins in Chicago. From time to time, the knee would buckle under him. Curt Bennett of St. Louis described the descent of hockey's best player this way: "Now you could chase him around the back of the net and catch him. Guys would be so surprised they'd done it they wouldn't know what to do next."

Orr said goodbye to the 1976–77 season after those 20 games, and in April consented to one more operation. Dr. Palmer called it major knee surgery, with removal of more bone chips and loose cartilage.

Bobby Orr night at Boston Garden on January 9, 1979.

Orr announced his retirement. He sat out the 1977–78 season and worked in the Chicago front office.

"I'd see Bobby coming out of an office out there in his three-piece suit," said Bruins trainer Dan Canney, "and I'd think, 'Wait a minute, this isn't right. He's not ready for three-piece suits.' "

Orr felt the same way, and in August of 1978 decided to give it one more try.

"Nobody tried to discourage me," he said. "They knew me too well."

But it was no use. There really was nothing left inside the left knee but air, and on Nov. 8, 1978, after 6 games with the Hawks and 2 goals, Orr called it a career.

"I'd need another operation," he said. "I have very little joint space in the knee. It's just bone on bone and chips keep breaking off."

Orr continued to work for Chicago, but on Jan. 9, 1979, came back to Boston for a day in his honor.

At a city hall celebration, Mayor Kevin White said, "He'll be described in years to come by people who never saw him play, as he passes from hero into legend."

Orr told the noontime crowd gathered at city hall, "I had tears in my eyes when I left Boston and I have tears in my eyes now."

He received a clock from the city. An inscription on the back read: "To Bobby Orr, who graced this city for too short a time, yet long enough to be remembered and revered for years to come. Thanks for memories which will last a lifetime."

That night, Orr was honored at the Garden, where once he had been king. When he shuffled onto the ice he was given an ovation that lasted more than six minutes.

"I love you all so much," he told the crowd. "The ten years I spent here were the best of my life." John Bucyk presented Orr with the familiar Number 4 jersey, and the crowd began a chant: "Put it on, put it on."

So he did, over the three-piece suit, and the Bruins sweater looked as natural as it had when he was performing his hockey magic.

In June of 1979, only seven months after his retirement, Orr was voted into Hockey's Hall of Fame. He was the youngest so honored.

Orr played 657 games in the National Hockey League, scoring 270 goals and 945 total points. In the play-offs he had 28 goals and 92 points.

But statistics will never be the way to measure the greatness of Bobby Orr. You won't find the grace of an Orr rush up-ice in a ledger, or the skill of an Orr pass in a calculator.

He was one of a kind, and to truly know what he was like as a hockey player, you had to be lucky enough to be there when he made it all happen.

CHAPTER 8

"MEN IN THE MIDDLE"

MILT SCHMIDT AND

PHIL ESPOSITO

"He hit to hurt."

—Con Smythe's analysis of
Milt Schmidt's style

"It's not how, but how many."

—Wayne Cashman's analysis of
Phil Esposito's style

Each was a big man and each played center for the Boston Bruins, but the similarities between Milt Schmidt and Phil Esposito stop right there.

The two performed in different eras, and the style of each was a reflection of their respective hockey generations.

Much of Schmidt's career was when the National Hockey League consisted of a 48-game schedule. In his time, the league had only six teams, the games were played close to the vest, and a center had damn well better know how to body-check.

Phil Esposito's heyday was a time of expansion. In his most productive seasons the NHL had jumped to a 78-game season and consisted of 16 teams. Something called the World Hockey League had obtained some topflight talent from the older NHL and the games were more wide open.

But each man's style was suited to his time, and each was the best in the league at what he did.

Schmidt came to the Bruins as the team opened training camp in St. John's, New Brunswick, for the 1936–37 season.

A somewhat shy seventeen-year-old, Schmidt, according to one story,

125

walked into the dressing room, told Win Green his name, and said that Mr. (Art) Ross had told him to ask for a new pair of skates.

Green said, "Just a minute," and checked out the request.

"There's a new kid here named Smith," the trainer said to the Bruins general manager and coach. "He says you sent him down for a pair of skates."

Replied Ross: "It's okay, Win, give him the skates. He'll be wearing them for a long time."

The story may be apocryphal, but Ross couldn't have been more right. Schmidt didn't hang up his Bruins skates until 1955. He played sixteen seasons with them, missing more than three others right in the middle of his career (mid-1942 through 1945) when he served in the Canadian Air Force.

He led the Bruins in scoring four times, in goals three times, and in assists twice. In 776 regular-season games he scored 229 goals. That may seem a piddling amount next to today's cash-register totals, but goals were not easily come by when Milt Schmidt was in his prime.

Anyway, numbers had little to do with his value on a rink. He was, in the best sense of the word, a presence, a force to be reckoned with.

"Milt Schmidt," observed longtime NHL president Clarence Campbell, "typifies everything a hockey player should be. He has heart, courage, speed, ability, and color, and provides inspiration to his team."

Schmidt grew up in Kitchener, Ontario, a town that had been called Berlin until World War I. During wartime, however, Teutonic names aroused strong anti-German feelings, and certain changes were made. Sauerkraut became "liberty cabbage," for example, and, through a similar thought process, Berlin, Ontario was renamed Kitchener, in honor of a famous British field marshal.

Kitchener was a hockey hotbed and the citizens were proud of its hometown team. Schmidt, when he was fifteen, was on the team and so were two other kids in town, players who would be identified with Schmidt for the next twenty years. Their names were Woody Dumart and Bobby Bauer, and the three would make up the most famous line in the Bruins' history, the formidable "Kraut line."

Bauer was left wing, Schmidt the center, and Dumart the right wing. The three played hockey together, socialized together, went off to war together, returned together.

Bauer and Dumart left Kitchener ahead of Schmidt, and joined the Boston Cubs in 1935. They kept touting Schmidt, a skinny sixteen-year-old, to Ross so much that Ross went to Niagara Falls to scout Schmidt in a game there.

Ross offered the last Kitchener kid a $2500 contract, but Schmidt said no thanks, he'd just as soon keep playing for Kitchener.

He signed the next year, but, after training camp, was farmed out to Providence. Bauer and Dumart, now with the Bruins, kept pestering Ross to bring their linemate up to the NHL. Finally, late in the season, the three were reunited, with Schmidt scoring 2 goals and 8 assists in the few games he played.

In his first full season, he had 13 goals and 14 assists, and in a couple of years he would, despite his youth, be a leader of an extremely talented group.

"Milt Schmidt typifies everything a hockey player should be."—Clarence Campbell, NHL president.

The Bruins of the late '30s and early '40s are rated by many as one of the three best hockey teams of all times, the other two being the Maple Leafs immediately following World War II and the Canadien teams that won five Stanley Cups between 1956 and 1960.

The Bruins of Schmidt's early years included such great veterans as the incomparable Eddie Shore, Dit Clapper, Cooney Weiland, and Tiny Thompson. They combined with such younger talent as Dumart, Bauer, Frankie (Mr. Zero) Brimsek, Mel (Sudden Death) Hill, Herb Cain, Flash Hollett, Jack Crawford, and Bill Cowley, a smooth, play-making center of whom sportswriter John Gilooly wrote, "He made more wings than Boeing."

As the 1930s wound down, the Bruins were obviously a team on the rise. They had finished first in their division in 1935, and second the next two seasons. They could not, however, sustain that excellence through post season play. They could not grab the handle of the Stanley Cup, and were, in fact, bounced out in the first round in each of those three seasons.

The Bruins had won the Cup only once, in 1928–29, when they skated past the Canadiens and Rangers without losing a game.

A decade after that, it would be the Bruins' turn again, and Schmidt was a big factor in the triumph. He will not, however, be remembered as much as Mel Hill, who beat the Rangers three times in the play-offs with sudden-death goals.

Schmidt, described as a hitter and a fighter with a prow of a nose, skated low to the ice.

"No other man skated at the tilt he did and was still able to make the play," said Art Ross. A quiet man off the ice, Schmidt never backed away from a confrontation.

When asked about his crushing body checks, he once replied: "I can't help it if those guys just keep running into my elbows."

Though he was a hard hitter, Schmidt was not highly penalized. The most penalty minutes he ever had in a season was fifty-seven.

Schmidt won the NHL scoring title in 1939–40 with 22 goals and 30 assists, and the Bruins, with a 31–12–5 record (20–3–1 at home) captured a division title for the third straight season. However, they would not repeat as Stanley Cup champions, losing to the Rangers in 6 games.

The Bruins came back in 1940–41 to once again roll over the league with a 27–8–13 record. This time, they kept going through the Stanley Cup competition, beating Toronto in a dramatic 7-game series and then wiping out the Red Wings in 4 straight.

The 1940–41 group would be the last Stanley Cup champions to represent Boston until the Orr–Esposito era.

Schmidt scored only 13 goals and 25 assists that season, but in the play-offs was the leading scorer, with 5 goals and 6 assists. His reputation as a hard-nosed player was well established by then.

"He has more guts than any player I ever saw," said referee Red Storey. "I'd take five Milt Schmidts, put my grandmother in the net, and we'd beat any team."

Hockey being the game it is, Schmidt's reputation as a hitter naturally got him into some pretty good scraps. Once he and Dickie Moore of the Canadiens went into the corner at the Montreal Forum, both going after the puck. Moore put his stick over Schmidt's head, whereupon the Bruins strong

1941 Stanley Cup team members at a Bruins' Old-Timers practice. Front: Milt Schmidt, Eddie Weisman. Rear: Dit Clapper, Frankie Brimsek, Woody Dumart, and Cooney Weiland.

man lifted the Canadien and his stick high into the air with one sweep, and dropped him on the ice.

Moore had to be removed on a stretcher, and Schmidt was showered with programs, boots, and other debris.

"I started to throw them back," he said, "but my arm wasn't in shape. Dickie had been giving it to me pretty good with his stick and I'd warned him a couple of times."

Schmidt and Black Jack Stewart of the Red Wings had a career-long feud.

"I never knew why he had it in for me," said Schmidt, "and one day I was told it was because I'd kneed him way back when I first came in the league. So help me, I don't remember that at all, but it certainly started something."

The feud got so bad that Art Ross once threatened to bench the Bruins center against the Wings. Schmidt would have none of that, however, knowing that when word got out that he'd been benched, he'd be a marked man. Milt Schmidt would duck no fights.

The feud was not particularly dirty—that is, there was no high-sticking or butt-ending. It was rather, according to one newspaper account, "just two railroad cars colliding."

The glory years of the Bruins ended with the triumph in 1941. The next season they slipped to third place, with Schmidt scoring 35 points in only 36 games. He didn't play a full season because in early 1942, the Kraut line enlisted in the Royal Canadian Air Force. They spent much of that time in the service together, with Schmidt serving as a physical training instructor.

In the Kraut line's last game, they piled up 8 points in an 8–1 shellacking of the Canadiens. At the finish, players from both teams carried Dumart, Schmidt, and Bauer around the rink as the organist played "Auld Lang Syne." There weren't too many dry eyes in the Garden.

During the war years, when the Bruins were struggling, a fan yelled at Ross, no longer the coach but still general manager: "Hey, Ross, where's your power play?"

The crusty Ross yelled back: "In France, England, and Germany."

Schmidt returned to play the 1945–46 season, and for the next ten years would be the brightest light on a team that never finished first in its division and only twice got to the Stanley Cup finals, losing to the Canadiens in 1946 and again in 1953.

Injuries took their toll, especially in 1947, '48, and '49, when Schmidt missed a total of 33 games and played hurt in many others. He played 9 games with a broken jaw and went into a play-off game against Toronto with a slightly dislocated shoulder, a torn knee ligament, and an injured wrist.

The team doctor said the problem was not getting Schmidt into a game, but keeping him out of one.

Hammy Moore, the Bruins trainer in 1951, estimated that he used 18 feet of adhesive tape on Schmidt's knee before every game.

"Milt Schmidt," wrote the *Globe*'s Jerry Nason, "gives a little piece of himself every time he goes onto a hockey rink."

From an individual standpoint, the 1950–51 season was Schmidt's greatest, even though the Bruins finished with a 22–30–18 record. He led the team in goals (22), assists (39), and points (61). Though the Bruins finished a shaky fourth, Schmidt was named the most valuable player in the NHL.

The Kraut line had been dismantled in 1947, when Bauer retired to enter the family sporting-goods business. There would, however, be a reunion in 1952, an emotional outpouring perhaps equalled only by the night Bobby Orr returned to the Garden to see his Number 4 retired.

On March 18, 1952, Bauer returned, signed a 1-game contract, to play against the Black Hawks at the Garden.

The occasion was a night to honor Schmidt and Dumart. The two were showered with gifts. Each received a $5000 check, plus such varied presents as golf shoes, watches, raincoats, tricycles, a case of peanut butter, sterling silver bowls, shirts, hats, a six-month supply of ice cream, and a shuffle-bowling machine.

Then the game began, and for the first time in five seasons, the Kraut line came over the boards and onto the ice together as the 12,658 fans went wild.

Midway through the second period, Schmidt got the puck out of the corner and snapped it to Bauer. Bauer slid it to Dumart, who passed to Schmidt for a 6-foot shot that blazed past Hawks goalie Harry Lumley. Just like old times, the public-address announcer boomed: "Boston goal by Schmidt. Assists to Bauer and Dumart. Time of goal, 12.56." It was Schmidt's 200th career goal. Later in the game, as the perfect exclamation point, Bauer scored on an assist from Schmidt.

Uncle Miltie's career was winding down by then. Age and injuries had taken their toll, and after scoring only 4 goals in limited duty during the 1954–55 season, Schmidt took off his player's skates and put on a coach's whistle.

Schmidt, who was elected to hockey's Hall of Fame in 1961, was not the success as a coach that he had been as a player, possibly because he didn't have Milt Schmidt types he could call upon.

Lynn Patrick, his predecessor as coach, said it best when he stepped down from the job: "Milt will never be as successful as I was as a coach because he'll never be able to look down the bench when the team's in trouble and say, 'Milt, get in there.' "

Schmidt, general manager of the Bruins in 1967, pulled off the deal that has always been referred to around Boston as the Brinks robbery of hockey. In it, the Bruins traded defenseman Gilles Marotte, forward Pit Martin, and sub goalie Jack Norris to the Black Hawks for center Fred Stanfield, winger Ken Hodge, and a black-haired, big-nosed, sad-eyed superstitious forward named Phil Esposito.

Esposito had been a player of promise in his three seasons with Chicago, averaging 25 goals and 33 assists as part of the "HEM line"—Bobby Hull, Esposito, and Chico Maki. But nobody was ready for what Esposito would accomplish as a Bruin. Nobody was prepared for the scoring machine he would become as the big bad Bruins of the late '60s and early '70s swaggered their way through a National Hockey League far different from the NHL of Eddie Shore and Milt Schmidt.

Esposito was the perfect complement to the finesse of Bobby and the belligerence of the rest of the team. The Bruins of those seasons were one

Phil Esposito—the jokester, the needler, and most of all, the scorer.

big, rollicking family, and Esposito was the jokester, the needler who made them laugh. And most of all, he was the scorer.

The numbers he rang up were unprecedented in the NHL. Hull and Rocket Richard and Gordie Howe had been the acknowledged scoring kings of the modern era, but now here was Esposito, burying their statistics under a mountain of goals and assists.

Working smoothly with linemates Hodge and Wayne Cashman, Espo had seven straight seasons of 40 or more goals. In five of those seasons he went over 50. He had six 100-point seasons, five in a row. One year, he had 550 shots on goal. In another year, he had a record 7 hat tricks, and in still another, a record 28 power-play goals.

"He shoots and shoots and shoots," said Montreal goalie Ken Dryden, "and I say to myself, 'Don't you ever get tired, won't your arms fall off?' But they don't and he just keeps on shooting."

Esposito was born to score goals.

"Listen to that music," he once said, "the puck making the strings move. That's what I love to hear."

He had his critics. His goals were cheap, they said. The shots came out of a crowd in front of the net. They were jabbed home, slithered in from a foot away. They were not works of art.

"Tell me about pretty goals," said Cashman, Esposito's longtime teammate. "I've never seen one that wasn't pretty, if it's your team that scores it."

Esposito would station himself in the slot and shake off the defensemen who came at him like Sherman tanks.

"Where he stands," columnist Jim Murray observed, "he could play in street shoes."

Sooner or later, Esposito's chance would come. He'd deflect a shot from the point, or pounce on a rebound, or get his stick in front of a stray puck, and the red light would flash behind the beaten goalkeeper.

Said Punch Imlach: "He can reach around the block with that stick."

Said goalie Rogie Vachon: 'I'd rather see Orr with the puck at the point than Esposito with the puck in the slot. It comes off his stick so fast you can't see it until it's behind you."

This angular man who would rewrite the hockey record book was born in Sault St. Marie, Ontario, on Feb. 20, 1942. He learned the rudiments of the game on a rink his father built in the back yard, with apple trees as the goal. His younger brother, Tony, who would later star in the nets for Chicago, was the goalie.

Esposito was not exactly a schoolboy Einstein, failing in ninth grade because, as he told Tim Moriarty in the book *Tony and Phil Esposito*: "I was a real jerk."

Esposito, who left high school in his senior year to play junior hockey, was not a big star in the amateurs. He played a year in Junior B in Sarnia, Ontario, and then was promoted to St. Catherine's, a team sponsored by the Hawks. When he turned pro he spent a year and a half with Chicago's Central League affiliate in St. Louis. Clearly, he was no phenom.

But Esposito learned a lot about how to put the puck in the net as a linemate of Hull's in Chicago. After three full seasons, he was beginning to feel an integral part of a team that had made the Stanley Cup play-offs for nine straight years.

Then, one night in the off season, while attending a sports celebrity banquet, his wife called to tell Esposito he'd been traded to Boston. He was

moving from a first-place team to one that had finished in the cellar six times in seven years. The news did not sit well with Esposito.

The Bruins of that time were pussycats, a team of small, nonhitting, nonscoring players. Oh, sure, the kid Orr had shown potential greatness in his rookie season, but still . . .

Esposito had no choice, however, so packed up and went to Boston. His first season he scored 36 goals and 49 assists as the Bruins moved from sixth to third and got into the play-offs for the first time in nine seasons. They were dispatched by the Canadiens in 4 straight, but Esposito predicted that in two years, the Bruins would win it all.

With a young man named Harry Sinden as coach, the Bruins put all their eggs in the offensive basket. Never mind what the other team scores, we'll score more. This wide-open hockey, with Orr at the throttle and Esposito leading the charge, brought the crowds back to Boston Garden and made the Bruins the number-one winter show.

"Before Phil," said Tom Johnson, who would be the coach for three of Esposito's seasons with the Bruins, "the main job of the center was play-making. He changed all that."

In Esposito's second season in Boston, he broke the all-time NHL scoring record, getting point number 98 on March 1 against the Rangers. The fans gave him such an ovation he had goose bumps. When the season had finished, he had pushed the record to 126 points on 49 goals and a record 77 assists, and was named the league's most valuable player.

Esposito was the first Bruin to lead the league in scoring since Herb Cain, twenty-five years previously.

The Bruins had a 42–18–16 record that season, best in a couple of decades, yet finished second to the powerful Canadiens. In the play-offs, Boston wiped out the Maple Leafs 4 straight, but fell to Montreal in the finals, 4 games to 2. In a game against the Leafs, Esposito scored 4 goals, the first time anyone had done this since Richard in 1945.

The best was yet to come for both the Bruins and their scoring machine. The Bruins won everything in 1969–70. They lost only 3 games at home, and in the struggle for the Cup, beat the Rangers, Black Hawks, and St. Louis Blues, losing only 2 games of the 14 played.

The season belonged to Orr, who was named MVP. Esposito had 43 goals and 56 assists, disappointing only when measured against his seemingly untouchable 126 points of the year before.

Untouchable? Esposito would smash his record to bits in the 1970–71 season, when he hammered home 76 goals and the same number of assists for 152 points. Esposito broke Hull's goal-scoring record of 58 by 18.

"I think I've put down all the skeptics," said Esposito on the night he broke the mark against the Los Angeles Kings.

"I know guys," said opponent Lou Nanne, "who couldn't score 76 goals if you counted the ones they made in practice."

Espo in the "slot" where he scored many of his 76 goals during the 1970–71 season.

Phil continued scoring for the Bruins until he was traded in 1975 to the New York Rangers.

Hull sent the new scoring king a telegram, which read: "See you break records as well as chandeliers," a reference to the time Esposito had broken a chandelier on a visit to Hull's house.

On the last day of the season, Esposito scored a hat trick against the Canadiens, and received a prolonged standing ovation, which he termed "the greatest moment an athlete can experience."

Schmidt, still the general manager, called the 76 goals "a completely unimaginable feat."

Slightly irreverent bumper stickers appeared on cars around Boston, reading: "Jesus Saves, but Esposito Scores on the Rebound."

The play-offs would be a disappointment to the Bruins in general and Esposito in particular. They lost in the first round in a 7-game shoot-out with the Canadiens, as goalie Dryden again and again frustrated the league's top shooter.

In 1971, amid rumors that he might be traded because he was asking for too much money, Esposito signed a four-year contract with the Bruins. He scored 66 goals and 67 assists as the Bruins once again dominated hockey, losing only 13 of 78 regular-season games and smashing the Maple Leafs, Blues, and Rangers to regain the Stanley Cup.

This team was the modern Bruins at their peak. It included Esposito, Cashman, the forever young John Bucyk, Hodge, Don Marcotte, feisty John McKenzie, rookie Terry O'Reilly, popular Derek Sanderson, Stanfield, Mike Walton, and Ed Westfall up front, Orr, Don Awrey, Ted Green, Dallas Smith,

and Carol Vadnais on defense, and Gerry Cheevers and Eddie Johnston as goalies.

Before the next season began, Esposito would have chalked up another accomplishment, leading Team Canada against the Soviet Union's national team.

The series got off badly for Canada, with the home forces, perhaps taking the Russians too lightly, being outskated and losing a couple of games.

The Canadian team took much criticism from their rabid fans, and it was then that Esposito went on national television. He asked his country to get behind the team and to realize that everybody was trying as hard as they could. He said the job was tougher than expected, but that they'd get it done.

The series then moved to Europe, and in a dramatic final game Team Canada, on a goal by Toronto's Henderson, beat the Soviets. Esposito was voted Canada's athlete of the year for his performance in that series.

"He was everything you'd want in a hockey player," said Sinden, who coached the team. "He rallied guys on and off the ice. He showed me sides of Phil Esposito I never knew existed. He killed penalties, won face-offs, played the power play. He convinced me then that he was the greatest center who had ever played the game."

Esposito continued his amazing scoring pace in the next three seasons, scoring 130, 145, and 126 points, but there would be no more Stanley Cup championships.

In 1972–73, the Bruins were bounced quickly by the Rangers. The next season, Esposito was named the league's MVP for the second time, an accomplishment all the more remarkable because he'd undergone preseason surgery to repair a torn left knee ligament, the result of a Ron Harris body check.

For seven weeks he wore a cast from under the shoulder to just below the knee, but he was ready when the season began and played in all 78 games. He scored 9 goals in 16 play-off games, but this was the year for the Philadelphia Flyers to win their first Stanley Cup. They beat the Bruins in the finals, 4 games to 2.

There was talk of Esposito jumping to Vancouver of the World Hockey League in 1974, but nothing came of the rumors. The team was showing signs of age and infirmity, however. Orr's injuries had slowed him down, and coach Bep Guidolin was having trouble corraling his free-spirited players.

The Bruins made the play-offs but lost in a preliminary best-of-3 set to Chicago, the earliest they'd been eliminated since Esposito joined the team.

Esposito signed a three-year contract in May of 1975 and then 12 games into the 1975–76 season came the bombshell.

On Oct. 25, Esposito told John Powers of the *Globe* that he was loose and quite happy under new coach Don Cherry. He said he didn't think he would ever be traded, but that if it happened, he would go quietly.

"Even though you're an institution here?" Powers asked.

"Institutions, when they get to a certain age," replied Esposito, "I guess they get torn down."

On Nov. 7, with the team in Oakland, the institution was indeed traded. Esposito and defenseman Vadnais were shipped to the Rangers for defensemen Brad Park and center Jean Ratelle, two New York institutions, plus minor leaguer Joe Zanussi, who wasn't an institution.

Punch Imlach, the veteran NHL coach and general manager, commented: "In my memory I can't think of the league's best scorer ever being traded. I think New York got the best of the deal."

That's what most of the Bruins fans thought, too. John Limoli of Tewksbury squawked, "It would have been better to give the Rangers Faneuil Hall."

General manager Sinden called it the most difficult decision he'd ever had to make in Boston.

Actually, the trade worked out for both teams. Park and Ratelle played well for Boston for many seasons. Espo and Vadnais did the same for New York.

Esposito scored 29, 34, 38, and 42 goals in his four seasons with New York, before retiring in January of 1981.

He spent as many years away from Boston, wearing an enemy uniform, as he did with the Bruins. And yet, when Esposito retired, it was as though a Bruin had said goodbye. His most exciting seasons were spent at the Boston Garden.

"He was a great competitor," said Cashman, his wingmate for all those glory years. "He was always laughing and full of fun, until game time."

Then Phil Esposito, the greatest goal scorer in the Bruins' history, got very serious.

CHAPTER 9

"THE EDMONTON EXPRESS"

"For sheer power and irresistible force, Eddie Shore stands alone."
—General Manager Frank Selke of
the Montreal Canadiens

Eddie Shore, they say, backed down from a battle only once. The story goes that King Clancy of the Toronto Maple Leafs once ran Shore into the boards, whereupon the Boston tough guy automatically put up his hands, routinely ready for the fisticuffs sure to follow.

However, Clancy, instead of fighting, grabbed Shore's hand and shook it, saying "Hello, Eddie, how are you?"

Shore, thrown off guard by this ploy, could only mumble, "Fine, King, and yourself?" as Clancy skated away.

However, one more fight was not needed to enhance the reputation of Eddie Shore. He was generally considered the best amalgamation of skill and toughness who ever laced on a pair of hockey boots. To paraphrase Rodney Dangerfield, Eddie Shore was so tough, his picture is in the dictionary under "tough."

"From the first time he put on skates," observed hockey writer Frank Orr, "Eddie Shore was in the middle of trouble."

Sometimes he came out of that trouble second best. By the time he'd dragged his battered body off the ice for the last time he had accumulated 978 stitches, an almost-severed ear, a dislocated hip, and a broken collarbone. He'd had his nose broken fourteen times and his jaw fractured five times, but, as they say, "You shoulda seen the other guys."

It can be said without exaggeration that Shore sold the Bruins to the citizens of Boston.

"If we hadn't got Eddie Shore," said Art Ross, the coach and general manager, "I doubt if the Bruins would have survived."

137

Eddie Shore—
"The Edmonton Express."

A far different brand of hockey was in vogue when Shore was in his prime, from 1924 through 1939. The accent wasn't on speed so much as it was on strength and waiting for an opening.

"I liked it better in the old days," Shore said many years after his retirement. "It was a 50–50 proposition then. You socked the other guy or the other guy socked you."

And yet, Shore's get-out-of-my-way, length-of-the-ice rushes had as much to do with speed as they did with brute strength.

"He was the only player I ever saw who had a whole arena standing every time he rushed down the ice," said Bruins trainer Hammy Moore. "When Shore carried the puck something happened. He would either end up bashing somebody or get into a fight or score a goal."

Shore never did anything on the ice the easy way, or for fun. He was hockey's equivalent of baseball's nasty immortal, Ty Cobb. The philosophy of both was simple, namely, "Here I am, you so and so. What are you gonna do about it?"

"In an era of stationary defensemen," wrote Roger Barry of the *Quincy Patriot–Ledger*, "Shore was a superlative skater and cold-blooded antagonist who would check an opponent by whatever means necessary."

The man who "built" the Boston Garden was born in Fort Qu'Appelle, Saskatchewan. He spent his childhood working hard on a farm, with his greatest fun the breaking of wild horses—ironic, because Shore was a wild horse nobody could break.

His future as a hockey immortal wasn't carved in granite. In fact, Shore didn't play the sport much until his brother talked him into trying out for the team at Manitoba Agricultural College in Winnipeg. He figured the game shouldn't be too hard and set out to teach himself how to play.

The challenge had been laid down and Shore would never refuse a challenge, neither at seventeen nor seventy. He taught himself the game, spending countless hours on outdoor rinks at temperatures that went as low as 40 below zero.

Shore had no thought of making a living at the game. His plans were to be, like his father before him, a farmer. But money problems at home forced his hand. He had to find a job, and the job he picked was playing ice hockey.

He began by joining the Melville Millionaires, an amateur team in Western Canada, in 1924. He moved on to Regina, Edmonton, and Victoria, throwing punches and taking punches, and establishing the reputation for toughness that would stay with him throughout his life. In Regina, he was called "the wildest, wooliest cowhand ever to lace on a skate."

A skate went through his leg in that period, a terrible injury. Two days later, on crutches, Shore boarded the ferry to Vancouver, en route to a game the next night. His teammates, clowning around to enliven the dull trip, threw his crutches overboard. Shore played hockey the next night.

The Pacific Coast Hockey League in which Shore played ended operations after the 1925 season, tossing a number of players onto the market. The Bruins, in the NHL only three seasons and not doing very well, signed several of these players, Shore among them.

Right away the Bruins veterans tested Shore, who, though twenty-four years old and with a reputation for nastiness, was nonetheless a rookie. He took a daily pounding in practice, and finally said to himself: "Eddie, my boy, the time has come to discover if they can take it the way you've been taking it." The next day he put his thoughts into action and after that things worked out fine.

The man Shore picked to retaliate against was a burly veteran named Billy Coutu, who had been taking daily runs at the rookie.

"All you Western guys think you're tough," Coutu told Shore.

"I'm here to get a job," Shore replied. "I don't want your job, I just want a job."

On the day of reckoning, Coutu began a rush down-ice and headed directly at Shore, who dug in and braced himself for the collision.

"He hit me, bounced about 8 feet, and went down," said Shore. "He got up and sank down, got up again, and went down again. This time he stayed there."

Shore had beaten down his tormenter. He had withstood the veteran and won the battle, but at a dear price. Coutu's head had smashed into Shore's left ear and split it from top to bottom. The ear was literally hanging to his head by a thread, a small piece of skin, with blood pouring from the wound.

Shore went to a doctor, who told him the ear would never grow back. The doctor said it would be impossible to sew back and suggested an amputation.

Shore would have none of that. He had the team trainer tape the ear to his head and sought a more flexible physician. Six hours later he found one willing to try to save the ear.

The doctor asked Shore what kind of anesthetic he preferred. Shore replied by asking for a mirror, so that he could see what was going on as the doctor worked. "Start sewing," he said, and when the job was done, he asked the doctor to take out the last stitch because he felt it puckered his ear.

Years later he was asked what his thoughts were as the doctor sewed his ear back on.

"I thought it hurt like hell," he said.

One last footnote to the incident. Billy Coutu lasted a half-season with the Bruins.

The salvaged-ear story was incorporated into the rapidly growing Shore legend for toughness. The legend, however, should not stifle the fact that Shore was a great hockey player, though statistics certainly won't bring that greatness to the surface.

In his career, Shore had 105 goals and 179 assists for 284 points, a goodly amount for a defenseman in that era. Indeed, in 1930–31 he scored 15 times to finish fifth among all goal scorers in the NHL's American Division. But it wasn't statistics that made Shore a hockey immortal, it was presence.

You could not attend a hockey game involving Shore and be neutral about him. You loved him or loathed him but you certainly noticed him.

"What makes Eddie Shore the greatest drawing card in hockey," wrote Kyle Chricton in *Collier's Magazine* in 1934, "is the hope—entertained by spectators in all cities but Boston—that he will some night be severely killed."

Ross, knowing he had a meal ticket for the next decade in this brash brawler, played up Shore's villain role. In Shore's first years, Ross occasionally used a hokey gimmick to stir up the Garden fans. The Bruins would skate onto the ice without Shore. Fans not wise to the trick would wonder where the great man was. Had he been hurt? Would he play?

Then a band would break into the strains of "Hail to the Chief" and Shore would skate onto the ice, bathed in a spotlight and wearing a matador's cloak. He would take a turn around the rink and then have the cloak removed by a valet. The great man was now ready to do battle and so was the partisan crowd.

Naturally, the opposing club was not thrilled about this inflammatory showmanship, and the New York Americans finally decided to strike back, using as their weapon a little forward named Rabbit McVeigh.

The Amerks followed Shore's act one night in Boston by coming out of the dressing room carrying a long red carpet. The players skated to the center of the rink, unrolled the carpet, and out popped McVeigh. The Rabbit leaped to his feet, pirouetted like someone in the chorus of Swan Lake, and tossed kisses to the gallery. That finished Shore's matador act.

When Shore joined the Bruins, the team played home games in the Boston Arena, whose limited seating capacity was still ample enough to contain the curious willing to plunk down money to see this lackluster team. But in a couple of seasons, after Shore had shown what he could do, the arena simply did not have enough seats. A main reason the Boston Garden was built was to accommodate the new hockey fans who wanted to catch Shore in action.

He was a dramatist who played to the audience. When he was knocked down, he would gesture to the crowd in the grand manner later used by wrestlers. He was the wronged man prevented from doing his job—which was, more often than not, running into an opponent at full speed.

Naturally his style earned him a hundred enemies. His fiercest battles were with the Montreal Maroons. In one, Shore had his cheek torn open and his lip sliced. In another he was felled by a punch, lost several teeth, was out cold for fourteen minutes, and had to be carried from the rink.

His number-one antagonist was Albert (Babe) Siebert. Siebert caught Shore in the face with a stick in 1929. Shore hit the ice and was unconscious for twenty minutes. He had a broken nose, three cracked teeth, a concussion, and two black eyes, and, naturally, played the next night.

It is entirely possible that Siebert had just cause for the mayhem, since Shore previously had slammed into Siebert behind the net, giving the Maroon defenseman a broken toe, bruised ribs, and a black eye.

Ironically, Siebert came to the Bruins in early 1934 as a replacement for Shore, who had been suspended after the frightening episode involving Irwin (Ace) Bailey of the Toronto Maple Leafs. The Shore–Bailey incident is not one of the brightest moments in NHL history, but it certainly is one of the better known.

On Dec. 2, 1933, the Leafs met the Bruins at the Boston Garden and from the start it was obvious the game would not be a tea party. Midway through the second period, Shore, starting a rush up-ice, was knocked off his skates by King Clancy, and slid into the boards.

Shore got up, looked around, and saw Bailey, who he assumed was the culprit who had upended him. The Edmonton Express thereupon gathered a head of steam and slammed into Bailey from behind, sending the Leaf forward high into the air. Bailey came down hard, hitting his head on the ice with a resounding crack.

Frank Selke, a member of the Toronto front office at the time, described the scene: "All of us in the press box heard a crack you might compare to the sound you remember from boyhood days of cracking a pumpkin with a baseball bat. Bailey's knees were raised, his legs were twitching, and his head was turned sideways."

Bailey lay still as death as the irate Leafs skated toward Shore. When defenseman Red Horner reached Shore, he threw a solid punch to the chin that knocked the Bruin tough guy down. Shore hit his head as he fell, and blood began oozing onto the ice.

Bailey was at death's door for a month. The Leafs' management made funeral arrangements. A Boston paper actually had his obituary on the front page of an edition that was recalled only moments before it hit the streets.

Bailey, a plate in his head, eventually recovered, but never played hockey again. An inquiry cleared Shore of malicious intent in the affair, though he was suspended for 16 games.

The first NHL all-star game was played in Toronto as a benefit for Bailey, and Shore visited him in the locker room, saying, "I'm sorry, Ace, I didn't mean to hurt you."

Bailey replied, "That's all right, Eddie, it's part of the game."

Just before the start of the game, the crowd gave the two of them a big ovation as they shook hands, but Shore gave no sign that he heard the applause. Said an observer: "That night, Eddie Shore was ice on ice."

Shore never regarded Bailey's injury as anything more than an accident. "I wouldn't be telling the truth if I said I've had to live with this thing throughout the years," he said later. "I never let it affect me."

An equally famous, if less gory and certainly less tragic, incident was Shore's wild ride through a raging blizzard from Boston to Montreal.

A snowstorm had snarled his cab on Boston streets, causing him to miss the overnight train that would bring the Bruins to Montreal for a game against the Canadiens. After much difficulty, however, Shore located a car and a chauffeur who agreed to drive him to the Canadian city.

The two started out, but sleet and snow made the visibility poor and the driving treacherous. The windshield wipers failed and the glass began to thicken with ice. The chauffeur, who wanted to turn back, refused to drive any longer, so Shore took the wheel.

The going got worse, and soon the car became stuck in the drifts along the side of the road. The two men could not free it by pushing, so Shore slashed branches from nearby trees with the tire jack, placed the branches in front of each wheel, and got enough traction to propel the car back onto the road.

Making only a few miles an hour, they drove all night and through the next day, finally procuring new wipers and a set of tire chains in a small Quebec town. In midafternoon, with Shore catching a catnap in the back seat, the car skidded into a ditch. Shore trudged a mile through the drifts to a farmhouse, where he hired a team of horses for eight dollars to pull the car out of the ditch.

Shore and his exhausted chauffeur arrived at the hotel in Montreal at six that night, three hundred miles and twenty-two hours after they'd begun the journey.

Here's the way Ross described his defenseman's appearance: "His eyes were bloodshot, his face frostbitten and windburned, his fingers bent and set like claws after gripping the wheel for so long, and he couldn't walk straight. I figure his legs were almost paralyzed from hitting the brake and clutch."

Shore went straight to his room and slept for an hour, awoke groggily, and took a cab to the Forum for the game. How could he possibly play after such an ordeal? Well, at 8.20 of the second period, after a typical length-of-the-ice rush, he fired a low hard shot into the right corner of the Montreal net. Final score—Bruins 1, Canadiens 0.

Here's another Shore story. He slammed into a goal post in a game at Madison Square Garden, breaking three ribs. He was taken to his hotel room and administered to by a doctor, who cautioned Shore to stay in bed while he went to register the injured player in a hospital.

The doctor had no sooner left the hotel than Shore did likewise. He took a cab to Grand Central station, where he caught a train to Montreal. He rejoined the Bruins there and that night had 2 goals and an assist.

Like Ty Cobb, to whom he was so often compared, Shore found little comradeship in his teammates, although they admired his courage and skill. He was frequently fined, and was a holdout at the beginning of almost every training camp.

But the Bruins always came to terms with him, because he was the franchise. Once a team offered to buy him, and Bruins owner Charles Adams, so the story goes, wired back: "You are so far from Shore you need a life preserver."

Cooney Weiland, his teammate for so many years, said of Shore: "He was a genius on defense, a great puck carrier and body checker, and a second goal tender. He'd meet the other man at the blue line and either force the man to pass or step into him."

Though the physical and violent part of Shore's career is always emphasized and is what has been passed on from generation to generation, he was not merely the nontalented bullyboy-type employed by so many teams in later generations to stir things up. He was voted the most valuable player in the league in four seasons and seven times he made the first all-star team.

Shore's last hurrah came in the 1939 Stanley Cup play-offs, when he was thirty-seven years old. In the semifinals against the Rangers, a brawl erupted after the Rangers' Phil Watson walloped Bruins defenseman Jack Portland with a punch. Shore led the charge off the bench, but unfortunately for him came in contact with the fist of Muzz Patrick, who not only was big but knew how to fight. Patrick hit Shore three times, breaking his nose, cutting his eye, and finally knocking him dizzy.

Shore went to the infirmary, was patched up, and returned for the final period. The Rangers won that game and the next 2, forcing the series to a seventh game. But in every one, Shore, the fired-up old man, was the best player on the ice.

He was in the penalty box—where else?—when Flash Hollett scored the clincher in the final Stanley Cup game against Toronto. He leaped out of the box and went straight to the dressing room with thirty-seven seconds remaining in the game, and did not reappear when the contest was over and the Bruins went into their victory skate.

However, the idolatrous Garden fans would have none of that. They knew they might be seeing the last of a breed and they wanted to give Shore one final ovation. At last, the great man, his Bruins sweater off and his underwear and suspenders showing, came out of the dressing room and back on the ice.

"I have never heard anything like the cheer that went up in the Garden when he came out," said Milt Schmidt, no stranger to the standing ovation.

Shore bought the minor league franchise in Springfield in 1939, for $42,000. His plan was to play and coach Springfield, and also to squeeze in some home games for the Bruins. It was obviously a situation that couldn't last, and early in January of 1940, Shore was traded to the New York Americans. His last goal for the Bruins was scored Dec. 5, 1939.

Coach Eddie Shore talks hockey with Gordie Howe.

Shore commuted between New York and Springfield that season, and then retired as an active player.

He did not retire from hockey, however, and his second life as a minor league franchise operator was, if possible, more bizarre than his playing career.

Shore, the hockey mogul, had ideas strange and wonderful, and sometimes not so wonderful. For example, he once advised a player at Springfield he'd be a better performer if he'd part his hair on the other side. Asked why he'd recommend such a ridiculous tactic, Shore replied: "Because it would give the player something to think about."

He ordered players to tap dance in hotel lobbies to improve their coordination. He had them run through ballet routines on the rink. He taped players' hands to their sticks during practice, so they'd grip the stick in the right spot and at the proper angle. He tied a goalie's legs together so he couldn't spread them apart and go down on the ice. Players sometimes even had to ask Shore's permission to put butter on their toast.

All hockey teams have a few players on the roster who are inactive for one reason or another. Those on Shore's Springfield team were called the "black aces" and had to perform such menial tasks as make popcorn, blow up balloons, and change light bulbs when they weren't playing but were still on the roster.

Shore, when he was past sixty years of age, had a fight with twenty-five-year-old Jacques Caron, his goalkeeper, following an argument over whether Caron could stay overnight with his wife in Toronto.

Caron had turned in a shutout in Buffalo that night and had planned to go to nearby Toronto. When Shore refused permission for the visit, Caron blew up and made some accusatory remarks to the owner–coach.

Shore promptly told the rest of the players to leave the dressing room and began to throw punches at the bewildered Caron.

Players under Shore's thumb learned to set their watches a half hour ahead (they called it Shore time), so they wouldn't be fined for being late to practice, even though by actual time they were early.

"My time is the only time," Shore told them.

You could never figure him out. The team would win a game and Shore would be angry because they hadn't played to his orders, or because some players had skated with their feet too far apart. Then they'd lose a big game and, though Shore wouldn't like it, he'd be happy because they'd played the style of hockey he liked.

Once Shore made a deal with Tulsa of the Central Hockey League. The player Shore traded for arrived with a broken arm, which made Shore somewhat angry, but perhaps not as upset as the man Shore dispatched to Tulsa. That player had a broken leg.

He once locked a referee out of his own dressing room at Springfield as punishment for what Shore considered bad officiating. Another time, incensed over some calls at the ice barn in West Springfield known as the Eastern States Coliseum, Shore came down from his owner's box to the public-address announcer's booth, grabbed the microphone, and proclaimed that the game would not continue because of the abominable officiating.

For all of that, Shore was an excellent judge of talent, and sent many players to the National Hockey League. A few even appreciated his eccentric methods. Kent Douglas, for example, who played many seasons on defense for the Maple Leafs, credited Shore for showing him things about the game nobody else mentioned.

"He showed me I didn't have to hit a man real hard, just get a piece of him. He showed me how to maneuver a man until he's off balance. Then you take the puck away."

Shore knew he was considered somewhat eccentric.

"Most of us are a little crazy one way or another," he said. "Some of us even admit it. But I'm not sorry about anything I've done in my life."

Eddie Shore never apologized for anything. He knew only one way to play and to live—"damn the torpedoes and full speed ahead." His way brought him hate and fear, admiration and respect, and a place in history as one of the greatest hockey players who ever lived.

PART IV

═INDIVIDUAL═
SPORTS

All athletes, in a sense, are individuals, engaged in one-on-one duels. It is the pitcher vs the batter, the runner vs the tackler, the shooter vs the defender.

Yet, beyond that individuality, these athletes are part of a team. They have help. Indeed, the games they play would make no sense without it.

However, certain sports are truly individual in nature. The boxer, the golfer, the tennis player, and the long-distance runner, though surrounded by the noise of fifty thousand fans, is truly alone.

These chapters are about three of that breed—boxer **Rocky Marciano** and marathoners **Johnny Kelley** and **Bill Rodgers**. There were many others, however, who stood out above the crowd, for example:

HAZEL WIGHTMAN—Winner of fifty national tennis championships, beginning with women's singles in 1909 . . . Was national singles champ four times and was still active as a player in the '70s . . . Her name remains alive as donor of Wightman Cup, competition between American and British players.

CLARENCE DEMAR—Seven-time winner of Boston Marathon.

JACK SHARKEY—Won heavyweight boxing championship of the world in 1932 by beating Max Schmeling . . . Lost championship to Primo Carnera a year later . . . Retired in 1936 with record of 35 wins, 12 losses, and 3 draws.

FRANCIS OUIMET—Considered the "father of American golf" . . . Won U.S. Open at the Country Club in Brookline in 1913 at age of twenty . . . Won national amateur the next year and again in 1932 . . . Won more Walker Cup matches than any golfer in history.

PAUL PENDER—Won middleweight championship of the world with 15-round decision over Sugar Ray Robinson in 1960 . . . Defended title successfully against Robinson later that year . . . Knocked out Terry Downes of England and decisioned Carmen Basilio in 1961 but lost title same year in rematch with Downes in London . . . Retired in 1963 with record of 49 wins, 6 defeats, and 2 draws.

TONY DEMARCO—Knocked out Johnny Saxton in fourteenth round in 1948 to win world welterweight title . . . Lost title to Carmen Basilio in Syracuse on twelfth-round knockout, and in rematch lost again . . . Retired in 1962 with record of 58 wins, 12 defeats, and 1 draw.

HENRI SALAUN—Many times U.S. and Canadian open squash champion . . . Also won Canadian amateur squash championship 7 times, U.S. title 4 times, and veterans crown 6 times . . . Was all-America soccer player at Wesleyan and number-one-ranked tennis player in New England for thirteen years.

TED BISHOP—Championship golfer who won national amateur title at Baltusrol in 1946, the last New Englander to do so.

CHAPTER 10

"THE ORIGINAL ROCKY"

ROCKY MARCIANO

"What could be any better than walking down any street in any city and knowing you are champion?"

—Rocky Marciano after defeating
Joe Walcott on Sept. 23, 1952, to
win the heavyweight boxing
championship of the world

His burning ambition was to be a major-league baseball player, a catcher with a strong right arm like Mickey Cochrane, the famous catcher of an earlier era from nearby East Bridgewater.

He wanted to be a slugger who would hear the roar of the crowd in the big league ball parks as he hit another one on the nose.

However, as is the way with most kid dreams, the baseball fantasy did not work out, and so Rocco Marchegiano had to settle for being the undefeated heavyweight boxing champion of the world.

And yet, in a way, the dream did come true. He was a catcher. Nobody caught more punches than he did and still persevered to become a champion. Nobody threw a baseball any better than Rocco threw a punch with his right arm.

And nobody hit any harder. He was a slugger, all right, for whom the crowd in Yankee Stadium roared every bit as much as it had for DiMaggio, Ruth, and Gehrig.

He hit several on the nose, not to mention the jaw and forehead and arms and belly and anywhere else his sledgehammer fists could land.

By that time, of course, nobody except his parents and those he'd grown up with in Brockton, Massachusetts, knew him as Rocco Marchegiano. By then he was Rocky Marciano, the most famous prize fighter in the world.

He was champion only a little longer than four years—a mere blink in the

149

Rocco Marchegiano—
the original "Rocky."

eye of boxing. He defended his title only 6 times, retiring after his ninth-round knockout of Archie Moore on Sept. 21, 1955.

The legend that is Rocky Marciano does not depend on longevity, but rather on the road he took to the championship and the type of fighter he was.

Some criticized the film "Rocky" as far-fetched and maudlin, unrealistic and made for Hollywood. But the saga of Rocky Balboa, gulping raw eggs and running the back streets of Philadelphia to train for his title bout with Apollo Creed is pretty straight stuff compared to the Cinderella tale of the real-life Rocky.

Consider the following scenario:

Subject is twenty-five years old and unemployed, with hand in cast. He has been turned down as ball player after try-out with Chicago Cubs farm team in Fayetteville, North Carolina. Subject had tried boxing in army, but was told he was too old to take it up as a career, plus he was built wrong to be any kind of boxer—football legs, short arms, fragile hand bones, and awkward as a penguin.

Only one who thinks subject has fistic possibilities is childhood friend, who writes letter touting subject to bigtime fight manager in New York City.

Bigtime manager answers letter, saying, "Bring your boy down, how can it hurt?" Subject and friend hitch ride to Big Apple, go to gym, and spar with local heavyweight. Fight manager is not impressed, but wily trainer sees something in awkward roughhouse style. Subject is told to go home and get in shape, and a bout will be arranged for him in nearby Providence.

Subject runs up impressive string of knockouts, but is still broke and still thumbing his way to New York to train, living in cheap rooming house. Two years later, he is fighting in Madison Square Garden. Three years later, he is beating Joe Louis and appearing on the Ed Sullivan television show. And four years later he is the heavyweight champion, one of the best-known names in the world, and a rich man.

The story is so corny it wouldn't get past the receptionist at Universal Studios. Yet it actually happened to Rocky Marciano, a generation before Rocky Balboa started punching those sides of beef in the South Philadelphia meat locker.

Marciano, the oldest of six children of Pasqualena and Pierino Marchegiano, was born Sept. 1, 1923, weighing in at 13 pounds, 6 ounces.

Growing up, he was just another kid who liked sports. Elizabeth Marshall, his fifth-grade teacher, remembered him as "a very small boy and a perfect gentleman." Margaret Sheehan, who had him in the sixth grade, later remarked: "If only a teacher could know in advance which of her pupils would become famous, she would watch him more carefully. There was nothing about Rocky that would arrest my attention, nothing to separate him from thirty-five or forty others."

Brockton was then the shoe capital of America, and it was hardly unusual for son to follow father into a shoe factory as soon as the mandatory school requirements had been completed.

But Rocky had other ideas. He was going to escape the drudgery of the mill. Sports was going to be his way out, and so his early years were filled with baseball and football on the James Edgar playground in Brockton's Ward Two.

In Everett Skehan's excellent biography, *Rocky Marciano: The Biography of a First Son*, Rocco's childhood friend Izzy Gold says: "The Rock never thought about being a boxer in those days. He didn't go to the YMCA or any of those places where they have kids involved in amateur boxing. Rock spent all his time practicing baseball. He never knew it was in the cards for him to be a fighter. If Rocky had ever suspected he was going to be a fighter he'd have been working at it from the time he was ten years old."

Marciano was a catcher on both the Brockton High and the St. Patrick's diocesan teams, but when his high school coach said he had to choose between them, Rocky quit the high school team. He was also a linebacker on the school football squad and when he was fifteen, intercepted a pass and ran it back 67 yards for a touchdown.

However, when he quit the baseball team, he also decided to quit school, on the somewhat shaky ground that if he couldn't play on the team, what was the point in continuing classes?

He went through jobs as a coal-truck loader and a candy mixer and a brush cutter, and, worst of all, in a shoe factory. And then, in March of 1943, Rocco Marchegiano, his thoughts still fixed on becoming a professional baseball player, was drafted into the army.

It was while stationed at Ft. Lewis, Washington, that Marciano laced on boxing gloves for the first time. He also put on 30 pounds and was noticeably overweight when he returned to Brockton for the first time in two years.

While on furlough, he fought in a local boxing show, embarrassing both himself and his friends by swinging himself into exhaustion and then, in desperation, kneeing his opponent. He was disqualified for fouling—his first defeat as a fighter.

But there had been some good moves, too, especially with the overhead right. Allie Colombo, who was Marciano's pal, began to have his own dreams for Rocky, and they were of boxing, not baseball.

Marciano returned to Ft. Lewis and entered the AAU championships in Portland, Oregon. He won 2 fights, but in the second hurt his left hand and was no match for Joe DeAngelis of Boston in the finals.

Rocky had bumped into the 6'3" DeAngelis in the cafeteria before the fight and had said that the best man would win, that he would knock Joey dead.

DeAngelis had replied, "You're right, the best man will win, and it will be me."

And it was. DeAngelis won all 3 rounds, and claims that the only punches Rocky landed were on the top of his head. The Boston fighter said Rocky then was a sarcastic and cocky guy who became a better and better fellow the higher he went on the fistic ladder.

"Rocky got the dough," DeAngelis quoted in the *Boston Globe* years later, "but I got the gold medal that shows I beat him."

If you'd asked anybody who saw Marciano fight in that tournament, they'd have assessed him as being too awkward and chunky to become a heavyweight of any distinction. Some were still saying that about him the day he retired. Marciano truly was not the graceful stuff from which legends usually grew.

After he beat Rex Layne in what was his first really bigtime fight, Layne commented, "Rocky is a good fighter but he's awful awkward."

Nobody knew more than Marciano that he wasn't a stylist and that the way he fought wasn't pretty. In 1950 he said, "I can hear the crowd laugh at me sometimes. I know I must look ridiculous when some of those things miss. All I hear is that word, 'Crude,' and all the time I think I'm doing pretty good."

However, veteran trainer Freddie Brown summed up Rocky's style pretty well. "He hits you with something that looks like a little tap to the crowd," said Brown, "but the guy who gets hit shakes right down to his legs."

Neatness never counted for much in boxing, and if Marciano never reminded anyone of the Ballet Russe, he got the job done most effectively.

Even before Rocco Marchegiano became Rocky Marciano he was Rocky Mack. That was his pseudonym in his first pro fight, at the Holyoke, Massachusetts, Valley Arena on St. Patrick's Day of 1947.

His pal Colombo set up the match, and Rocky Mack won, as he would every tight he was paid for. He kayoed Lee Epperson in the third round, though Epperson made a punching bag of Rocky's face en route.

Marciano was supposed to receive $50 as his share of the purse, but the promoters coughed up only $35, and this much only after a large beef from Rocky, who showed his soon-to-be-legendary regard for a buck by offering to clean out the joint if he didn't get his share.

The Holyoke fight was merely an interlude. "Rocky Mack" may have turned pro but Rocco Marchegiano was still an amateur and still burning to be a baseball player, even though twenty-four was an ancient age for somebody who'd never played a game as a pro.

That's when the Cubs gave him the try-out in Fayetteville, and though he showed some promise as a hitter, he needed a bus to run the bases and a slingshot to help him throw. Perhaps in today's game, Marciano would have survived as a designated hitter, but in 1947 he was back in Brockton after a few weeks, the dream gone and no new one to take its place.

He won the Golden Gloves heavyweight championship in Lowell and represented New England in the all-East bouts in New York City. He was paired in his first bout with Coley Wallace, a Joe Louis lookalike who would, in fact, play the title role in the film story of the Brown Bomber's life many years later.

Wallace was a highly regarded amateur who never went very far as a pro. But this night he won a controversial decision, defeat number three in Rocky's brief career.

In the spring of 1948, Marciano fought in the AAU Olympic try-outs at the Boston Garden, the only time he appeared there. He lost just once, a 3-round decision to Bob Girard of Lynn. It would be the last time anybody wearing gloves beat him.

Marciano kept training early in 1948, though his boxing future seemed as bleak as a Brockton winter. He had a broken hand, an empty wallet, and no job—not exactly the perfect combination for a twenty-five-year-old man with what many felt were delusions of grandeur.

This is when fact became stranger than fiction. This is when Allie Colombo wrote the letter to Al Weill and the drive to the championship began.

The odds against anything coming as a result of the letter were astronomical. Would Casey Stengel have invited somebody down to the Stadium for a try-out on the strength of a letter touting a twenty-five-year-old catcher who hit .400 in a Brockton semipro league? Would Red Auerbach have opened the doors to a twenty-five-year-old who was scoring 22 points a game in a Brockton YMCA Seniors League?

But boxing was different. Boxing didn't have scouting systems or minor leagues. Boxing was sports' version of flying by the seat of the pants. The new champ might be anywhere. He might be somebody tossing garbage cans around in Duluth, or working in a steel mill in Pittsburgh. Or he might be an awkward, unemployed twenty-five-year-old Italian-American from Brockton, Massachusetts. You just never knew.

Weill called Colombo and said to bring Marciano to New York for a try-out.

Weill and trainer Charley Goldman took Marciano to a gym and had him go 3 rounds with heavyweight Wade Chancey. They saw what everyone else saw—a roughhouser who didn't know the first thing about boxing but whose punch would fell a grizzly. In short, they saw possibilities—that is, Goldman did. To Weill, Marciano was just another clumsy oaf good for filling out a prelim card somewhere.

The New York manager called Boston promoter Sam Silverman and asked him to give this guy from Brockton some fights in Providence.

"He thought so little of this kid," Silverman told Jerry Nason of the *Boston Globe* years later, "that he won't risk $10 a week on him for a room at the

YMCA in New York. Weill spent all his time trying to push some stumblebum from Little Rock and he's got the future heavyweight champion of the world stuck away in Providence."

Of course, Marciano had made no impression on Silverman either, when the promoter had seen Rocky fight as an amateur a few years before. "He didn't impress me," said Subway Sam. "I can't even remember who he fought or how he fought."

It wasn't until Rocky's third fight in Providence that Silverman recognized there was a diamond buried in that Brockton rough.

"Rocky was supposed to be cannon fodder for a kid named Bobby Quinn, who was unbeaten in 13 bouts," said Sam. "Marciano knocked him out in the third round and I started to get interested."

Marciano and Colombo were still training in New York, and often still hitching rides to get there.

"Once they came down on a fruit truck," said Charley Goldman. "I hope the cabbages on that truck don't look as bad as Rocky and Allie did. They looked like they'd come down to sweep the place up."

Goldman might have had a hard time distinguishing between a fruit and a vegetable, but he hadn't been in the fight game almost fifty years without knowing something about boxing, and he worked hard with Marciano.

Said Rocky, "Gee, he's only a little guy, but something tells you that when you talk to him he knows all the answers, and you're a little afraid of him."

Said Goldman about Rocky, "In every fight and before every fight, he learns something new."

Goldman saw him in Providence for the first time in August of 1948, when Rocky knocked out Jimmy Weeks in the first round. Weill caught Rocky's act in Washington when he kayoed Gil Cardione in thirty-six seconds. Cardione, according to newspaper accounts, was unconscious for ten minutes. Rocky received $200 for the bout, plus a broken hand that kept him out five weeks. He punched so hard he was apt to hurt himself as much as an opponent.

About this time, he became known as Marciano. The ring announcer in Providence was having trouble with his last name, so the "heg" in the middle was wiped out and Rocky Marciano was born.

Marciano swept through 1948 and half of 1949, with injuries doing more damage to him than opponents. He had a bad back early in 1949, and his doctor said he would need surgery for a slipped disc and should stop boxing for at least a year.

But the twenty-six-year-old Marciano couldn't afford that luxury. The brass ring was hanging out there, and he wasn't about to get off the merry-go-round now.

Marciano had become so accustomed to early knockouts that when somebody named Don Mogard lasted 10 rounds with him, Rocky became depressed and felt he might be slipping.

Colombo told him to be realistic, that he couldn't expect to knock everybody out. Marciano could never reconcile himself to that logic.

In those days, Madison Square Garden was the showcase, just as, a generation before, performing at the Palace had been the goal of every vaudevillian.

Marciano made the Madison Square Garden on Dec. 2, 1949, and knocked out Irish Pat Richards in the second round. This earned him a ten-rounder against Carmine Vingo on Dec. 30, a fight that would establish Marciano's reputation as a relentless instrument of destruction.

Carmine Vingo was a twenty-year-old heavyweight from the Bronx. He was 6'4" and 189 pounds, 5 inches taller than Marciano and 8 pounds heavier. Rocky's record was 24–0, 22 knockouts and 2 decisions. Vingo, who had been a pro since he was seventeen, was 30–3.

As usual, Marciano took a dressing-room nap before the fight. No matter how big the bout, he had the knack of being so relaxed he could catch forty winks at a time most fighters are so nervous they are pacing up and down, with the adrenalin flowing.

In the first round, Marciano floored Vingo for a nine count with two solid left hooks. In the second, Vingo was on the canvas again for another nine count.

But Vingo got off the deck, and though blood was streaming from his nose

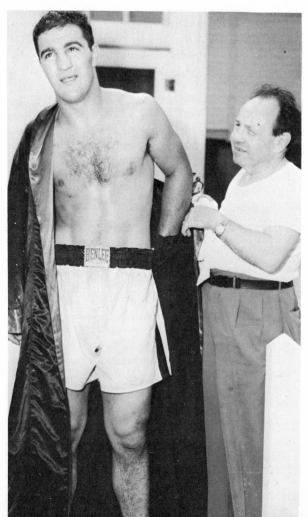

Rocky and his trainer, Charley Goldman.

and from a cut over his right eye, he rocked Marciano with a series of rights. By the end of the round, the Brockton fighter seemed on the verge of going down.

The furious pace slackened a bit through the fifth round, and referee Harry Ebbets warned Marciano for a low blow early in the sixth.

Then, with startling suddenness, the bout ended. At 1.46 of the sixth round, Marciano hit Vingo with a left hook to the chin and the Bronx fighter toppled to the floor.

Vingo lay motionless as Ebbets raised Marciano's right hand high in triumph. The fallen Vingo was obviously badly hurt, but no ambulance was available, so he was wrapped in blankets and carried the two blocks to St. Clare's Hospital.

His injury was diagnosed as a contusion, or swelling of the brain. He was put on the critical list and was given the last rites of the Catholic church.

James P. Dawson of the *New York Times*, in his account of the fight the next morning, wrote: " ... torrid slugging during the third, fourth and fifth rounds until it seemed human endurance could stand no more. One or the other must drop from the combination of punches and exhaustion."

Vingo was in and out of consciousness for several days before showing signs of improvement. He gradually recovered, but never fought again. The injury to his opponent worried Marciano, who paid several visits to Vingo in the hospital. But if Rocky had any thoughts about quitting the ring because of what had happened, they were soon put out of mind.

Boxing fans couldn't wait to see "the Animal" again. Three months after the Vingo fight, Marciano met Roland LaStarza at the Garden. For the first time, Rock was in a feature bout in New York.

LaStarza and Marciano were opposites. The former was a twenty-two-year-old college kid, a counterpuncher and a boxer. Marciano? Well, everyone knew what he was in the ring by now. The two had one thing in common. They were both unbeaten. LaStarza had notched 37 straight victories, Marciano 25.

The fight was on theater television, in forty-five theaters at about $4 a ticket, with a total gate of more than $300,000. The live gate—13,658 paid their way to the Garden—came to $53,723.

It was Rocky's first big payday. The fight itself was a waltz compared to the war with Vingo. Marciano knocked LaStarza down in the fourth and the bell rang at the count of eight with LaStarza still on one knee.

Later, Marciano was charged with a foul and it was evident when the ten-rounder ended that it was anybody's fight. The judges split their votes, so it was Jack Watson who would decide it. Watson gave each fighter 5 rounds, but scored 3 points for Marciano and 6 for LaStarza.

Rocky had escaped the first blot on his professional record by 3 thin points.

He was obviously a contender now. He scored an eighth-round TKO over Keene Simmons early in 1951 but suffered a cut eye and had to sit out several weeks. When he was ready to spar again, he went to Greenwood Lake in the Ramapo Mountains of New York State to train for Rex Layne.

Layne, a cumbersome sort from Utah with a big punch, had a 35–1 record with 24 knockouts. He was a 17–10 choice despite Marciano's 35 straight victories over what *New York Tribune* writer Jesse Abramson called "a string of hamdonnies."

Rocky demolished Layne, opening up a gash over the big man's eye in the second and finishing him off in the sixth. Accounts of the fight in the newspapers the next day described the many combinations Marciano had used to punish the lumbering Layne.

"That was the first time I was credited with doing anything like that," said Marciano, who was becoming, for all his lunging and awkwardness, an adequate boxer.

The crowd went wild over the Layne victory and so did the city of Brockton. Rocky had been married the previous December, and he and his bride, the former Barbara Cousins, rode in a limousine through the streets of Brockton. The mayor gave him the key to the city. The shoemaker's son was somebody at last.

Marciano took his quest for the world heavyweight championship seriously. He lived the life of a monk while in training. The last month before the fight he wouldn't write a letter. The last ten days he wouldn't look at mail, receive a phone call, or meet anybody new. The week before the fight he wouldn't shake hands with anybody or go for a ride in a car.

Nobody could get into his kitchen in that last week except the chefs, and no new foods were introduced or prepared.

Marciano ate very well, however, while in training. His breakfast the morning of the second Walcott fight, for example, was two lamb chops, cereal, three soft-boiled eggs, once slice of toast, and two glasses of milk.

Charley Goldman was asked if there was anything unusual in such a meal.

"Yeah," the trainer replied. "He ususaly has four eggs and three lamb chops."

"Once in a while when I'm in training," Marciano said, "the thought occurs, 'Suppose this guy does lick me, what then? What about all my grand plans?' But I never believe it could happen, really. It's just a passing thought and it passes quickly."

Marciano figured he had only one fight to go before getting a title match with Walcott. He had to beat the Brown Bomber, the aging Joe Louis. Louis was thirty-seven years old and well past his prime, but still dangerous. Walcott had taken his title away, and Louis had retired, but he needed the money, so had made a comeback.

Rocky gave away eight inches in reach to Louis when they fought in New York on Oct. 26, 1951, before a crowd of 17,241. Marciano was slightly ahead going into the eighth round when he belted Joe with a short left hook. Louis took an eight count and when he got to his feet, Marciano swarmed all over him. A solid right sent Louis through the ropes, with his feet sprawled awkwardly on the apron.

"I saw the right hand coming but couldn't do anything about it," said Louis. "When Rocky defeated me I think it hurt him more than it did me."

Brockton got out the drums and the speeches once more. There was a parade and a celebration at Marciano's old stamping grounds, the James Edgar playground.

But the title fight had to wait and an impatient Marciano was forced to take on thirty-six-year-old Lee Savold on Feb. 13, 1952.

It was a terrible fight. Savold was clumsy, Marciano had a virus, and by the sixth round Savold's face looked like last week's hamburger. Marciano won the fight when Savold failed to answer the bell for the seventh round, but the performance was far from Rocky at his best.

Coming off the Louis victory, Marciano had been given a big build-up, and the fight was a disappointment to the small crowd of 9243, who booed lustily. They wanted destruction from Marciano, not technical knockouts.

Clif Keane of the *Globe*, who covered the fight, described Marciano as "being as wide open as Franklin Park after he throws a punch."

Nevertheless, the next day Savold, the fighter Rocky was supposed to have had such a tough time with, went into the hospital with the inside of his mouth ripped open, both lips split, and gashes above both eyes, and in a state of shock.

There was one more pretitle bout, this an easy second-round knockout of light heavyweight pretender Kid Mathews on July 28, 1952. Marciano could no longer be denied his shot at Walcott, the champion.

The fight was scheduled for Sept. 23 in Philadelphia's Municipal Stadium. Marciano trained at Grossinger's in the Catskills for the bout, which was one of the bloodiest battles in heavyweight history.

Walcott, who had beaten Ezzard Charles for the title, was 2 inches taller and 10 pounds heavier than Rocky. And at the age of thirty-eight, he was the oldest heavyweight champion ever. But any doubt as to whether he could still punch was dispelled when, in the first round, Jersey Joe slammed a thundering left hook to Marciano's jaw.

Marciano, the unfloorable Rocky, went down for the first time in his career, for a count of four. He staggered to his feet, blood dripping from his nose, and a puzzled look on his face, as if to say, "Did he really do that? Is this really happening to me?"

The crowd of 40,379 was in an absolute frenzy as they watched Walcott try to finish off the muscular challenger. But Marciano survived the round, and the next and the next. Pretty soon he was again the aggressor, and Walcott was in trouble. The champ was cut badly above the left eye in the sixth and only the bell saved him. Rocky was also cut and had trouble seeing as Walcott kept flicking a left into his face.

The two bumped heads during the furious infighting and a gash opened up just above Marciano's hairline. In addition, Rocky's eyes smarted after coming in contact with a substance that had been rubbed on Walcott's neck and shoulders.

As the fight moved through the tenth and eleventh rounds, it became more and more obvious that barring a dramatic turnaround, Marciano was about to suffer the first defeat of his professional career at a time he could least afford it.

In the eleventh, Walcott hit Marciano with a devastating right to the heart and followed with a combination to the head that opened a cut over Rocky's right eye.

When the bell rang to end the twelfth, Marciano asked Allie Colombo how matters stood.

"You are losing," replied his friend. "You have to knock him out to win."

Forty-three seconds later, the fight was over. The frustrated baseball catcher from Brockton had done what Colombo said he had to. He had knocked out Jersey Joe Walcott and won the heavyweight championship of the world. The punch that did it was a short right to the jaw.

Walcott said afterward that he thought Marciano was finished, but the cut that had reopened over Joe's left eye obscured his vision to the point that he never saw the right hand that put his lights out.

Said Marciano: "I never hit a guy harder in my life. I felt the punch down to my heels."

Jersey Joe's face went blank, his mouth hung open, and his mouthpiece dribbled from his lips as referee Charlie Daggert tolled the count. At the count of five, Walcott went from his knees and elbows onto his face, and Massachusetts had its first heavyweight champion since John L. Sullivan sixty-two years before.

The sudden and dramatic ending precipitated a new riot as wild-eyed spectators rushed the police at ringside in their efforts to get near the new champion.

The city of Brockton had its third Marciano celebration a month later, and really went all out. A throng of a hundred thousand, twice the city's population, welcomed their champion home. It was a greater turnout than when President Roosevelt and Vice President Harry Truman had visited the Shoe City.

Globe reporter Jerry Sullivan covered the homecoming and began his account this way: "Brockton's sole may be in its shoes, but today its heart belongs to Rocky."

Crowds were eight to ten deep along Belmont, Brook, and Main streets. Marciano was made a life member of the Kiwanis Club. His boxing shoes were gilded and presented to him. He was given a Cadillac with a license plate that read "KAYO."

He received the Edward Neil Plaque as fighter of the year, the *Ring Magazine* "Best Fighter Award," and the Ray Hickok Belt as pro athlete of 1952.

There were some less welcome gifts as the result of the battle with Walcott. Marciano needed fourteen stitches to close the cuts on his face and forehead.

His share of the purse was $94,035, his biggest financial reward yet. He received almost twice as much for the rematch—$166,038—but Walcott, though no longer the champ, was guaranteed $250,000. The fight, in Chicago, drew only 13,266, and was over in such a hurry that on a prorated basis, Jersey Joe made $100,000 a minute.

The bout had been postponed for six weeks while Marciano recuperated from a nose injury suffered in training. But when the rematch was held on

May 15, 1953, Walcott quickly showed what eight months and the first beating had done to his thirty-nine-year-old reflexes.

Marciano hit Walcott with a light left to the head and a hard right to the chin, and stepped back as the aged challenger fell to the floor. Walcott waited on one knee until referee Frank Sikora's count reached eight. He then attempted to rise, but before he could make it, Sikora had intoned, "Nine, ten, and you're out."

Walcott didn't seem to comprehend that Sikora had counted him out. He put his gloves up so the referee could brush resin from them. Walcott's trainer, the controversial Felix Bocchiccio, raged that it had been a fast count and that his fighter had been cheated.

It was a sorry ending to twenty-three years of boxing for Walcott, who left the ring with boos ringing in his ears.

"It was a good punch," said Marciano of the blow that decked Jersey Joe, "but I couldn't quite believe it was that good."

Rocky still hadn't won the wholehearted respect of the boxing world, which admitted to the dynamite in his fist, but still harped on his clumsiness.

Still, the new champ had developed a left jab and a left hook and a short right. Once he had flopped around like a stranded sea cow when he missed a punch. Now, he still missed often, but recovered in a hurry.

Ezzard Charles, who twice would be a future victim, remarked that Marciano was "better than people think. They keep laughing at him and he keeps knocking 'em dead."

A month after the second Walcott victory, the guy who had once had to hook a ride on a truck to get to New York City had luncheon at the White House with President Dwight Eisenhower and forty-three other leading athletes of the day.

Al Weill, the manager who had thought of Marciano as preliminary fodder a few years before, was now describing him as "the hardest puncher in history." At 2.25 of the first round, Marciano's second victory over Walcott was the sixth fastest in heavyweight title history.

Now, instead of Marciano waiting for his turn, the others were getting in line for their shot at the big money. Roland LaStarza, the young boxer from the Bronx, from whom Marciano had had so much trouble winning a 15-round decision a few years earlier, was first at the door.

Rocky was a 5–1 favorite this time as the two went at it before 44,562 at the Polo Grounds in New York. And again Marciano had difficulty with LaStarza's style. Referee Ruby Goldstein had to warn the champ six times for low punches, for elbowing, and for butting, and at the end of six rounds, LaStarza was ahead on points.

Then Marciano changed his style. From the seventh until Goldstein stopped the bout in the eleventh, Rocky forgot about the knockout punch and concentrated instead on hooks and combinations. LaStarza went down for a count of nine early in the eleventh, and midway through the round, Goldstein had seen enough.

"He is five times as good a fighter as the last time we fought," said LaStarza, whose left arm was numb from absorbing sledgehammer punches.

Marciano won a decision over Charles on June 17, 1954, before 47,585 in Yankee Stadium in what the Rock called his toughest fight. It was the only one of his 7 title bouts that went the fifteen-round distance.

Marciano hit Charles eighteen straight punches at the end of the sixth round and twenty-three straight at the end of the bout but never could connect with one of his Brockton blockbusters. On seven occasions, the two fought it out toe to toe, with neither giving an inch.

Marciano made $248,038 in the first Charles bout, but only $178,608 in the rematch. The return fight, postponed a day because of Hurricane Edna, was held at Yankee Stadium, with only 34,330 looking on. And, as was the case with LaStarza and Walcott, the rematch didn't take as long as the original, though there were some anxious moments for the champion.

He knocked Charles down in the second, but in the sixth Charles surprised by opening a big cut on Rocky's nose. Marciano finished Charles off in the eighth, twenty-four seconds before the round ended. Sam Silverman always maintained that if Charles had been able to survive the round, he would have been awarded a TKO, because the cut on Marciano's nose was so bad he wouldn't have been allowed to continue.

In after-fight photos, Marciano has the battered look of a loser but the joyful grin of a winner. He called it the best fight of his career.

Wrote *Herald–Tribune* columnist Red Smith the next morning, "Rocky had to make his best fight to win. In doing so he exhibited the two qualities for which he has been chiefly distinguished in the past, his incredible indifference to pain and the numbing force of his punch."

The thrill of the chase was lessening for Marciano, however. He had reached the pinnacle of his profession, and the challenge of staying there was wearing thin.

The monk-like training methods that separated him from his wife and new daughter were getting to him. At Marciano's wedding party, Al Weill, in toasting the bride, had said: "Remember, Barbara, Rocky's boxing future comes first. This marriage has to play second fiddle because he will have to pay strict attention to me."

And that's the way it was. Boxing did come first, but to Marciano it no longer seemed that important.

There was also worry over his physical well-being. Though he always won, he also never backed away from a punch. The blows were taking their toll. The stitches and the lumps were mounting, and there had to be an end to that.

Marciano would fight only twice more. He knocked out Englishman Don Cockell on May 16, 1955, in the ninth round of a brawl in San Francisco, and then came the grand finale, another ninth-round knockout, this time of Archie Moore on Sept. 21, 1955, at Yankee Stadium.

The colorful Moore, then pushing forty, had to promote himself to even get the fight. He sent out "Wanted" posters, with a drawing of Marciano dressed up as a convict. The poster read: "$100,000 reward for anybody who can get Marciano into a ring. Notify sheriff Archie Moore."

The resultant publicity made the fight a much-anticipated event that drew

61,574 people and a live gate of $948,117, both personal highs for Marciano.

His take-home pay was $470,887, by far the largest purse of his career.

Once again, the fight wasn't easy. For Marciano, it seldom was. Moore knocked the champion on his tail with a solid right to the jaw in the second round. It was the second knockdown of Marciano's career, and his last.

Moore always claimed that referee Harry Kessler saved Marciano. When Rocky got up at the count of two, Kessler grabbed Rocky's gloves and wiped them off, counting to five as he did.

"If a man is on his feet," said Moore in Peter Heller's book, *In This Corner,* "he is automatically a target. It cost me the heavyweight title. I never take any credit from Rocky, because I think Rocky was one of the greatest fighters that ever lived, and one of the nicest fellows that ever lived."

Once Marciano got past that early crisis, the danger was over. He floored Moore in the sixth for a count of four, and again for a count of eight.

"I hit Rocky Marciano some shots that would have taken the head off the average guy," said Moore, "but he kept piling up on top of me."

In the eighth, Archie hit the deck again, but the bell saved him. When he went down for the fourth time, in round nine, the gallant old man of boxing was finished.

Rocky Marciano and Muhammad Ali-Cassius Clay mix it up in the true "Battle of the Century"—the world-famous computerized fifteen-round television fight that was produced to determine the greatest heavyweight champion of all time.

Nobody knew it that night, but so was Rocky Marciano.

Since winning the title from Walcott, Marciano had defended it six times. Counting the first Walcott fight, he'd won 5 by knockouts, 1 by a TKO, and 1, the first Charles bout, by a unanimous decision.

His share of the receipts from those seven fights had come to $1,462,961. Not bad for a shoemaker's son with a weak throwing arm. But now it was time to get out of the business that had brought him fame and fortune.

He made the announcement in April of 1956, citing his desire to spend more time with his family, plus his increasing distaste for training, plus a back that was bothering him more and more, plus an unwillingness to fall into the "one more fight" trap that catches so many champions.

In short, the drive and single-mindedness that had pushed him to the top were no longer there.

"I am confortably fixed and not afraid of the future," he said. "I've studied boxing and boxing's mistakes and was as sorry as anyone to see Joe Louis, one of the greatest fighters who ever lived, make his comeback. I could win 60 in a row, but what would that prove?"

Marciano, freed from the rigors of training, started to live the good life. He put on 35 pounds and started investing his money in different businesses, many of them bad.

Stories surfaced concerning his inordinate frugality, or, to use a perhaps more accurate expression, his penny-pinching. It was said that money had become such an obsession he would tape it to the inside of a toilet tank in his hotel room, or squirrel it away inside a light fixture.

Three years after his retirement, Marciano began training in Ocala, Florida, for a possible comeback. He was serious, cutting down to two meals a day and running several miles.

But the comeback never materialized. During his career, boxing had come first, last, and always, but now business interfered. He could never settle into a routine. He'd work out a few days, then fly to New York for a meeting. After a month, Marciano called off the comeback.

In 1960, Rocky had to pay $5000 after being sued by a magazine writer for allegedly striking the writer after an argument in a restaurant.

Said the writer, Gene Schoor: "I passed out and bells have been ringing in my head ever since and I had a fuzzy feeling for weeks. When a heavyweight champ hits you, it doesn't have to be more than once."

In awarding for the writer, the judge commented, "The stronger the man the more important the man, the more restraint he must exercise."

Rumors continued to float around that Marciano would make a comeback, even when he was forty-three years old and young Cassius Clay was the champion.

Well, the Rock did make one, sort of. In the summer of 1969, he went into training so that he and Clay, now known as Muhammad Ali, could film some fight action that could be developed into a simulated title bout.

Marciano dropped 50 pounds and "boxed" seventy rounds with Ali in a film studio. Seven different endings were filmed, with the one finally decided upon kept secret. The movie, shown in 1970, had Marciano knocking out Ali in the fourteenth round and then being declared by computer the greatest heavyweight in history.

But Marciano never lived to see the film. On Sept. 21, 1969, he was a passenger in a single-engine Cessna that took off from Midway Airport in Chicago en route to a business meeting in Des Moines. From Des Moines, Marciano planned to head for home in Ft. Lauderdale, Florida, where his wife, Barbara, his sixteen-year-old daughter, Mary Ann, and seventeen-month-old son, Rocky Jr., were waiting. The next day was Marciano's forty-sixth birthday, and they were planning a party.

Marciano never made it even to Des Moines. Flying too low in a heavy fog, the plane smashed into an oak tree and crashed in Newton, Iowa.

The shoemaker's son with the punch of a stevedore and the heart of a lion was dead at forty-six.

Jimmy Cannon, the great New York sports columnist, once wrote: "Rocky Marciano stood out like a rose in a garbage dump."

In the sordid business that boxing was, is, and maybe always will be, that is epitaph enough.

CHAPTER 11

"THE MARATHON MEN"

JOHNNY KELLEY AND BILL RODGERS

"It seems as if I've spent a lot of my life running up Commonwealth Ave."
—Johnny Kelley

One ran his first Boston Marathon in the days of Al Capone and bathtub gin. The other began when men were landing on the moon and athletes were paid in six figures.

The careers of Johnny Kelley and Bill Rodgers started almost fifty years apart, yet the two shared a common bond. They were both caught up in the battle between body and spirit, the struggle between endurance and fatigue. For Kelley and Rodgers, marathon running held a fascination that does not diminish with age. For them the loneliness of the long distance runner became a siren song of the open road, calling them back one more time.

When twenty-one-year-old Johnny Kelley went to the starting line in Hopkinton in April 1928, long distance runners were considered about on an entertainment par with sword swallowers and six-day bicycle riders. Jogging was not only unfashionable, it was virtually unheard of.

But by the time twenty-five-year-old Bill Rodgers made his Boston Marathon debut in 1973, roadrunners were as common as the housefly. Joggers clogged suburban streets. Serious runners thought nothing of going a hundred miles a week, and you were nobody if you didn't own at least one pair of striped running shoes.

Kelley won the Boston Marathon in 1935 and 1945, and through 1981 had run in an incredible fifty of them. Rodgers won in 1975, 1978, 1979, and 1980, and was considered the best in the world in that stretch of time.

However, neither Kelley nor Rodgers finished their first Boston race. Kelley had run a marathon in Rhode Island in 1928, to get some experience.

165

Johnny Kelley, winner of the 1945 Boston Marathon (which he had also won in 1935).

He was with the leaders all the way to Woonsocket, but when he started the return journey to Pawtucket, something odd occurred.

"I could see Pawtucket out there in the distance," he told Chris Warner of the *Boston Herald–American* many years later, "but as I ran towards it, I just never seemed to get any closer. I fell way back and finished seventeenth."

With that under his belt, Kelley joined the Patriots' Day crowd at Hopkinton a month later. He ran 22 miles, to Coolidge Corner in Brookline Village, and could go no further. When a man offered him a ride the rest of the way, Kelley took it, on the day when Clarence DeMar won his sixth Marathon.

Rodgers trained for his first marathon by finishing third in a twenty-mile race in February of 1973. He placed highly in two shorter races and felt confident he would do well in Boston. The confidence was misplaced, and Rodgers later admitted there was plenty he didn't know about running a marathon.

He was hardly a jogging fashion plate in his blue jeans, and, after 7 miles, he got a stitch in his side and dropped out. He dropped back in shortly afterward, but had to stop several times before finally quitting for good on the Newton Hills, 21 miles into the race.

Neither Kelley nor Rodgers gave any indication of things to come by their showings in their first marathons.

But before they were done, Kelley would be known as the grand old man of marathoning and Rodgers would be considered the one who brought both notoriety and prosperity to a sport as old as Athens and as demanding as a dictator.

John Adelbert Kelley was born in West Medford, Massachusetts, on Sept. 6, 1907. His father, a mail carrier, had been an athlete, and once entered an early Boston Marathon. Johnny's favorite sport as a kid was baseball, but by the age of twelve, when he weighed only 95 pounds, it was apparent that he would not be a ball player of distinction.

In 1920, he began competing in youth track meets at Playstead Park in West Medford, and, for the rest of his life, never stopped running. He was captain of the cross-country team at Arlington High in 1927, and entered his first road race that year, finishing second in a 5-miler in Rockland.

Nobody made money from running marathons in Kelley's heyday. There were no running boutiques selling $80 shoes and fancy outfits. In Kelley's time, it was sneakers and shorts and away you went.

"In those days," he said, "we didn't train every day because we were afraid we'd get stale. We wouldn't push ourselves for fear we'd get hurt. Now we've found that the human body can stand that punishment, and in fact thrives on it."

After Kelley's 1928 dropout, he didn't run the Boston Marathon again until 1932. He made a name for himself locally by competing in shorter races, ten-milers and six-milers. In 1932, he tried Boston again, but after staying with the leaders through Wellesley, he once more had to quit, this time because of blisters.

Johnny Kelley didn't make "big money," but he won many trophies.

Kelley ran many races other than marathons—ranging from three to fifteen miles.

Johnny Kelley crosses the finish line after competing in his fiftieth Boston Marathon.

In the next forty-nine years, Kelley failed to finish only 2 other Boston Marathons—in 1956 when he hurt a leg, and in 1968 when he couldn't compete because of a hernia.

Kelley finished in the top ten in Boston 19 times. Seven times he was runner-up, including heartbreakers in 1944 and 1946. In '46, he was edged at the finish line by Stylianos Kriakides of Greece. After the race, as the hollow-cheeked Greek told reporters how he had raced and won to publicize the plight of his starving countrymen, Kelley listened with tears running down his face.

"B-b-b-y gosh," the American sobbed, "I'm g-g-glad you beat me, Stanley."

Kelley, weakened by the flu, finished 37th in 1933. The next year he finished second, and then, in 1935, he came pounding through Kenmore Square all alone, the champion at last.

"I really expected to win," he said. "I'd won a twenty-mile race in Medford shortly before and was in great shape. I just felt it in my bones that I was going to win."

The 1935 victory wasn't easy, not that any Marathon champion has a waltz from Hopkinton to the Back Bay of Boston. Only 190 runners, a far cry from the 6000 who would try the race two generations later, were entered in 1935.

Kelley was fourth as the pack loped through the six-mile mark at Framingham and had dropped to sixth in Natick, 11 miles out. But a few miles later, in Wellesley, he took over the lead for good, and in the process wore out Dave Komonen, a Finn from Ontario who had been his conqueror the previous year.

Komonen was at Kelley's side going past Wellesley College, but coming into the square, the Finn began walking. He resumed running a short time later, but went less than a half-mile before quitting for good.

Komonen was given a ride into Boston and was so sure Kelley would break the tape first that he left the little man a note of congratulation before leaving for Ontario. With Komonen out of the race, the only challenge Kelley would get was from Pat Dengis, a swarthy runner from Baltimore.

Tony Paskell of Lynn had taken the early lead, but it was obvious the pace would be too much for him, and, indeed, it was. He finished by grabbing a bus ride back to town.

Dengis held the lead briefly at the twelve-mile mark, but just before the Wellesley Hills Kelley caught him, and the two-man race to the finish line began. With ten miles left Kelley had opened up a 25-yard lead, which he gradually increased to 100 yards in Newtonville.

Through Lake Street, Kelley was ahead by 300 yards and seemingly had victory locked up. However, there were signs that the Newton Hills had taken their toll on Kelley. His face was strained and haggard, his shirt was soaked with sweat, he was gasping for breath, and there were still 4 miles to go.

Yet, at Coolidge Corner, Kelley led by 500 yards as he headed into the home stretch, urged on by the cheering thousands along Beacon Street.

Then, in Kenmore Square, Kelley gave the throng a jolt by stopping in the street and doubling over with nausea. Glucose tablets, which he had taken for stimulation, had given him stomach cramps.

Dengis cut 100 yards off the lead as Kelley bent over in agony. The little man from Arlington resumed running, but went only 10 yards more before he stopped again. It seemed as though once more his body had betrayed him just before the finish.

But with Dengis now only 250 yards away and coming closer every second, Kelley, in an act that perhaps was inelegant but which also won him the race, threw up. He then broke once more into stride and kept the 250 yards between him and Dengis until he staggered across the finish line at Exeter Street and collapsed into the arms of his father.

Kelley ran that marathon in 2.32.07 and the delay undoubtedly cost him the record, which at the time was held by Les Pawson of Pawtucket at 2.31.01.

It would be a decade before Kelley won the Boston Marathon again.

He was the favorite in 1936, but finished fifth in what he called his biggest marathon disappointment. In Newton he had caught Tarzan Brown, the leader, patting him on the back as he went past. But Brown sprinted into the lead again and fought off Kelley for the next two miles. At Beacon Street Kelley got a case of the staggers and barely made it to the end.

He and Walter Young of Quebec dueled for twenty-three miles on a sun-baked course in 1937, but the late going got Kelley again and he finished a badly beaten second, six minutes behind Young. He was third to Pawson in 1938, once more fading in the last few miles.

By now Kelley had a reputation as a runner who could be caught. He did nothing to disprove the label in 1940, when Gerard Cote of St. Hyacinthe, Quebec, overtook him at the twenty-two mile mark on Beacon Street. Kelley had his best time in 1941—2.31.26—but Pawson, his close friend, beat him.

In 1943 and 1944 he finished second to Cote. The '44 race was excruciating for Kelley, who battled Cote shoulder to shoulder through the Newton Hills and all the way to the home stretch. Seven hundred yards from home Cote began to edge away, beating Kelley to the tape by only 60 yards. It was the sixth time Kelley had finished second.

It was beginning to look as though he would never again win a Boston Marathon. He was, after all, thirty-seven years old, an advanced age to hope to stay with the younger runners for that considerable distance.

The age business was mentioned to him before the start of the 1945 race, and Kelley replied that life began at forty, so he had three years to go before he even got started. He then proceeded to run what he always thought was his most strategic and satisfying race. He paced himself well, being content to let Clayton Farrar of the coast guard set the pace.

"My legs weren't limber, but I felt okay coming through Wellesley," Kelley said. Then, as he pounded through Auburndale, he got his second wind and felt just fine.

He was fifth, perhaps a half-mile behind Farrar, as the runners turned into the Newton Hills. But as Jerry Nason of the *Boston Globe*, long recognized as the premier chronicler of the marathon, wrote in his description of this race:

"Nobody in the business can run over the craggy part of the course in Newton as can Kelley, the pony boy of the marathon. He was like a string of firecrackers popping off. The first upward sweep toward Brae Burn Country Club ignited him."

Kelley passed two runners and now had only Farrar and Lloyd Bairstow, another coast guardsman, to catch. He didn't overtake Farrar so much as Farrar came back to him. At the bottom of Heartbreak Hill, Farrar, the pace setter, simply ran out of gas.

Coolidge Corner, three miles from home, had often been Kelley's downfall in the past. It was the spot where he ran out of gas. This time it was the point where he knew he was the winner.

Bairstow was still running smoothly, but Kelley was simply a whirlwind that could not be contained. He came into the homestretch at Kenmore Square in far different condition than in his first victory a decade before. This time he was fresh and exultant, and afterward, when asked about his finish, he said: "What a feeling to come over the bridge into Kenmore and see nobody ahead of me. Hot damn."

Kelley was on three U.S. Olympic teams. He ran in Berlin in 1936 (the Jesse Owens–Adolph Hilter confrontation Olympics) and was eighteenth, the only American to finish.

"They had a rule at the Berlin games," he said, "that when an athlete finished his event he had to get out of the stadium. I didn't know about the rule and so when I finished I collapsed on the grass. I was just tired. The next thing I knew, two big German soldiers had me, one by each arm, and they hauled me off. They didn't mean any harm. They just wanted me out of there."

Kelley qualified for the Olympics in 1940, but they weren't held because of World War II. He made the team again in 1948, at the age of forty-one, and finished 21st in London. A year later he finished 4th in an international meet in Oslo.

Kelley held every New England title from three miles to fifteen miles, which was his favorite event. He also won 7 national AAU championships, and by 1980 figured he'd run the equivalent of three times around the world.

He was a model of consistency. In 1933, he ran a marathon in 2 hours and 50 minutes. Thirty years later, his time was 2.48, and in 1969, when he was sixty-one years old, he ran the 26 miles, 385 yards in 3.03.

Though his last win was in 1945, it was hardly Kelley's final Boston Marathon. In 1958, when he was fifty, he finished ninth. The newspapers began referring to him as Johnny Kelley the Elder, to distinguish him from a younger John Kelley from Manchester, Connecticut, who won the marathon in 1958.

By 1960, the chance to be number one was not the reason he ran. As he told Francis Rosa of the *Boston Globe*: "It's not pleasant to stand at the starting line and know you can't win. I run for sentimental reasons now."

And more and more, as the marathon went from being a regional to a national competition and in the process became a media event, Kelley was the sentimental favorite of the ever-increasing crowds along the route.

In 1981, at the age of seventy-three, Kelley was still averaging seventy miles a week out of his retirement home in Dennis on Cape Cod. Most of his running was done at 5:30 in the morning, on cape beaches or sandy roads through the woods.

"If I don't run for two or three days," he said, "I feel as if something's been stolen from me."

In April of 1981, he competed in his fiftieth marathon, finishing in 4.01.25, and afterwards called it "my easiest race in years."

As he came around the corner of Commonwealth Avenue and turned up Hereford Street toward the Prudential Building, the cheering began for the man race director Will Cloney called "the spirit of the Marathon."

The front runners had finished long ago. The winners had been photographed and interviewed and had gone about their business. The remaining spectators were there for only one reason—to welcome this gray-haired, bandy-legged running machine. Emotions surged over Kelley when he heard the huge ovation.

"They made me cry and some of them were crying, too," he said, "and yelling for me, and blowing kisses. It made me feel wonderful."

Kelley estimated he'd run more than thirteen hundred road races of a mile or more, yet said he'd never made a nickel from his endeavors.

"Running has always cost me money," he said. "Once a clothing store in Boston wanted to give me a suit in exchange for the use of my name, but under the rules I couldn't do it. Now nobody really gives a damn. It's all gotten so big. Every manufacturer sends me shoes."

No doubt about it, times had changed by the time Bill Rodgers became known as the world's top marathoner, and Rodgers himself had the most to do with changing them.

In 1975, Rodgers became the first Greater Bostonian to win the marathon since Kelley's triumph the year before. The events leading up to that improbable victory sound like something concocted by a script writer—a bad script writer.

Rodgers, born Dec. 23, 1947, had grown up in Newington, Connecticut, and had always liked to run.

"It suited my personality," he wrote in his autobiography, *Marathoning*, done in collaboration with Joe Concannon. "I chased butterflies as a kid. I loved the sensation that running through the fields and running on grass gave me."

Rodgers specialized in the two-mile run at Wesleyan University in Middletown, Connecticut, where he roomed with Amby Burfoot. Burfoot had won the Boston Marathon in 1968.

"Amby's win impressed me," said Rodgers, "but at that time I really didn't understand road racing, or what it took to win a marathon."

Burfoot told him he'd be a good runner if he became serious about it, but the fact is that Rodgers had a difficult time becoming serious about anything except the Vietnam War.

"I used to try to get him to stop drinking beer on Friday nights, and come out to train with me on Saturday mornings," said Burfoot years later. "But he wanted to go to the discos and drink beer. Now he's serious and I'm the one drinking the beer."

The Vietnam War was escalating and that dirty business made running seem terribly unimportant to Rodgers. By 1970, after a period of running in the morning, partying at night, and smoking cigarettes all day, he stopped working out altogether. He was still interested enough to enjoy watching races, but he no longer ran.

"I was totally up in the air," he said, "with no goals. My major occupation was dictated by the federal government regarding the war in Vietnam. I was a conscientious objector and a subsitute letter carrier in Hartford."

Rodgers moved to Boston, lived in a sleazy room in the Back Bay, went to BC graduate school, and took a job as an escort messenger at Peter Bent Brigham Hospital. His functions included wheeling patients to appointments, carrying blood samples, and wheeling dead-bodies to the morgue. His take-home pay was $75 a week, and his only fun was going into bars.

So many of life's decisions hinge on one seemingly inconsequential moment, and so it was with Rodgers. In 1972, somebody stole the motorbike he rode to work, so he began running the mile and a half to the hospital every day. And one day, after a sixty-year-old beat him in an informal race, he quit smoking. He expanded his running to 10 miles a day, and then to 100 miles a week. One week he ran 124 miles.

In 1973, when he was twenty-three years old and out of a job, Rodgers entered his first Boston Marathon. He wasn't ready for it, even though he'd placed third in a twenty-miler two months before. After stopping several times, he dropped out of the marathon after twenty-one miles.

The failure, if that's what it was, discouraged Rodgers. He thought about moving to California, but instead returned to Connecticut, where for two

Bill Rodgers with
Special Olympics winners.

Rodgers was coached by Bill Squires, but here, Jock Semple shouts information and encouragement to him at Lake Street.

months he did not train at all. He picked up again, however, and, in October, won the Bay State Marathon.

About that time, life carved out another lesson for Rodgers. He returned to the Boston area and took an attendant's job with the Fernald School in Waltham, where he learned what it was like to deal with the true inequities of life.

Rodgers later told Paul Katzeff of the *Boston Herald:* "I saw people who were not very retarded and some who were severely retarded. I saw people who happened to have been hit by a car at age five and had to live with brain damage for the rest of their lives. I saw people who had been hammered by life.

"How can you feel tired after a five-mile run when you've seen that? How can you think running is painful after seeing these people? Working there had a gigantic effect on me."

Rodgers really began to get serious about his running. He joined the Greater Boston Track Club, with Bill Squires as coach, and got some discipline into his training. He finished fourteenth in the 1974 marathon, but was fourth until leg cramps got him at Heartbreak Hill.

Rodgers was still learning, and he was not yet convinced that he had what it took to be a marathoner. He didn't know if he had the stamina and desire to gut it out on the hot, foot-ripping macadam roads, when every muscle in his body was urging him to quit.

He finished third in New York in 1974, won a race in Philadelphia, captured the Woods Hole–to–Falmouth 7.3-mile race, and, in what rated as one of his big accomplishments, won the bronze medal for finishing third in the world cross-country championships in Rabat, Morocco.

Still, the 5'9" 130-pounder was hardly among the favorites as the 1975 marathon approached. Even Rodgers himself didn't think much of his chances. Ernie Roberts of the *Boston Globe* was the only newsman to mention him at any length prior to the race.

Roberts asked Rodgers how he'd feel if somehow he won the 79th Boston edition. Replied Rodgers, "I would totally amaze myself. I'd be in a complete state of shock."

The temperature hovered around 50 degrees that April, with a northwest wind. It was weather that would come to be known as perfect for Bill Rodgers. After six miles, Jerome Drayton, Mario Cuevas, and Rodgers were battling for the lead. Cuevas dropped back after nine, but Drayton, a Canadian, hung right at Rodgers's elbow.

"I heard somebody yell, 'Go Jerome, go Jerome,' and that depressed me," said Rodgers.

Then, at the ten-mile mark, near Natick, Rodgers took off the gloves given to him by his brother Charlie and spurted into the lead. He was out front, still holding the gloves, the rest of the way.

Rodgers looked back only twice and never faltered in his stride. He did stop twice, once in Newton Lower Falls to accept a cup of water, and again in Newton to tie a shoelace.

"Why there?" he was asked in the postrace interview. "Because it seemed like a good spot to do it," the unflappable and refreshing Rodgers replied.

He also said that he felt like quitting several times, but spectators along the route, noting the GBTC stitched on his jersey, kept yelling, "C'mon, Boston, keep going, keep going."

Rodgers finished in 2.09.55, an American record, and of course, a Boston Marathon mark. When he was told of the winning time, he mumbled, "Are you sure, are you sure? This is absurd. I can't run that fast. This is ridiculous. I must be dreaming the whole thing."

The victory in 1975 brought marathon running into the spotlight and began a chain of events that made Rodgers an international sports celebrity.

Bill Rodgers meets with the press after one of his many marathon wins.

He didn't finish his next marathon, in Enschede, Holland, but then came in third in the prestigious Fukuoka, Japan, race with a time of 2.11.26.

Rodgers didn't defend his Boston championship in 1976 because he was in serious training for the Olympics to be held that August in Montreal. Rodgers was consumed with the thought of winning an Olympic medal, and his failure to do so in Montreal was perhaps the biggest disappointment of his career.

"If you put a stack of a million dollars over here, and an Olympic medal over there," Rodgers told Steve Harris of the *Boston Herald American*, "and said to pick one, I'd take the medal. Keep the million. Anyone can make a million bucks. I'd take one of those medals."

Rodgers was among the leaders in Montreal for about 20 kilometers, but even then knew it was not going to be a good race for him. He had injured a foot shortly before the race, and it bothered him. So did the wet, muggy day. Rodgers finished a nondescript fortieth, as East German Waldemar Cierpinski won in 2.09.55.

After Montreal, Rodgers felt somehow as if his running career had finished on a downbeat. "Words just can't convey the utter feeling of losing," he said.

However, he came back strong by winning in New York in 1976, thus getting reams of big-city publicity. However, the next spring in Boston was a disaster. On a 90-degree day, when spectators and runners alike were dropping from the heat, a dehydrated, overtrained Rodgers failed to finish. He had dueled with Drayton again in the early stages, but this time it was Rodgers who was wiped out.

"I just got blown away," he said after the race. "The heat and the pace killed me."

That defeat would be his last for a long while, because Rodgers then put together a most remarkable string of victories. He won 17 in a row, including 3 straight firsts in New York, 2 in Boston, and 2 in Fukuoka—the 3 most prestigious marathons in the world.

"He just destroyed people," said racing guru Tommy Leonard.

Rodgers became a hero in Japan after winning in 2.10.55, the fastest marathon time in 1977. In New York, he beat Frank Shorter, always the name linked with his, by 3 minutes.

Rodgers was making off-the-road news as well. Always outspoken, he had begun to challenge what to him was the outdated amateur code that kept roadrunners from profiting from their talent.

"We're living under a system of hypocrisy," Rodgers said. "I've talked to runners from all over the world and a lot of people have the mistaken belief that amateur athletics and poverty go hand in hand. That's just not so any more."

To back up his beliefs and to capitalize on his notoriety, Rodgers opened a store in Cleveland Circle, directly on the Boston Marathon route, that specialized in running gear. The store clicked immediately, and he later opened branches in other cities.

The 1978 Boston Marathon was a memorable one, with Rodgers beating out Jeff Wells of Texas by only 2 seconds, in the closest finish in history.

"I thought I had it won easily," said Rodgers. "We ran the last 100 yards like a dash." His time was 2.10.13, the second fastest Boston mark.

After winning in New York in 1978 for his seventeenth straight, Rodgers's streak came to an end when he was sixth in Fukuoka, despite a 2.12.51 clocking.

Rodgers leaped into the headlines again before the 1979 Boston Marathon when he criticized the venerable institution for being behind the times.

"I'm not sure I would run Boston if I had a chance to go somewhere else, where I would be well taken care of," he said. "If they want it to be a truly great marathon, they should invite runners from all over the world. It should be commercial. Corporations should sponsor American amateurs. They benefit and the runners benefit. I'm in favor of open sport."

Rodgers was proud of his accomplishments and decried what he felt was a lack of respect given marathoners by the general public.

"I'm a better athlete than Joe Namath," he said. "I'll be running over his grave."

After one of Rodger's New York victories, *Globe* writer Joe Concannon noted the disparity in money and adulation by commenting, "Julius Erving left this city a millionaire. Before Bill Rodgers left it, he had his car towed and it cost $90 to get it back."

But Rodgers noted that at least the New York Road Runners Club had paid that bill. "If that had happened in Boston," he said, "I'd have paid for it. I don't know if I'll run there again if there's not something in it."

However, the pull back to the race that had first brought his name before the public was too strong. Rodgers ran in Boston again in 1979 and set an American record of 2.09.27.

Perhaps this was his most competitive marathon. He trailed for eighteen miles and had to fight against the urge to put on an early burst of speed, a foolhardly move that would have meant big trouble for him in Newton.

The weather was chilly that day, with the temperature at 42 degrees, so Rodgers wore a wool cap. Tom Fleming led early, then Gary Bjorklund took over. But at Heartbreak Hill, Toshihiko Seko of Japan and Rodgers made it a two-man race.

After Rodgers took the lead, he wasn't sure how far Seko was behind him, and had visions of a repeat of the 1978 sprint to the finish with Wells. But as he went past the Eliot Lounge on Commonwealth Avenue he saw Seko 200 yards behind and knew that victory was his.

Rodgers thus became only the fourth man to win 3 marathons, and the next year became the only one besides 7-time winner Clarence DeMar to capture 4 championships.

President Jimmy Carter, a jogger himself, had called to congratulate Rodgers in 1979, and Rodgers and his wife had later been guests at the White House. But there was no call in 1980, because of a marked difference of opinion between the president and the athlete over the pull-out of the United States from the 1980 Olympics, scheduled that summer in Moscow.

Rodgers called the boycott "the blackest day in United States Olympic history," and charged the Olympic committee with selling its athletes down the river.

The boycott, seethed Rodgers, "is a blatant, disgusting applying of pressure by a president whose main motive is to be reelected."

Rodgers scoffed at the paragraph in a news report that read, "The United States will not send an Olympic team to Moscow."

"When did the United States ever send an Olympic team anywhere?" he wanted to know. "The country doesn't spend a nickel on its Olympic athletes."

Rodgers further told newsmen, "When appearance money is an accepted fact, all you guys will have to write about is what we do in a race and not how much we supposedly made from it."

The Olympic boycott seemed to take the edge off Rodgers's performance, and after winning in Boston, he didn't fare well in his next few 1980 appearances. The usual "is he over the hill?" stories surfaced, but Rodgers quieted them by winning in New York for the fourth straight time, catching teenager Kirk Pfeffer at the twenty-three-mile mark and cruising home.

At the age of thirty-three, Rodgers finished third to Seko in the 1981 Boston Marathon, with the strong time of 2.10.34, his fifth best all-time effort.

Rodgers's record is amazing. Starting with the Boston win in 1975, he ran 9 marathons in less than 2.12, 4 more than anyone else. At one time he owned the four fastest times by an American citizen. In one stretch, from Jan. 1, 1977, to Oct. 23, 1978, Rodgers ran 55 races and won 50 of them.

Rodgers finishing third in the 1981 Boston Marathon.

Johnny Kelley, when this was written, had been running long distance races for fifty-four years. Rodgers had been competing in them for only nine. The Boston Marathon had changed greatly in the years spanned by these two great runners.

But marathon running remained the same. You picked 'em up and put 'em down as fast as you could for 26 miles, 385 yards. You battled blisters and cramps and exhaustion and bad weather and one another, and most of all, you battled yourself.

Few, if any, did it better than Johnny Kelley and Bill Rodgers.

PART V

━━THE OLYMPICS━━

They are paid nothing for their talents. They receive minimal support from the government and the public. They train long lonely hours for what usually amounts to a once-in-a-lifetime long shot, namely, the opportunity to represent the United States in international athletic competition.

And yet, Olympic champions occupy a unique place in American sport. To win an Olympic medal, even in today's politically controlled atmosphere, is still considered the highest form of athletic achievement.

Massachusetts has had many athletes who have mounted the victory pedestal in an Olympic stadium, heard the strains of the national anthem, and had a gold, silver, or bronze medal placed around their necks.

The Boston Athletic Association sent five track-and-field men to Athens in 1896—sprinter Tom Burke, hurdler Thomas Curtis, jumper Ellery Clark, pole vaulter Welles Hoyt, and distance runner Arthur Blake. Burke won the 100- and 400-meter dashes, Curtis the 110-meter hurdles, and Clark the broad jump.

James B. Connolly, who dropped out of Harvard to compete, was the very first gold medal winner in the modern Olympics, winning the hop, step, and jump competition in 1896.

"It was," wrote Connolly, "a moment to inspire."

In the modern, modern Olympics, that is, the games after World War II, many others from Massachusetts have excelled.

CHAPTER 12

"THE OLYMPIANS"

ALBRIGHT, JENKINS, CONNOLLY, THOMAS, HEMERY, 1960 AND 1980 HOCKEY TEAMS

"Just being part of the Olympics has affected my whole life."
—Tenley Albright

Tenley Albright, of Newton Centre, skating to the strains of a Jacques Offenbach medley in a Cortina, Italy, ice palace before a crowd of ten thousand, won the Olympic figure-skating gold medal on February 2, 1956. The victory was the exclamation point on a dramatic story of a twenty-year-old athlete who overcame polio, suffered at the age of eleven, to become a skating champion.

Albright had started skating at the age of eight, when her father, Dr. Hollis Albright, flooded the yard behind the house. She became so proficient that her parents decided to take her to the Boston Skating Club for lessons. After she became world champion, she estimated it had cost her parents $50,000 for the lessons that had helped make her the best.

But Albright didn't become dedicated to skating until after the polio attack. Young Tenley, on Sept. 13, 1946, was holding a baby in her arms when she began to have strange sensations.

"My arms," she said. "They won't hold anything. They feel as though all the skin is coming off."

She was taken, with a temperature of 102, to Haney Memorial Hospital, where the diagnosis of polio was made.

"She knew where she was, all right," said her father. "There was a big sign, 'Polio Floor', right above the door."

After the fever has subsided, it was established that Albright, though the illness was serious enough, would not have permanent paralysis. She exercised faithfully to regain her muscle tone, so much so that her parents worried that she might be trying too much too fast.

"It took remarkable will power and concentration for a child to go on with her exercises as she did," commented Dr. Robert H. Morris, a Boston therapist.

Twice when she was starting to walk again, Albright toppled over, unable to control her leg muscles.

"She was very determined," said Willie Frick, instructor at the Boston Skating Club. "She took a lot of falls, but she'd pick herself up and start over."

Tenley Albright was the United States figure-skating champion from 1952 through 1956, won the women's world championships at Davos, Switzerland, in 1953, and repeated the feat in Vienna in 1955. She was the first American to win a world figure-skating title.

Maribel Vinson Owen, the famous skater and teacher who later died in a tragic crash that also took the life of the U.S. skating team, helped tutor Albright in her rise to the top. Said Mrs. Owen: "As a pupil she was serious, receptive, and diligent, and displayed enormous powers of concentration."

The year before her world triumph in Vienna, Albright had finished second in the competition, losing out in Oslo to Gundi Busch of Germany.

"There I was coming out of a double jump when my skate slipped," she told reporters. "I was so angry. I do that jump hundreds of times. When I finished I had to do it by myself again and again just to prove I could do it. Losing something makes you appreciate winning even more."

Albright, then sixteen, had finished second to Barbara Ann Scott of Canada in the 1952 Olympics. Since then, however, her national and world championships had put her on the cover of *Sports Illustrated* and made her a favorite in the 1956 competition at Cortina.

A practice injury almost ruined Albright's chances. On Jan. 19, 1956, her skate caught a hole in the ice and, as she was falling, the point of the blade hit her right ankle. She was carried from the rink to the hotel, where a doctor made her walk a few steps so her leg wouldn't stiffen.

Albright turned in a remarkable performance to beat out sixteen-year-old Carol Heiss of Ozone Park, New York. She won even though her ankle was not fully healed. As close as two days before the finals she had been unable to do some of the trickier jumps in her program. In the finals, it hurt every time she put her full weight on the toe of her right foot.

"I don't care if the ankle bursts wide open," Tenley said before the competition. "All I care is that it holds me for four minutes."

The victory was not without controversy. Albright had piled up a considerable lead in compulsory figures and when she averaged 5.6 points out of a maximum 6 on the final day's performance, the lead was too much for Miss Heiss to overcome.

However, the 100-pound teenager received enthusiastic applause from the crowd, with fans yelling "sei, sei" to the judges, imploring them to award Carol the maximum 6 points. After Heiss finished her free-skating routine, she avoided photographers' attempts to take her picture with the gold medal

Tenley Albright, at 13, was the 1949 New England Junior figure skating champion.

winner. The awkward interlude was the culmination of the tension that had built between the two because of Olympic pressures.

Albright graduated from Harvard Medical School when she was twenty-four, and began studying surgery at Beverly Hospital in 1961. As Dr. Tenley Albright, she received the gold plate award in 1976 from the American Academy of Achievement, and served as team doctor for the Olympic team in Innsbruck, Austria.

Charlie Jenkins was another Olympic winner from Massachusettts in 1956. A lithe sprinter from Rindge Tech in Cambridge, he won the 400-meter in Melbourne that summer.

Jenkins, born in New York City, moved to Cambridge when he was a year old. At fourteen, when his mother died, he went to Wilmington, Delaware, to live with relatives, but a year later returned to Cambridge to live with his aunt.

Jenkins had no special feeling for track at that age. In fact, he used to watch the runners working out and laugh at them. His sport was basketball, and he planned to try out for the team at Rindge. But a friend who was a member of the track team challenged him to go out for that sport.

"I told him running was silly," Jenkins said, "so he challenged me to run faster then he could."

Jenkins won the state 600-yard championship two years in a row and, as a

Charlie Jenkins shows one of his two Olympic gold medals upon arrival at Logan Airport.

quarter-miler, was unbeaten outdoors. Twice he won the national AAU schoolboy title in Madison Square Garden.

Even then, though he had come to regard running as fun, he would rather have been a high-jumper.

"If I could really jump high," he said, "I'd stop running in a minute."

Tom Duffy, Jenkins's coach, wasn't about to let his protegé become a high-jumper. Duffy knew he had a potential Olympian in tow.

In January of 1955, Jenkins, by then a student at Villanova, won the third fastest indoor 600-yard dash in history (1.10) in the K. of C. Meet at Boston Garden. It was taken for granted he would be on the 1956 Olympic team. The question was, which event would he run? There was no 600-yard run, Jenkins's specialty, in the Olympics. There was a 400-meter and an 800-meter, and Jenkins opted for the shorter distance. It was a wise move.

On November 28, 1956, Jenkins, not given a big chance for a gold medal, qualified for the 400-meter finals by winning his heat in a 46.1 clocking, a remarkable time under the bitter-cold, windy running conditions.

In the finals, he was in the third lane and got off to a fast start. Lou Jones of New Rochelle, New York, the world record holder, set the early pace, but Russia's Ardalion Ignatiev caught Jones at the last curve. Ignatiev, in taking over the lead, had also blown past Jenkins.

"When he went flying by me," Jenkins said after the race, "I froze for a moment, and then I started out to catch him. All I ever thought about was running as hard as I knew how." The thought was father to the act. Jenkins overtook the Russian 25 yards from the wire, fought off Karl Haas of Germany, and won the race in 46.7 seconds, not close to a record, but plenty good enough considering the bad weather conditions.

"Jenkins was in perfect physical and mental condition for this great race," said Duffy, who had set up his protegé's pre-Olympic training routine.

Later in the same Olympics, Jenkins won a second gold medal as part of the American 1600-meter relay team.

As the first Olympic running champion from Massachusetts in fifty years, Jenkins came home to a tumultuous welcome and a hundred-car motorcade in Cambridge. The champion talked of the challenge of the 1960 Olympics in Rome, where he hoped to compete in the 800-meter run.

But it was not to be. By 1958, the competitive fires had burned out, and Charlie Jenkins, only twenty-four years old, retired from competitive racing.

Much was made in those days—and is made in present days too, for that matter—of American–Soviet competition. Daily point standings ran in the papers, and, whenever athletes from the Soviet Union competed in a final with Americans, the event took on an added dimension.

Harold Connolly, a Boston College athlete, made front page news when in the 1956 Olympics in Melbourne; he beat out Russia's Mikhail Krivosonov to win the hammer throw.

Harold Connolly, 1945 Olympic gold medal winner in the hammer throw, demonstrates his throwing ability in Berlin during a goodwill tour of Europe.

Connolly, whose left arm had been slightly withered since birth, began tossing the hammer back to the regular throwers on the BC track team, as an exercise for strengthening his arm. When he discovered he could throw the iron ball further than the varsity, he took it up seriously.

Krivosonov, the world record holder, was a slight favorite to win the event, but Connolly was so determined to beat the Russian he kept a photo of his adversary on the windshield visor of his car as a reminder.

All six finalists in the hammer throw qualified for their last three tosses by breaking the Olympic mark. Then, on his second toss of the final competition, Connolly threw the hammer 207' 3 1/2", 6 inches beyond Krivosonov's best.

"Man, was I nervous," Connolly said after the world-record-breaking toss. "My hands were sweating so bad I could hardly hang on to the handle. But Krivosonov was nervous too."

Connolly was a favorite to repeat in 1960 in Rome, as he'd upped the world record to 230' 9" in California a month before the Olympic competition. But a performance in Bern, Switzerland, two weeks before the Olympic games, may have been a tip-off that his concentration was not what it had once been. He barely won the Bern event, and branded the trip as a silly sightseeing tour.

In the 1960 Olympics, Connolly, saying he simply ran out of gas, was a badly beaten eighth.

John Thomas, a high-jumper from Boston, made a bittersweet story in the summer Olympics of 1960. Thomas, considered the greatest high-jumper in American history, went 7 feet or better 191 times in his career. He held every American record available, and for a time, was the world record holder.

When he was nineteen, he set that world mark of 7' 3 3/4" to win the U.S. Olympic trials, and if there was one certainty for a gold medal in that Rome extravaganza, the introspective student from Boston University was it.

Jerry Nason of the *Globe*, one of the premier track experts in the United States, wrote, prior to the 1960 Olympics: "Perhaps the most prohibitive favorite in the history of the modern Olympiads is John Curtis Thomas, 19, of Cambridge and Boston University—the most gifted high jumper the world has ever known."

But Thomas didn't win in Rome. He finished third to Robert Shavlakadzke and Valery Brumel, both of the Soviet Union. He cleared 7' 1/4", but the two Russians went 7' 1".

What happened to Thomas in those 1960 Olympics was as searing an example of how the pressures of sport—not merely the pressures of competition but the outside distractions—can affect the outcome of an event.

In the same story in which Nason had crowned Thomas the champion in advance, the writer had sensed what might happen. Wrote Nason: "There are elements present for an emotional crackup under the weight of pressures that build up in the days and hours leading to the ultimate struggle for the gold medal."

And so it was in Rome. The quiet Thomas, poised and confident in his American competition, had trouble coping in Rome. A few days before the

John Thomas clearing 7'2½" at Madison Square Garden in New York.

games began, there was talk that Thomas would have to be isolated from the crowds.

"This boy is undergoing torture." said Larry Snyder, the head track coach for the Americans. "He can't eat. He can't sleep. He never gets any privacy. He never gets any rest. People crowd him all day long, going into his bedroom, hanging over his elbows at the lunch table, mobbing him on the practice field. He's the most sought-after athlete in the entire village."

An Associated Press dispatch on Aug. 30, 1960, described Thomas as having tears in his eyes as he described his futile attempts to salvage some privacy.

Even so, Thomas remained a heavy favorite as the high-jump preliminaries began at nine in the morning of Sept. 1. Ten hours later, he had failed three times at 7'1". Let the words of Arthur Daley, Pulitizer-Prize-winning columnist of the *New York Times*, describe the moment:

"The third try came amid the funereal silence of 70,000 breath-holding witnesses. The bar toppled into the sawdust pit with him. The silence was split by a deafening roar. The invincible one had met with defeat. Slowly he arose, sawdust matting his uniform shirt, for the long grief-stricken walk to the sidelines."

The aftermath of the finish was worse than the event itself. Thomas could go nowhere without being asked for an accounting of how it could have happened. Americans accused him of being overconfident. The Soviets said just the opposite, that the youngster was suffering from a bad case of nerves.

The episode left a deep scar on the nineteen-year-old. In his mind, all his previous accomplishments had been forgotten by fellow Americans quick to pin the donkey's tail on him for what had happened in Rome.

Four years later, while preparing for the 1964 Olympics in Tokyo, Thomas said: "I don't care what the people think. If I win, they're with me. If I lose, they're the first to desert me and call me a bum . . . They don't give credit to a man for trying."

Thomas said he felt proud to have won a bronze medal in Rome but that people treated him as though he had the plague.

He was right in many ways. We do tend to come down hard on athletes who don't live up to our/their expectations. We do take it personally. We do feel a sense of disappointment, as though we've somehow been let down.

But time takes care of many wounds, and time has given us a better perspective on what a marvelous athlete John Thomas was, gold medal or not.

Thomas came out of the same Rindge Tech High School as Charlie Jenkins and said he became a track man because everybody in the neighborhood who went to Rindge went out for track.

Mrs. John Thomas, the athlete's mother, once said that the first indication that John would be something special as a jumper came when neighbors noticed the youngster leaping over a four-foot picket fence around his house.

"He was so crazy about high-jumping," she said. "He read every book in the library on it."

When Thomas entered Rindge he was 5'6" tall. By the time he began at Boston University, he was 6'5" and a high-jumping phenomenon. He first came to national attention when he cleared 7' 1¼" in the 1959 Millrose games in New York, a world indoor record.

A month later, Thomas's career was in jeopardy after his left foot was mangled in an elevator accident at his BU dormitory. Thomas was operating the elevator as part of a work detail during the school's spring vacation. He was sitting on a stool when his foot became wedged between the elevator and shaft while the cage was in motion. No bones were broken, but the injury forced him to forego high-jumping for ten months.

His comeback, at the age of eighteen, was electrifying. On Feb. 1, 1960, he pushed his indoor record to 7' 1½" at the Millrose games, the third time he'd gone over 7' since returning to competition. Three weeks later, he upped the record to 7' 2". In March he went a half-inch higher in Chicago, and also broke the world outdoor mark with a 7' 1½" jump in Philadelphia. He topped that in May with a 7' 1¾" success at MIT.

Then came the 7' 3¾" leap in Bakersfield, California, in the Olympic trials. Little wonder that the question as he prepared for Rome was not whether he would win but how high he would jump.

It took some time for Thomas to regain his competitive edge after the

Olympic disappointment. From March through July of 1961 he was beaten four times, and that included three more victories for Valery Brumel, the Russian who had finished second in the Olympics, but who had since gone on to become the world's best.

Brumel came to Boston on Feb. 18 and beat Thomas with a jump of 7' 3". A week later in New York, the Soviet made it three in a row with a 7' 2"-to-7' 0" victory.

In May of 1961, Thomas had his best jump since before the Olympics, 7' 2⅜", in a quandrangular meet at Brandeis. He leaped 7'2" in Philadelphia in June, and then went to Moscow to battle Brumel on the Russian's home turf. A crowd of seventy thousand turned out in Lenin Stadium, and once again the nineteen-year-old Brumel, jumping in the rain, beat the American in the closest battle they'd had since the Olympics.

Brumel went 7' 4" on his last try to break Thomas's world record. Thomas cleared 7' 2¼", and barely scraped the bar on his last try at 7' 4".

Thomas continued to compete in college meets, as well as in the most prestigious American competitions. He was aiming for one last hurrah, the 1964 Olympics in Tokyo.

He had finally beaten Brumel in February of 1963. Thomas, now an "aging" twenty-three years old, continued to leap at least 7' in every meet. He won four straight in the indoor season of 1964 including a record 7' 2" in the Millrose games.

Thomas went to Tokyo in circumstances far different from 1960.

"I'm a nobody now and it's wonderful," he told Will Grimsley of the Associated Press. The tension and edginess of 1960 were gone. Thomas was relaxed and friendly, and, when asked what his expectations were, replied: "I'll go out there and do the best I can and if I do that, I'll be happy with myself. As for what everybody else thinks, to hell with them."

Thomas jumped as high as Brumel (7' 1") in Tokyo, but the gold medal still eluded him. Brumel got it on the basis of fewer misses, and Thomas settled for the silver.

"I wasn't outjumped," he said. "On paper, I was as good as there was. I'm as good as there is in the world at this time and that makes me feel good."

No apologies made, no apologies needed, for John Curtis Thomas, the best high-jumper in American history.

Dave Hemery, another Boston University Olympian, running, however, for Great Britain, would strike gold four years later, in Mexico City. Hemery, a transplanted Britisher who had lived in Braintree since he was fourteen, won a gold medal in the 400-meter hurdles in 1968, then took a bronze and a silver in 1972.

Hemery grew up on the English seacoast, where he spent long hours running on the sand and hurdling the boards that had been set up to keep the beach from eroding. His father had been the schoolboy long-jump champion in Australia. Hemery came to the United States with his family when he was twelve. He'd attended Thayer Academy in Braintree, and then Boston University.

"When I first saw him," said Billy Smith, Hemery's coach at BU, "I didn't see how he could miss as a hurdler."

The long-legged Hemery, 6'1½" and 173 pounds, was twenty-four years old when he won at Mexico City. He had trained in the summer of 1967 in the surf and on the sand at Duxbury Beach, hoping to repair a leg muscle damaged so badly there was a possibility he would not race competitively again.

The rehabilitation worked and Hemery felt fit as his race approached in Mexico City. Smith told him that if he ran a 48.1 or 48.2 no one would come close.

And that's what happened. Hemery ran a 48.1 in the 400-meter finals, more than a second under the existing Olympic record. He was 4 yards ahead of his nearest competitor.

In his book, *Another Hurdle: The Making of an Olympic Champion,* Hemery describes the magic moment:

"With every muscle in me, I forced my stride length and speed. I ripped at the line and two strides afterward, tipped my head to the right to see if [Ron] Whitney was coming by. I could not see him and my hands went to my knees. I was not 100 percent sure I had won. I think the gradual confirmation came when the BBC cameramen raced forward for an interview."

Dave Hemery
showing Olympic form
over the hurdles.

Hemery was twenty-eight, out of college for four years and living in England when he went back to the Olympics in 1972 and won the bronze in the 400-meter hurdles and a silver in the 1600-meter relay.

Shortly after that performance, he shook up the Olympic committee with some revolutionary ideas for the future of the games. He suggested that athletes be allowed to receive appearance money without damaging their status, that the Olympics be split into four separate meets, each in a different country, that the flag-raising ceremonies should be abolished, and that all medals should be presented at the end of the games, with only the Olympic flag flying.

None of Hemery's suggestions, logical as they seemed then and now, have been adopted at this writing.

The flag consciousness that Hemery sought to downplay was very much in evidence in both the 1960 and 1980 winter Olympics, when several Massachusetts athletes had a big part in two of the great Olympic triumphs of all times.

Both *hockey gold-medal victories* were held in this country, the 1960 edition at Squaw Valley, California, and the 1980 one at Lake Placid, New York.

Going into the competition at Squaw Valley, the American team was given only an outside chance of winning even a bronze medal. Canada and the Soviet Union figured to battle for the gold, and if things broke just right, the U.S. could take third place ahead of Czechoslovakia.

History gave the Americans no reason to be optimistic. The United States, in seven previous winter Olympics, had never won a hockey gold medal.

The sport, after all, was the national game in Canada. It was played everywhere in that immense country, whereas in the U.S., it was big only in New England, the Minnesota–Northern Michigan area, and upper New York State.

The defending champion Soviet Union subsidized the best hockey players in the nation and put them in the military. There, they practiced as a unit twelve months a year, polishing a passing style that would eventually change the way the game was played, even in the NHL.

The American team, which included a fireman, a soldier, two carpenters, and two insurance agents, had four men from greater Boston on its roster— Capt. Jack Kirrane of Brookline, Dick Rodenhiser of Malden, and the Cleary brothers, Bill, of Cambridge, and Bob, from Westwood. In addition, Jack Riley, the coach, was from Medford, and the trainer, Ben Bertini, was from Lexington.

The U.S. squad opened with 6–3 and 9–1 wins over Sweden and Germany, respectively, with Billy Cleary scoring 4 goals and Bobby 1 against the Germans. But Sweden and Germany were the two weakest teams in the event. The rocky road lay dead ahead.

Canada quickly established itself as the clear favorite for the gold by shutting out Germany, 12–0, and Czechoslovakia, 4–0.

But the Americans had beaten Canada in 1956 and so weren't awed by the team from the north when the two clashed in game number three. The contest was scoreless until midway through the first period. Then Bobby

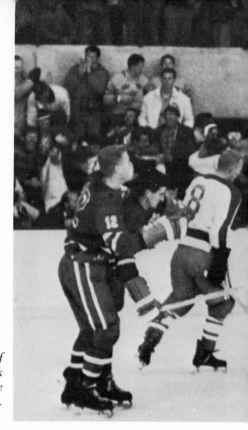

Squaw Valley, California: Rodney Paavola of the U.S. hockey team throws his hockey stick into the air after the final second of their game with the U.S.S.R.

Cleary took a pass from John Maytasich of Minnesota and slid the puck into the net. On the ice for Canada at the time, playing defense, was Harry Sinden, who would one day coach the Stanley Cup champion Bruins and later become general manager of the team.

With Jack McCartan brilliant in goal with 39 saves, the U.S. hung on to beat Canada, 2–1.

Television in 1960 was not the all-seeing eye it has since become, but enough footage filtered through to the nation so that the team suddenly became the darling of America.

And so millions watched as the U.S. team went against the powerful Soviets. The Russians were an experienced team, with many players, including the goalie, veterans of the 1956 Olympic titlists. A U.S. hockey team had never beaten a Russian team.

"I don't know how many people came up to me after we got home and said they were glued to the TV set that day," said Billy Cleary, who scored first for the Americans.

The Russians led 2–1 at the end of a period, but midway through the second period, Bill Christian scored. Then, with six minutes left, Bill and Roger Christian and Tommy Williams, who would later play professionally with the Bruins, combined on a goal that won the game. Bill Christian scored it, as the ten thousand partisans in the Squaw Valley arena went wild. The Americans had done it. They had beaten the unbeatable champions and clinched at least a tie for the gold medal.

But there remained the final game against the Czechs, a disappointing but still strong team. They proved they were tough by taking a 4–3 lead at the end of two periods against an American team that seemed mentally and physically exhausted by the rigors and tensions of its two previous games.

However, the Americans had become known as a third-period team and proved it against the Czechs by pouring through 6 unanswered goals in the final period to win 9–4. Bobby Cleary scored 2 of those and brother Billy put the finishing touch on the great victory with the final goal.

The last player cut from that 1960 team before it went to Squaw Valley was Herb Brooks of the University of Minnesota. Brooks, however, later surfaced as coach of the Cinderella team that captured America's heart by winning the gold medal at Lake Placid in 1980.

There were several parallels between the 1960 and 1980 champions. Again the Soviet Union was the principal adversary. Again the Americans were underdogs. Dave Christian of the 1980 team was the son of Bill and nephew of Roger, both of whom had starred at Squaw Valley.

And again, four players from Greater Boston would play key roles, with one of them again being captain. This time the names were Capt. Mike Eruzione of Winthrop, Jack O'Callahan of Charlestown, Dave Silk of Scituate, and goalie Jim Craig of Easton.

And as the competition progressed, it was obvious that Craig would play the same key role in his team's success as had goalie Jack McCartan twenty years before.

Also in the U.S. team's favor was the fact that the games were again held on American soil.

"When you are home and get that crowd behind you," said Bill Cleary, the 1960 high scorer, "it can do great things."

Realistically, the American team figured to finish no better than fifth. Since the last U.S. triumph, Soviet skaters had won four straight gold medals, and had progressed to the point where they more than held their own with the best in the National Hockey League in a series of exhibitions.

The U.S. team played a grueling pre-Olympic schedule, trying to accustom itself to the Brooks system, which combined the best of the Russians' passing style with the more physical NHL game. The Americans finished the tour at Madison Square Garden, where they were overwhelmed by the Russians, 10–3. It simply was no contest.

Shortly before the Olympic opener against Sweden, O'Callahan suffered a knee injury and was lost for the first two games.

The Lake Placid arena was far from filled for the game with Sweden. Silk scored to tie it at 1–1 in the second period, and, with twenty-seven seconds left in the game, with Sweden again out front, 2–1, defenseman Bill Baker whistled a 55-foot blast into the nets for the tying goal.

This started the American rooters on an emotional binge that lasted for a week, a ground swell of enthusiasm that built until the entire country was caught up in it.

The Americans pulled a huge surprise by beating Czechoslovakia, the second-rated team, 7–3, with Craig outstanding in the goal. Next came a 5–1 win over Norway, with Eruzione's goal early in the second period the catalyst. Silk also scored. The streak continued with a 7–2 victory over outclassed Rumania.

By now there wasn't a ticket to be had when the boys of winter skated onto the Lake Placid rink.

The last game in the preliminary round robin was against West Germany. The U.S. had already qualified for the final four. Win big against West Germany, that is, by 7 or more goals, and the team would not have to play the Soviets until the final game.

"We were talking in the locker room about all the possibilities," said O'Callahan, "and all we could decide was that they were too confusing."

The West Germans were also confusing. They would not be in the final four, but played that first period like champions, taking a 2–0 lead.

"Let's forget about the goal differential and go at the West Germans," said Eruzione. "Let's win the game."

They did win it, 4–2, with the chant of "U-S-A, U-S-A" coming from the jubilant flag wavers in the stands.

On Feb. 22—the birthday of George Washington, who never played hockey but knew something about patriotism—the United States took on the Soviet Union. Scalpers were getting $150 a ticket. Standing room was going for $25, if any of those tickets could be found.

The first period appeared over with Russia ahead, 2–1, but with a second left, Mark Johnson of Minnesota slipped the puck past goalie Vladislav

Mike Eruzione,
Captain of the 1980 U.S.
Olympic hockey team.

Tretiak to tie the game. When the second period began, Tretiak, punished for his last-second indiscretion, was not in goal. Substitute Vladimir Myshkin was.

The Soviets moved ahead 3–1, and were kept from breaking the game open only because of Craig's spectacular goaltending. Then, at 8:39 of the third period, Scituate's Silk passed to Johnson 5 feet in front of the net, and Johnson slammed the puck past Myshkin for a 3–3 tie.

A minute, twenty-one seconds later, Eruzione sent chills up the spines of millions of Americans watching the delayed television showing of the game, many of whom thought they were too sophisticated and too blasé to be moved by such matters.

The former Boston University star fired a 25-footer past Myshkin for the go-ahead goal. From there to the end, it was the Jim Craig show. Craig, also a former BU player, was sensational in goal, kicking away shot after shot as the seconds ticked off.

The Americans had beaten the Russians, the same team that had embarrassed them a month earlier. It was an incredible victory, and time, rather than diminishing the accomplishment, has only enhanced it.

The United States, however, still had to deal with Finland. If the Americans lost the final game by a large margin, they could end up as far down as fourth. A medal, even a bronze, was not yet a certainty.

Once again, the U.S. found itself behind early, with Finland on top, 1–0, at the end of a period. The Finns led 2–1 at the end of two. The drama and tension were building to a sizzling finish.

The Americans tied the score at 2.25 of the third period. Rob McClanahan of Minnesota put them ahead at 6.05, and at 16.25, Johnson clinched the victory with a short-handed goal.

Craig again was unbeatable in the last period, and in the final minute, with the crowd counting down the seconds, he thrust his gloved hand high over his head in a victory salute.

When the game ended, the players tossed gloves and sticks into the crowd and fans rushed onto the ice. Craig, an American flag wrapped around his exhausted body, was seen on television by millions, scanning the stands in the midst of the pandemonium, anxiously searching out his father, as he did after every game.

The victory aftermath was a procession of parties, parades, celebrity functions, and command performances. The players went to the White House to meet President Jimmy Carter. They were given the keys to the city in hometown celebrations and it was weeks before America came down from its patriotic high.

The capture of the gold medal by the 1980 American hockey team was an incredible victory. The triumph was great for those who played in the games and was equally fulfilling for America.

Strange as it may seem, an international sports championship was a terrific emotional pickup to a country that had been having trouble feeling good about itself.

PART VI

═COLLEGE═ SPORTS

College athletes come and go quickly, their time in the sun a brief one; only a relative few of the many thousands who perform on the collegiate playing fields leave a mark that lasts far beyond their years.

Harry Agganis of Boston University, the subject of Chapter 13 was one of those. Joe Bellino of Winchester, who won the Heisman Trophy in 1954 while playing for the Naval Academy also left his mark, and so did the following:

From Harvard—Barry Wood, a great all-round back in the late '20s and early '30s; Dick Clasby, backfield star in the '50s; Torby McDonald, a great runner who later was elected to the U.S. House of Representatives; Endicott (Chub) Peabody, an all-American tackle on the 1941 team and later the Governor of Massachusetts; Dick Button, Olympic figure-skating gold medalist in 1948 and 1952, and Chet Boulris, halfback selected to the all-Ivy-League football team of the '60s.

From Boston College—Charlie O'Rourke, passer on the unbeaten (11–0) Sugar Bowl champions of 1940; Edward (Butch) Songin, a football and hockey star who later played in the Canadian Football League and who was the first quarterback for the Boston Patriots; Mike Holovak, captain and fullback on bowl teams in 1941 and 1943, and later coach of BC and the Patriots; Art Donovan, star guard, who went on to a long career with the Baltimore Colts; Ernie Stautner, a star lineman who played fifteen years with the Pittsburgh Steelers and then became a defensive coordinator for the Dallas Cowboys.

Also, Art Graham and Jim Colclough, outstanding pass catchers who later starred with the Patriots; John Austin, the all-time basketball point maker; Jack Concannon, a quarterback who later played with the Chicago Bears; Tim Sheehy, a hockey star who played professionally with several teams; Mike Esposito, a halfback who holds several career rushing records, and Larry Eisenhauer, a defensive end who was a Patriots star for many seasons.

From Boston University—Mickey Cochrane, baseball Hall of Famer from East Bridgewater who caught for the Athletics and Tigers; Tom Gastall, quarterback and catcher whose major league baseball career with the Baltimore Orioles ended in a plane crash; Jack Garrity, twice an all-American hockey player who was on the 1948 Olympic team; Gary Famigletti, fullback who was all-pro three times with the Chicago Bears in the early '40s; John Kastan, fullback and Agganis' teammate who still holds many of BU's scoring records, and Bruce Taylor, best defensive back ever to play for the Terriers, who starred for nine seasons with the San Francisco '49ers.

From Holy Cross—Bill Osmanski, fullback who later starred with the Chicago Bears; golfer Willie Turnesa, who won the U.S. Open in 1938; George Kaftan, center on the great basketball teams of the late '40s; Paul Harney, who became a big-money winner on the pro golf tour; Ronnie Cahill, sensational passer of the late '30s; Ron Perry, basketball and baseball star who later became director of athletics at the Cross; Togo Palazzi, great point maker who played pro basketball for several seasons; Bob Dee, defensive end who later starred on the early Patriot teams, and Jack Foley, sensational shooter on basketball teams in the early '60s.

CHAPTER 13

"THE GOLDEN GREEK"

HARRY AGGANIS

"Today, the roads all runners come, Shoulder high, we bring you home,
And set you at your threshold down, Townsman of a stiller town."
—"To an Athlete Dying Young,"
by A. E. Housman

They came by the thousands to his funeral that June day in 1955—famous people who did not really know him and plain people who did. They filled St. George's Greek Orthodox Church in Lynn, Massachusetts, and the overflow gathered silently on the common outside.

Thirty thousand mourners had come to his wake and now a thousand jammed the church, with three thousand more in an adjacent hall and six thousand outside. Twenty thousand lined the route to the cemetery, where he was buried on a hillside overlooking Manning Bowl, the high school field he had once starred upon.

The thousands had come to say goodbye to Harry Agganis, who had captured their imagination and their hearts with his athletic ability and who had died long before his time.

Agganis had been the embodiment of every sports-minded boy's dreams. He was a schoolboy sensation, called the best high school athlete ever to come out of Greater Boston. He was a college all-American in the finest Frank Merriwell tradition—a one-man team pulling games out of the fire in the last minute, leading the underdog against unbeatable odds, laughing at adversity.

He had become a professional baseball player and in two seasons was in the major leagues, playing in Boston, ten miles from his hometown and a mile down the road from where he had been a college football star.

The well-built (6'1" 195 lbs.) Agganis was modest, handsome, strong, and good to his mother. He remembered old friends, always gave 100 percent, and was the ultimate team player. He was the too-good-to-be-true athlete come to life.

He had everything to live for and was seemingly indestructible and then, just like that, on June 26, 1955, Harry Agganis died of a blood clot.

He was twenty-six years old.

How can someone whose career had barely begun be included as one of Boston's greatest athletes? Perhaps, as George Sullivan suggested in the *Boston Globe*, "You had to have seen Harry Agganis to have believed him."

For those not fortunate enough to have caught a glimpse of this gifted performer in action, the memories of his contemporaries and the words written about him during his brief but marvelous career will shed some light on just how great he was.

Buff Donelli, who coached Agganis at Boston University, called him a coach's dream and the greatest football player he'd ever seen.

Harry Agganis was a schoolboy standout at Lynn Classical.

Jerry Nason, who covered college games for a quarter of a century for the *Boston Globe*, rated only three players as unforgettable—Bill Osmanski of Holy Cross, Doc Blanchard of Army, and Agganis.

Notre Dame coach Frank Leahy said, after viewing high school films of Agganis, "He's the finest football prospect I've ever seen." Benny Friedman, a former great college passer, called the Golden Greek better than Sid Luckman, Sammy Baugh, and Frankie Albert.

And yet, it was baseball that Agganis picked as a career. Paul Brown, coach of the Cleveland Browns, had made him the number-one draft choice in 1954 and had him figured as the quarterback successor to Otto Graham. But Agganis turned down a reported $50,000 offer from Brown to sign with the Red Sox.

In picking baseball over football, he was giving up a wide super-highway for the single-track road into the tangled forest. He'd been a college football sensation and the red carpet was out for him in the NFL. In baseball, he was an unknown quantity and would have to prove himself every day, which is precisely why he took the gamble.

The boy who would become known as the Golden Greek began throwing a football around with his brothers, James, Demosthenes, Philip, and Paul, when he was twelve. At Breed Junior High in Lynn he worked after school, first buffing shoes for $6 a week and then in a bakery for $10. He played legion baseball and also independent ball for the Lynn Frasers, and once got two hits off major leaguer Hugh (Losing Pitcher) Mulcahy, who was pitching for the Ft. Devens team.

There was little doubt Agganis would be a schoolboy standout, and he lived up to expectations in his years at Lynn Classical.

He warmed up by throwing 8 touchdown passes in his sophomore year. He upped that to 29 as a junior and had 20 more in his senior season. For his high school career, Agganis completed 326 passes in 509 attempts for 4099 yards.

He led Lynn Classical to an 11–0–1 season in 1946, climaxed by a 21–14 victory over Granby, Virginia, in the Orange Bowl schoolboy game. Granby, led by future major league pitcher Chuck Stobbs, had won 32 in a row.

Lynn Classical was upset by Peabody in the 1947 football opener, 7–6, as Agganis was reluctant to pass.

"Why not let some of the guys run?" he asked coach Bill Joyce as the team prepared for Gloucester High.

"You come out of there if you don't pass," Joyce warned.

So Agganis did, completing 23 of 32 as the largest crowd in Gloucester football history to that time saw its team lose, 27–0. When Agganis came off the field, he said to his coach: "Now can we start running the ball again?"

Agganis was old for his age, as the saying goes, and even in high school was a coach on the field. He had a fan club in high school and was captain of the schoolboy all-American football team in 1947.

He played in high school all-star baseball games in Chicago, New York, and Boston and after graduation, hit .300 in the summer of 1947 for the Augusta Millionaires semipro team.

The drums didn't beat as loudly for high school phenoms in those days as they would a generation later. College scouts didn't promise the world to kids who could throw a football or dunk a basketball. Even so, the colleges certainly had heard of Agganis. The offers flocked in and he could have written his ticket at any of a hundred schools.

The ticket he wrote was to Boston University, a heavily enrolled sidewalk school where football most definitely was not king. Agganis picked BU because he wanted to be near his widowed mother and because he wanted to make a name in the city in which he planned to live.

Agganis put smalltime BU football into the bigtime. The Terriers made the first sports page, not just in Boston but throughout the country. Before his college days were finished he would be featured several times on the covers of national magazines and would be generally acclaimed as the best all-round college football player in America.

Sometimes sports writers go overboard in acclaiming the latest sensation, who is back in the minors or on the bench before the ink is dry on the headline. But Agganis was no public-relations man's dream. He was the real thing.

Agganis was a quadruple threat, a rarity even then and unheard of in later days of specialization. He could pass, run, and kick, and was also a sensational defensive halfback. In his junior year he intercepted 15 passes. He was also durable, averaging fifty minutes a game for his college career and suffering only one serious injury.

The Golden Greek had something no coach could teach, namely, a feel for the game, a sense of the way things were and what should be done.

"When I'm going back to pass," he once said, "it's as though I can see everything at once. I see the fans all worked up, the coaches worrying on the bench. I see the expression on the faces of the guys trying to get me and on those trying to get out in the clear."

He had another God-given quality, that of being able to improvise. Against West Virginia, Agganis called a simple dive play to open the game, but without saying a word to his team, he faked the hand-off and ran 60 yards to West Virginia's 4-yard line. Asked why he would do such a thing without telling his teammates, he replied that he knew he'd get a better fake from the rest of the team if they carried out their original dive play assignments.

Agganis stayed cool when all around him was panic.

"I remember being on the plane going to Syracuse in 1949," Buff Donelli said, "and I was worried about the game. I had my tie loosened and was shuffling my play sheets when I felt a tap on my shoulder. It was Harry, who was only a sophomore."

"You worried, coach?" he asked me. "Don't worry, everything will work out okay. We'll take 'em." BU won the game, 33–21.

Once Donelli chided his quarterback about not passing enough and Agganis replied: "Coach, I pass when I think a pass is the right play. Otherwise I don't."

With Agganis directing the attack, BU, which had always been a whipping boy for the few major powers it scheduled, now became a force to contend with. During Agganis's time in school, BU played such bigtime football schools as North Carolina State, Kansas, Maryland, Navy, West Virginia, Oregon, College of the Pacific, Penn State, and Syracuse.

In his sophomore year, Agganis led the Terriers to six wins in a row. He completed 55 of 108 passes that season, with 15 touchdown throws. He ran for a 5.4 average and punted for a 46.5 average, the best in the country.

"Harry was like a pitcher," said Bob Whelan, a good running back on the 1949 team. "He could mix up the throws. Sting it. Float it. Anything. You go out, make your cut, look up, put your hands out, and . . . bang, there's the ball, right where you want it."

Agganis was already touted as the best in the country as the 1950 season approached, but in September, instead of reporting to BU, he reported to the Marine Corps boot camp at Camp Lejeune, North Carolina.

The story goes that Agganis was sitting on the BU bench before practice one afternoon, eating peaches out of a tin can, when he got word of the Marine call-up. Without him, BU's record was 3–5. With him, the Camp Lejeune football team won the sixth naval district championship.

Agganis was discharged from the Marines a year later, only forty-eight hours before Boston University's first game of 1951, against William and Mary. He studied the BU plays with assistant coach John Toner on the plane to Williamsburg, Virginia, then completed 10 of 23 passes, 2 for touchdowns, and ran for another score.

He also averaged 46 yards per punt. The Terriers lost, 34–25, but in recalling the game, Donelli said, "You can't believe the show Harry put on after being away for a year."

BU lost again the next week to Penn State, 40–34, but Agganis once more had a great day, throwing for 262 yards. Ernie Roberts, who covered the game for the *Boston Globe*, called it Harry's best performance.

Joe Yukica, who later would coach at Boston College and Dartmouth, was an injured member of that Penn State team, and thirty years later remembers Agganis's play that afternoon as one of the greatest individual performances he's ever witnessed.

In two games, BU had scored 59 points, yet had an 0–2 record. The next week, against a University of Louisville quarterbacked by a crew-cut kid named John Unitas, the Terriers again had no trouble scoring, but this time the defense also did its job. BU beat Louisville 39–7, with a balanced attack that included fewer passes.

BU beat Camp Lejeune, Agganis's "alma mater," and then upset powerful College of the Pacific, the nation's number-one offensive machine. The Terriers lost to Temple in what Donelli said was about as close to a bad game as Agganis ever had. Then came easy wins over NYU, 52–6, Oregon, 35–6, and Wichita, 39–6.

"By this time," said Donelli, "everyone who saw him knew this was a player who came along once in fifty years."

Agganis and BU finished his greatest season on a downer, a 26–14 loss to powerful Syracuse, a game in which Agganis was constantly pressured by the bulky but quick Syracuse line.

The BU star won all-America honors in 1951, completing 104 passes in 185 attempts for 1401 yards and 14 touchdowns. He was a runaway winner of the Bulger Award as the best college player in New England, and many thought he also should have won the Heisman Trophy, given to the man named the best college football player in the land.

Dick Kazmaier of Princeton, certainly no slouch, won the award, which prompted the outspoken and quite possibly biased Donelli to comment, "Kazmaier couldn't carry Agganis's shoes."

Agganis missed three games because of injury in his 5–4–1 senior year, but still completed 67 of 125 for 5 touchdowns. The sub-par season did not diminish his value in what would become known as the Agganis auction.

Agganis was a southpaw passer and punter. There haven't been many great left-handed passers in football history. Frankie Albert of Stamford and the '49ers, and Kenny Stabler of Alabama and the Oakland Raiders, are generally considered the two all-time best.

Agganis had a classic style and a textbook passing stance, the kind you see in publicity stills, but which usually disappears when the defensive line is making its charge.

He said he patterned his style after Sammy Baugh, the legendary Washington Redskins right-hander, who also cocked the ball behind his ear and threw with a graceful overhand motion. Agganis even wore 33, Baugh's number.

Which was Harry Agganis's best performance? He had so many that opinions vary, but the following are generally considered the top four. They were all against nationally ranked opponents, and two of the four were BU defeats.

NOV. 12, 1949—Boston University has won six in a row and is playing a big, strong Maryland team at Fenway Park before a crowd of 30,263, largest ever to watch the Terriers play football.

It is a game that has captured the imagination of New England fans: North vs. South, bigtime football machine vs undefeated smalltime school.

Maryland scores first, but BU, featuring Bob Whelan, end runs on pitchouts from Agganis, comes back. Agganis runs 17 yards on a keeper in a 56-yard march that ends in a Terrier touchdown.

BU misses the extra point, however, and Maryland still leads. In the third period, Agganis intercepts a pass at midfield and a few moments later BU scores to take the lead, 13–7.

In the fourth quarter, Agganis, mixing his plays like a veteran, takes BU to the Maryland four. But a line plunge is stopped a foot short of a first down. Maryland takes over and later thunders on an 81-yard march to win the game, 14–13.

Agganis throws only 12 times, completing 8, but it is the heady play calling and generalship of the sophomore quarterback that impresses the experts.

SEPT. 29, 1951—Agganis, in his second game after getting out of the Marines, completes 10 of 14 passes for 211 yards and 2 touchdowns and punts for a 48-yard average in a 40–34 loss to Penn State.

At halftime, BU leads, 14–7, in an exciting but not unusual game at State College, Pennsylvania. Then, midway through the third period, both sides say goodbye to defense and hello to offense. In seventeen minutes, the lead changes hands five times as the teams total 55 points. For the game, each team gains 400 yards, and there are 11 touchdowns scored.

Behind by 6 with a minute to go, BU takes over on its own 17 and begins a desperation march. With thirty seconds left, Agganis hits halfback Bob Capuano with a pass to the BU 35. With fifteen seconds remaining, he connects with John Kastan, who earlier has scored 4 touchdowns.

The ball is now on Penn State's 43, with time for one more play. Agganis pitches out to Joe Terrani, in the game for this one play, and Terrani flings a wobbly aerial that Capuano grabs on the Penn State 9. His knee touches the ground, however, and he is not allowed to get up and run. The game finishes with the Terriers 9 yards short of a tie.

OCT. 19, 1951—College of the Pacific comes to town with a great reputation as a beefy team with a terrific ground attack. Donelli, during the pre-game build-up, calls C.O.P. "the best team to appear here in the last ten years." A BU player comments that when the Pacific players came out of their clubhouse, Fenway Park tilted.

The previous season, Pacific had hammered BU, minus Agganis, 55–7.

The *Boston Globe*'s Clif Keane, after BU upsets the muscular visitors, 27–12, writes: "They insist that no one man means the difference in a football game, but the Golden Greek was the sole difference last night against a team that looked like a lot of Sherman tanks barging through the line.

"Their backs were broken by the ex-Marine, who blinded them on land and in the air, and had the highly-touted unbeaten coast club all at sea."

The game, however, does not start out well for Agganis. BU moves from its 26 to C.O.P.'s 7, only to have an Agganis pass intercepted in the end zone. This is the last time Pacific stops him.

Later in the period, Agganis runs 41 yards to Pacific's 43. He hits Tom Oates twice for 23 yards total and then finds Kastan on the Pacific 1. Kastan goes over for the score on the next play.

Pacific marches to the BU 13 after the kickoff, only to have Agganis stop the drive by knocking down an end-zone pass. Early in the second period, C.O.P moves to the BU 11, but again Agganis stops them, this time with a goal-line interception. He runs the ball out to the BU 36, and in eight plays BU has another touchdown, with the biggest play a 26-yard pass from Agganis to Oates.

In the first minutes of the third period, Agganis clicks on passes to Kastan, Capuano, and Oates. Then, with the ball on the enemy 10, he fakes a hand-off and runs in for a touchdown. Shortly afterward, he wafts a 13-yarder to Capuano for another score, and BU leads, 27–0. C.O.P.'s two meaningless touchdowns would come in the final minutes.

"I keep adding 'em all up," the *Globe*'s Jerry Nason would say many years later, "and nothing comes out equal to Agannis the night College of Pacific showed up in this town."

OCT. 10, 1952—Boston University beats Miami 9–7 at Fenway Park in what Nason calls "an astonishing upset engineered by an incredible effort by Harry Agganis."

The quarterback's passing sets up the BU first-quarter touchdown, his kicking protects the lead into the final period, and then a 64-yard spiral goes out of bounds on the Miami 5, setting up the game-winning safety.

Miami is a 12-point favorite over a BU team that had been shut out at Marquette the previous week in a game in which Agganis did not distinguish himself.

Criticized all week for his mediocre play against Marquette, Agganis is brilliant against the hard-charging Miami line. Time and again, he dodges in the backfield with the ball on his hip until his receivers can break free. He hits 11 of 22 passes and 6 others are dropped. In addition he is in on 14 tackles and intercepts 2 passes. Donelli always felt the Miami game was Agganis's best.

That opinion excludes the 1953 Senior Bowl, the showcase for players who hope to play professional football. Agganis played fifty-nine minutes in the game, threw for 2 touchdowns, intercepted 2 passes and was named the game's most valuable player. Red Grange, perhaps the greatest college runner in history, said afterward that Agganis was the best college player in America.

The Senior Bowl game, scouted by every professional team, boosted Agganis's stock higher than ever. No one was surprised when Paul Brown, coach of the Cleveland Browns, who had drafted Agganis when the quarterback was a junior, offered him $50,000 to sign.

He was a can't-miss prospect, heading into a system in which the quarterback was king. The Browns' offense was perfect for him, so it came as a rather large shock when Agganis turned down Brown's offer and signed with the Red Sox for a reported $30,000 bonus.

Baseball? Sure, everyone knew Agganis was a good ball player. The stories of his prowess as a teenager and his participation in the schoolboy all-star games were well known. Yet he had barely hit .300 for Boston University, and professional pitching would certainly be tougher than the collegiate variety.

Agganis was aware of this, but something else made him choose baseball, something that might be considered naive in today's grab-it-while-you-can world.

"I've already proven myself in football," Agganis replied when asked about his surprising choice. "I don't know if I can make good in baseball but I have the confidence that I can."

Confidence. He always had that. He always felt the next pass would produce a touchdown, the next defensive play would cause a fumble or an interception. He loved—square as it sounds—the next challenge.

The Red Sox signed Agganis in November of 1952 and the next spring sent him to Louisville. He spent the season there, where he made the American Association all-star team.

Agganis trained with the Red Sox in the spring of 1954 in Sarasota, Florida. His competition for the first base job was Dick Gernert, a power-hitting right-handed batter who had totaled 40 homers the previous two seasons. In a

The Golden Greek was acclaimed the best all-round football player in America.

letter to Donelli, Agganis wrote that he was being given the rookie freeze-out treatment and would have to perform twice as well as Gernert to win the job.

His analysis of the situation may have been a rookie reaction, but the fact is, Agganis did win the job, playing 132 games at first base for the '54 Red Sox. The kid from Lynn—though he never seemed a kid, always having the poise of a veteran—had come back home.

Agganis got his bachelor's degree from Boston University that June and went to commencement at BU field after hitting a game-winning home run that afternoon at Fenway Park. He had 11 homers that season, including 8 at

Harry with his mother, Georgiana Agganis, after signing with the Red Sox.

Fenway, the most there by a left-handed batter in twenty-five years, excepting, of course, Ted Williams.

But the Golden Greek had batted only .251, and that disappointed him. He felt he was a .300 hitter, so set that as his goal for 1955.

Agganis still had to fight for the first base job that spring. Gernert was gone, but in his place was 6'4", 220-pound rookie Norb Zauchin. The two became good friends and roommates. Zauchin started the first five games of the season, but when he failed to hit, Agganis replaced him.

In early May, when Agganis was over .300, he was stricken with pneumonia and spent ten days in Boston's Sancta Maria hospital. Zauchin took over first base and did well, but when Agganis was released from the hospital he immediately rejoined the Red Sox as they began a western swing in Chicago. He was given his job back and had three hits to boost his average to .313.

On June 4, when the Red Sox arrived in Kansas City, Agganis complained of chest pains and fever. He was sent back to Boston and readmitted to Sancta Maria. By now, it was apparent that his illness was more severe than originally suspected and the Red Sox put him on the voluntarily retired list. This meant he could not go back on the roster for sixty days.

Dr. Eugene O'Neill, one of Agganis's physicians, stated that "Harry began playing too soon after his first hospitalization, and this time, he'll wait longer before being returned to the active list."

The diagnosis was a severe pulmonary infection, complicated by phlebitis. But severe did not mean critical. Severe did not mean fatal. No one talked, at least for publication, about the possibility of Harry Agganis dying.

Some put forth the conjecture that a chest injury suffered in a physically punishing 34–7 defeat by Maryland in his senior year was the cause of Agganis's illness. He did not play the rest of that game, but instead of getting immediate treatment, he kept tossing a football back and forth on the sidelines. He missed three games and then returned to action with a heavy cast on his chest.

Buff Donelli disagreed with these thoughts. "Any talk that the injury contributed to Harry's death is completely out of line," the coach told Nason. "I've been assured by one of his physicians that such rumors are ridiculous."

On June 22, Agganis phoned Donelli and barked out some BU signals in a kidding manner.

"Harry," laughed the coach, "you must be feeling better."

Sunday night, June 25, Harold Zimman, a former coach and good friend from Lynn, visisted Agganis at Sancta Maria. There was a no-visitors sign on the door, but when Zimman and his wife introduced themselves, the nurse said, "Good, Harry wants to see you."

The Zimmans and Agganis watched the Ed Sullivan show on television, and talked about Harry's plan to spend $10,000 to fix up his mother's home on Waterhill Street in Lynn.

They spent about a half hour together.

"He wasn't down," Zimman would say at the end of that interminable week. "He'd had this phlebitis in his knee for some time, and he had a bad night Saturday, but Sunday he was feeling better."

At 11 o'clock the next morning, June 26, Harry Agganis died of a massive pulmonary embolism, a blood clot.

The Golden Greek, the superb and seemingly indestructible gladiator who would always win over all, was gone.

He died suddenly and too soon. There were miles to go before he slept, but he never got to walk them. Yet he left a Boston sports legacy that may never be equalled.

"In the time he had," Harold Zimman told the *Boston Globe*'s Harold Kaese, "Harry Agganis was great."

"BEHIND THE HEROES"

This book is about those who played the games and excelled in them. But there would have been no games, no arenas, and no championships, without front offices to provide the necessary players and men on the bench to direct them.

No book on Boston sports would be complete without a tip of the pen to the giants behind the scenes.

The Bruins came into being because of the perseverance and vision of a one-time grocery boy named *Charles F. Adams*, who founded the Boston hockey team in 1924.

Two years later, Adams built the foundation for the future by buying many stars, including Eddie Shore, from the financially distressed Western Canada League.

That same year, he put up a half-million dollars to help build Boston Garden. Adams, a member of hockey's Hall of Fame, died in 1947.

Another key figure in the Bruins' early years was *Art Ross*, the coach and general manager who created a Bruins powerhouse in the late '20s and '30s with such stars as Shore, Dit Clapper, Cooney Weiland, Bill Cowley, Frank Brimsek, and the Kraut line.

Ross was also a hockey innovator who redesigned the puck and the net. He also is in hockey's Hall of Fame.

In more recent times, the big name has been *Harry Sinden*, who never made it to the NHL as a player, but who has been a force with the Bruins, first as a coach and then as the general manager.

Sinden's Bruins won the Stanley Cup in 1970. After two years in private business, Sinden returned to the Bruins as general manager in 1972, and through 1981, the team has reached the Stanley Cup finals three times.

Sinden also coached Team Canada in its dramatic series against the Soviet Union in 1973.

No name has meant more to Boston sports over the years than that of *Thomas Austin Yawkey*. Yawkey, a wealthy sportsman only thirty years old, bought the struggling Red Sox franchise in 1933. He rebuilt both Fenway Park and the ball club, purchasing the contracts of such stars as Jimmy Foxx, Lefty Grove, and Joe Cronin. Soon the franchise became one of the strongest and most respected in baseball.

Yawkey-owned teams won three pennants (1946, 1967, and 1975), but each time lost the World Series in seven games. He was called a player's owner and was sometimes criticized for being too soft with his athletes. Yawkey, after forty-four years of ownership, died in 1976. Five years later he was inducted into baseball's Hall of Fame.

Joe Cronin was one of Yawkey's, and Boston's, favorite people. He came to the city after managing Washington to a pennant, and was the Red Sox playing manager from 1935 through 1947. Nobody before or since managed the club for so long a span. He won the pennant in 1946 and finished second four other seasons.

In 1948, Cronin replaced Eddie Collins as general manager of the Red Sox and stayed in that post until 1959, when he was named president of the American League. He retired as American League president in 1967. Cronin was elected to baseball's Hall of Fame in 1956.

Professional football, a sport without a long Boston tradition, came to the city to stay in 1960, when the Patriots were granted a franchise in the new American Football League.

The principal architect of the Patriots, and the only man who has been associated with the franchise since it began is *Billy Sullivan*.

Sullivan, former publicity director at Boston College and then of the Boston Braves, has been a tenacious keeper of the Patriots flame, both when it burned brightly and when it was at its dimmest. Through the years he has been controversial, voluble, impulsive, stubborn, and sentimental. But above all, Sullivan has been a fighter, and without him, the Patriots would have fled New England long ago.

Walter Brown was stubborn, too, or he would not have hung on to the Celtics at a time when they weren't drawing enough customers to pay the rent. He had founded the team in 1946, but had to take out second mortgages and borrow money to keep the team going in the early years.

Brown became the first NBA owner to pick a Black in the NBA draft when he selected Chuck Cooper in 1950. He was a sportsman in an era when such creatures were becoming extinct. Brown died of a heart attack a few days before the start of training camp in 1964, and his Number 1 insignia was hoisted to the Garden rafters on opening night that season.

And finally, *Arnold (Red) Auerbach*. He was born in Brooklyn and got his pro coaching start in Washington, but Auerbach is as much a part of Boston lore as the Bunker Hill Monument or Back Bay.

He was named coach of the Boston Celtics in 1950, and, together with a court magician named Cousy, taught the citizens of Boston to like basketball.

He won his first NBA championship with the Celtics in 1956–57, and in thirteen years would capture eleven titles, as the Celtics created the greatest dynasty in pro-sports history.

With Auerbach as general manager, the Celtics also won championships in 1972, 1976, and 1981. Brash, arrogant, shrewd, tough, rude, and tenacious, he is a great judge of talent and a master at staying a step ahead of his peers. You have to rise very early in the morning to put one over on Red Auerbach.

"STATS"

TED WILLIAMS

WILLIAMS, THEODORE SAMUEL
(The Splendid Splinter, The Thumper)
B. Aug 30, 1918, San Diego, Calif.
Manager 1969–72.
Hall of Fame 1966.
Height, 6.04. Weight 198. Greenish-brown eyes and brown hair.
Throws right and bats lefthanded
Hobbies—Hunting, fishing and golf

YEAR CLUB	LEAGUE	POS.	G.	AB.	R.	H.	2B.	3B.	HR.	RBI.	BA.	PO.	A.	E.	FA.
1936—San Diego	P.C.	OF	42	107	18	29	8	2	0	11	.271	64	5	2	.972
1937—San Diego	P.C.	OF	138	454	66	132	24	2	23	98	.291	213	10	7	.970
1938—Minneapolis	A.A.	OF	148	528	°130	193	30	9	°43	°142	.366	289	17	11	.963
1939—Boston	Amer.	OF	149	565	131	185	44	11	31	°145	.327	248	11	°19	.945
1940—Boston	Amer.	OF-P	144	561	°134	193	43	14	23	113	.344	302	15	13	.961
1941—Boston	Amer.	OF	143	456	°135	185	33	3	°37	120	°.406	262	11	11	.961
1942—Boston	Amer.	OF	150	522	°141	186	34	5	°36	°137	.356	313	15	4	.968
1943-44-45—Boston	Amer.							(In Military Service)							
1946—Boston	Amer.	OF	150	514	°142	176	37	8	38	123	.342	325	7	10	.971
1947—Boston	Amer.	OF	156	528	°125	181	40	9	°32	°114	°.343	347	10	9	.975
1948—Boston	Amer.	OF	137	509	124	188	°44	3	25	127	.369	189	9	5	.983
1949—Boston	Amer.	OF	°155	566	°150	194	°39	3	°43	°159	.343	337	12	6	.983
1950—Boston†	Amer.	OF	89	334	82	106	24	1	28	97	.317	165	7	8	.956
1951—Boston	Amer.	OF	148	531	109	169	28	4	30	126	.318	315	12	4	.988
1952—Boston‡	Amer.	OF	6	10	2	4	0	1	1	3	.400	4	0	0	1.000
1953—Boston‡	Amer.	OF	37	91	17	37	6	0	13	34	.407	31	1	1	.970
1954—Boston	Amer.	OF	117	386	93	133	23	1	29	89	.345	213	5	4	.982
1955—Boston	Amer.	OF	98	320	77	114	21	3	28	83	.356	170	5	2	.989
1956—Boston	Amer.	OF	136	400	71	138	28	2	24	82	.345	174	7	5	.973
1957—Boston	Amer.	OF	132	420	96	163	28	1	38	87	°.388	215	2	1	.995
1958—Boston	Amer.	OF	129	411	81	135	23	2	26	85	°.328	154	3	7	.957
1959—Boston	Amer.	OF	103	272	32	69	15	0	10	43	.254	94	4	3	.970
1960—Boston	Amer.	OF	113	310	56	98	15	0	29	72	.316	131	6	1	.963
Major League Totals			2292	7706	1798	2654	525	71	521	1839	.344	4159	142	113	.974

PITCHING RECORD

YEAR	CLUB	LEAGUE	G.	IP.	W.	L.	Pct.	H.	R.	ER.	SO.	BB.	Ave.
1940—Boston		Amer.	1	2	0	0	.000	3	1	1	1	0	.450

WORLD SERIES RECORD

YEAR	CLUB	LEAGUE	Pos.	G.	AB.	R.	H.	2B.	3B.	HR.	RBI.	B.A.	PO.	A.	E.	FA.
1946—Boston		Amer.	OF	7	25	2	5	0	0	0	1	.200	16	2	0	1.000

† Suffered fractured left elbow when he crashed into the left field wall making catch in first inning of All-Star Game at Chicago, July 11, 1950; despite injury he stayed in game until ninth inning. Williams had played 70 American League games up to the All-Star affair—but appeared in only 19 more contests with the Red Sox for the rest of the season. Played in 18 All-Star Games.

‡ In Military Service most of season.

*Led League.

These statistics courtesy of The Sporting News.

CARL MICHAEL YASTRZEMSKI (Yaz)
#8   OF-1B-DH

Born: August 22, 1939, Southampton, L.I., N.Y. Ht.: 5-11; Wt.: 185 lbs. Brown eyes. Brown hair. Bats: Left; Throws: Right. Home: Highland Beach, Fla. Signed by Scout "Bots" Nekola, November 28, 1958. Married Carolann Casper. Children: Mary Ann 9/21/60. C. Michael Jr. 8/16/61. Suzann 6/15/66, Carolyn 4/15/69.

Length of M.L. Service—21 yrs.

1981: Became 2nd all-time in games, 3,058, 1st in the A.L. . . . Missed his 1st Opening Day with back muscle spasms . . . Did not play in the OF . . . Had 19 game-tying or go-ahead RBI, 11 in Season II and led the club with 10 game-winning RBI . . . All 7 of his HR either tied the score or put the Sox ahead . . . Drove in 16 of 22 (.727) runners on 3rd with less than 2 outs . . . Hit .300 in Aug. (18-60) and had 17 RBI in Sept. . . . The lists on the next page show his rankings in the all-time top 20's.

CAREER: In 1980 became the 1st A.L. player to have 20 straight years of 100 or more games, the 3rd player with 100 hits for 20 yrs. (Aaron 21, Cobb 20) and the only one to do it his first 20 . . . A fracture rib Aug. 30 caused him to miss 32 of the last 35 games and stopped his best hitting surge of 1980 (17-43 .395) . . . Played 1B-LF-CF-RF-DH . . . In 1979 reached 3,000 hits . . . Aaron, Mays and Musial are the only others with 3,000-400 . . . Also won the A.L.'s Joe Cronin Award in 1979 . . . Only the 2nd A.L. player since 1925 to reach 3,000 hits along with Al Kaline . . . Has lifetime .286 avg. with 6 .300 marks . . . In 1978 he had 6 HR and 19 RBI in Sept. stretch drive . . . That included a homer in the second inning of the playoff vs. the Yankees for a 1-0 lead off Guidry and an RBI single in the 8th beofre fouling out to end the season . . . In 1977 he won his 7th Gold Glove while leading A.L. outfielders with 16 assists (the 7th time to extend his own M.L. mark) and no errors in 140 games . . . That year he became the 5th oldest player to have a 100-RBI year (Cobb, Banks, Ruth, Honus Wagner) . . . Hit 3 HR in Det. May 19, 1976 and then hit 2 more in N.Y. the next night to tie the M.L. record of 5 in 2 games . . . Has started the All Star game in LF, CF and 1B . . . Has 195 OF assists with high of 19 in 1964.

BACKGROUND: Signed with Red Sox as a shortstop after his freshman year at Notre Dame . . . Later obtained a degree from Merrimack College in Business Administration . . . Played 2B-SS at Raleigh in 1959 but moved to the OF the next year under manager Gene Mauch in Minneapolis . . . is an avid fisherman . . . Son Mike is a junior at Florida State and a member of the baseball team.

YEAR	CLUB	AVG.	G	AB	R	H	2B	3B	HR	RBI	BB	SO	E	SB
1959	Raleigh	.377°	120	451	87	170°	34°	6	15	100	78	49	45°	16
1960	Minneapolis	.399	148	570	84	193°	36	8	7	69	47	65	5	16
1961	Boston	.266	148	583	71	155	31	6	11	80	50	96	10°	6
1962	Boston	.296	160	646	99	191	43	6	19	94	66	82	11°	7
1963	Boston	.321°	151	570	91	183°	40°	3	14	68	95°	72	6	8
1964	Boston	.289	151	567	77	164	29	9	15	67	75	90	11	6
1965	Boston	.312	133	494	78	154	45†	3	20	72	70	58	3	7
1966	Boston	.278	160	594	81	165	39°	2	16	80	84	60	5	8
1967	Boston	.326°	161	579	112°	189°	31	4	44†	121°	91	69	7	10
1968	Boston	.301°	157	539	90	162	32	2	23	74	119°	90	3	13
1969	Boston	.255	162†	603	96	154	28	0	40	111	101	91	6	15
1970	Boston	.329	161	566	125°	186	29	2	40	102	128	66	14	23
1971	Boston	.254	148	508	75	129	21	2	15	70	106	60	2	8
1972	Boston-a	.264	125	455	70	120	18	2	12	68	67	44	8	5
1973	Boston	.296	152	540	82	160	25	4	19	95	105	58	18	9
1974	Boston	.301	148	515	93°	155	25	2	15	79	104	48	6	12
1975	Boston	.269	149	543	91	146	30	1	14	60	87	67	5	8
1976	Boston	.267	155	546	71	165	23	2	21	102	80	67	4	5
1977	Boston	.296	150	558	99	165	27	3	28	102	73	40	0	11
1978	Boston	.277	144	523	70	145	21	2	17	81	76	44	5	4
1979	Boston	.270	147	518	69	140	28	1	21	87	62	46	4	3
1980	Boston	.275	105	364	49	100	21	1	15	50	44	38	4	0
1981	Boston	.246	91	338	36	83	14	1	7	53	49	28	3	0
M.L. Totals		.286	3058	11149	1725	3192	600	58	426	1776	1732	1314	135	168

G-W RBI: 1980—8; 1981—10. Total: 18. (Red Sox Career—99) (Since 1971)
a-On Disabled List May 9 to June 9, 1972 with injured right knee.

CHAMPIONSHIP SERIES RECORD

YEAR	CLUB	AVG.	G	AB	R	H	2B	3B	HR	RBI	BB	SO	E
1975	Boston vs. Oak.	.455	3	11	4	5	1	0	1	2	1	1	0

CARL MICHAEL YASTRZEMSKI (Yaz) (Cont.)

WORLD SERIES RECORD

YEAR	CLUB	AVG.	G	AB	R	H	2B	3B	HR	RBI	BB	SO	E
1967	Boston vs. St. L.	.400	7	25	4	10	2	0	3	5	4	1	0
1975	Boston vs. Cin.	.310	7	29	7	9	0	0	0	4	4	1	0
W.S. Totals		.352	14	54	11	19	2	0	3	9	8	2	0

ALL-STAR GAME RECORD

YEAR	LEAGUE	POS.	AVG.	AB	R	H	2B	3B	HR	RBI	BB	SO	E
1963	A.L., Bos.	LF	.000	2	0	0	0	0	0	0	0	1	0
1965	A.L., Bos.				Replaced due to injury								
1966	A.L., Bos.				Did not play								
1967	A.L., Bos.	LF	.750	4	0	3	1	0	0	0	2	1	0
1968	A.L., Bos.	CF-LF	.000	4	0	0	0	0	0	0	0	2	0
1969	A.L., Bos.	LF	.000	1	0	0	0	0	0	0	0	0	0
1970	A.L., Bos.	CF-1B	.667	6	1	4	1	0	0	1	1	0	0
1971	A.L., Bos.	LF	.000	3	0	0	0	0	0	0	0	1	0
1972	A.L., Bos.	LF	.000	3	0	0	0	0	0	0	0	0	0
1973	A.L., Bos.				Replaced due to injury								
1974	A.L., Bos.	1B	.000	1	0	0	0	0	0	0	1	0	0
1975	A.L., Bos.	PH	1.000	1	1	1	0	0	1	3	0	0	0
1976	A.L., Bos.	LF	.000	2	0	0	0	0	0	0	0	0	0
1977	A.L., Bos.	CF	.000	2	0	0	0	0	0	0	0	1	0
1978	A.L., Bos.				Replaced due to injury								
1979	A.L., Bos.	1B	.667	3	0	2	0	0	0	1	0	0	0
A.S.G. Totals			.313	32	2	10	2	0	1	5	4	6	0

°led league   † tied for league lead

YAZ CAREER RECORD

	AVG.	AB	H	HR	RBI
CAREER	.286	11,149	3192	426	1716
BOSTON	.308	5540	1707	224	992
AWAY	.265	5609	1485	202	724
vs. Balt.	.299	1161	347	32	160
Calif.	.285	926	264	34	151
Chi.	.287	961	276	29	152
Clev.	.275	1175	323	48	187
Det.	.289	1220	353	63	233
K.C. A's	.259	456	118	12	57
K.C. Roy.	.288	473	136	19	70
Milw.°	.282	616	174	23	103
Minn.	.297	1033	307	43	153
N.Y.	.278	1204	335	51	156
Oak.	.272	547	149	24	81
Seattle	.283	159	45	3	31
Texas	.307	375	115	9	57
Toronto	.282	174	49	9	28
Wash.	.300	669	201	27	97
vs. Left	.244	2898	707	74	405
Right	.301	8251	2485	352	1311
Pinch Hit	.185	27	5	1	3
Des. Hit	.246	729	179	22	110
April	.269	1231	331	42	195
May	.282	1892	534	83	304
June	.295	1961	579	89	339
July	.292	2013	588	77	288
Aug.	.282	2116	596	60	291
Sept.	.292	1866	544	72	288
Oct.	.286	70	20	3	11

Hit Streak—16 games (1963)

°Includes 1969 vs. Seattle Pilots

CHECKING YAZ ON THE ALL-TIME RANKINGS

		ALL-TIME RANK	ACTIVE RANK	
Games	3058	2nd	1st	(Rose 2937)
AB	11,149	4th	2nd	(Rose 11,910)
Runs	1725	16th	2nd	(Rose 1915)
Hits	3192	10th	2nd	(Rose 3697)
2B	600	9th	2nd	(Rose 672)
HR	426	16th-Tied	2nd	(Stargell 472)
RBI	1716	12th	1st	(Stargell 1523, Perez 1501)
BB	1732	4th	1st	(Morgan 1625, Rose 1292)
TB	5186	7th	1st	(Rose 5078)
XBH	1084	11th	1st	(Rose 949, Stargell 946)
Singles	2108	23rd-Tied	2nd	(Rose 2748)

YASTRZEMSKI CAREER HIGHLIGHTS

Most Games, Lifetime, A.L., 3,058

Joe Cronin A.L. Award for Significant Achievement, 1979

Most Valuable Player, A.L., 1967

Sporting News A.L. Player of Year, 1967

Sporting News No. 1 Major League Player, 1967

Gold Glove OF Selections 1963-65-67-68-69-71-77

Led A.L. OF in Assists 1962-63-64-66-69-71-77

Led A.L. in Slugging Pct 1965 (.536), '67 (.622), '70 (.592)

Led A.L. in Total Bases 1967 (360), '70 (335)

Led A.L. in Sac. Flies 1972 (9), '77 (11)

Holds A.L. Record, Int. Walks, Career, 178

Tied M.L. Record, HR 2 Consec. Games, 5, May 19-20, 1976

Tied M.L. Record OF Fielding Pct., 1.000, 1977

Won A.L. Triple Crown, 1967

Holds M.L. Record, Most Yrs. Leading League, OF Assists, 7

Selected Outstanding Player of 1970 All Star Game

Holds 7th Longest OF Consecutive Errorless Game Streak, A.L., 167 Games, 7/28/76 thru 4/7/78 (354 chances)

First A.L. Player with 400 HR and 3000 hits

Named Most Valuable Player Carolina League, 1959

A.L. Record Most Consecutive Seasons 100 or More Games, 20

3rd Player To Get 100 Hits 20 Years

Only Player to Get 100 Hits First 20 Years

CARL MICHAEL YASTRZEMSKI (Yaz) (Cont.)

YAZ: 3,000 HITS & 400 HOME RUNS

Hits

NO.	DATE	OPP. & PLACE	TYPE	PITCHER
1	4/11/61 (Opening Day)	K.C. A's-Fenway	Single	Ray Herbert—1st at bat, went 1-5
1000	9/15/66	Chi. in Fenway	Single	Jack Lamabe, went 2-4
2000	6/9/73	In Texas	RBI Single	Steve Foucault—7th inng, went 1-4
2500	7/26/76	Clev. in Fenway	RBI Double	Stan Thomas—1st inng., went 1-4
3000	9/12/79	N.Y. in Fenway	Single	Jim Beattie—8th inng., went 1-4

Home Runs

NO.	DATE	OPP. & PLACE	PITCHER
1	5/9/61	L.A. Angels, Wrigley Field	Jerry Casale
100	5/16/67	Balt. in Fenway	Eddie Fisher
200	9/23/69	N.Y. in Fenway	Mel Stottlemyre
300	7/25/74	In Detroit	Mickey Lolich
400	7/24/79	Oak in Fenway	Mike Morgan

These statistics courtesy of The Sporting News.

Born August 9, 1928 at New York, N.Y.   Height 6:01.   Weight 175.
High School—Queens, N.Y., Andrew Jackson.
College—Holy Cross College, Worcester, Mass.
Drafted by Tri-Cities on first round, 1950.
Traded by Tri-Cities to Chicago for Gene Vance, 1950.
NBA rights drawn out of a hat by Boston for $8,500 in dispersal of Chicago franchise, 1950.

ROBERT JOSEPH COUSY (Bob)

—COLLEGIATE PLAYING RECORD—

YEAR	G.	MIN.	FGA	FGM	PCT.	FTA	FTM	PCT.	REB.	PTS.	AVG.
46-47	30	...	...	91	...	...	45	.667	...	227	7.6
47-48	30	...	...	207	...	108	72	.672	...	486	16.2
48-49	27	...	...	195	...	134	90	.754	...	480	17.8
49-50	30	...	659	216	.328	199	150	...	...	582	19.4
Totals	117	...	...	709	...	...	357	...	...	1775	15.2

NBA REGULAR SEASON RECORD

SEA.—TEAM	G.	MIN.	FGA	FGM	PCT.	FTA	FTM	PCT.	REB.	AST.	PF	DISQ.	PTS.	AVG.
50-51—Boston	69	...	1138	401	.352	365	276	.756	474	341	185	2	1078	15.6
51-52—Boston	66	2681	1388	512	.369	506	409	.808	421	441	190	5	1433	21.7
52-53—Boston	71	2945	1320	464	.352	587	479	.816	449	547	227	4	1407	19.8
53-54—Boston	72	2857	1262	486	.385	522	411	.787	394	518	201	3	1383	19.2
54-55—Boston	71	2747	1316	522	.397	570	460	.807	424	557	165	1	1504	21.2
55-56—Boston	72	2767	1223	440	.360	564	476	.844	492	642	206	2	1356	18.8
56-57—Boston	64	2364	1264	478	.378	442	363	.821	309	478	134	0	1319	20.6
57-58—Boston	65	2222	1262	445	.353	326	277	.850	322	463	136	1	1167	18.0
58-59—Boston	65	2403	1260	484	.384	385	329	.855	359	557	135	0	1297	20.0
59-60—Boston	75	2588	1481	568	.383	403	319	.791	352	715	146	2	1455	19.4
60-61—Boston	76	2468	1382	513	.371	452	352	.779	331	587	196	0	1378	18.1
61-62—Boston	75	2114	1181	462	.391	333	251	.754	261	584	135	0	1175	15.7
62-63—Boston	76	1975	998	392	.397	298	219	.735	193	515	175	0	1003	13.2
63-64 through 68-69								Voluntarily Retired						
69-70—Cincinnati	7	34	3	1	.333	3	3	1.000	5	10	11	0	5	0.7
Totals	924	...	16468	6168	.375	5756	4624	.803	4786	6955	2242	20	16960	18.4

ROBERT JOSEPH COUSY (Bob) (Cont.)

NBA PLAYOFF RECORD

SEA.–TEAM	G.	MIN.	FGA	FGM	PCT.	FTA	FTM	PCT.	REB.	AST.	PF	DISQ.	PTS.	AVG.
50-51—Boston	2	...	42	9	.214	12	10	.833	15	12	8	...	28	14.0
51-52—Boston	3	138	65	26	.400	44	41	.932	12	19	13	...	93	31.0
52-53—Boston	6	270	120	46	.383	73	61	.836	25	37	21	1	153	25.5
53-54—Boston	6	260	116	33	.284	75	60	.800	32	38	20	0	126	21.0
54-55—Boston	7	299	139	53	.381	48	46	.958	43	65	26	0	152	21.7
55-56—Boston	3	124	56	28	.500	25	23	.920	24	26	4	0	79	26.3
56-57—Boston	10	440	207	67	.324	91	68	.747	61	93	27	0	202	20.2
57-58—Boston	11	457	196	67	.342	75	64	.853	71	82	20	0	198	18.0
58-59—Boston	11	460	221	72	.326	94	70	.745	76	119	28	0	214	19.5
59-60—Boston	13	468	262	80	.305	51	39	.765	48	116	27	0	199	15.3
60-61—Boston	10	337	147	50	.340	88	67	.761	43	91	33	1	167	16.7
61-62—Boston	14	474	241	86	.357	76	52	.684	64	123	43	0	224	16.0
62-63—Boston	13	413	204	72	.353	47	39	.830	32	116	44	2	183	14.1
Totals	109	...	2016	689	.326	799	640	.801	546	937	314	4	2018	18.5

NBA ALL-STAR GAME RECORD

SEASON–TEAM	MIN.	FGA	FGM	PCT.	FTA	FTM	PCT.	REB.	AST.	PF	DISQ.	PTS.
1951—Boston	...	12	2	.167	5	4	.800	9	8	3	0	8
1952—Boston	33	14	4	.286	2	1	.500	4	13	3	0	9
1953—Boston	36	11	4	.364	7	7	1.000	5	3	1	0	15
1954—Boston	34	15	6	.400	8	8	1.000	11	4	1	0	20
1955—Boston	35	14	7	.500	7	6	.857	9	5	6	0	20
1956—Boston	24	8	2	.250	4	3	.750	7	2	0	1	7
1957—Boston	28	14	4	.286	2	2	1.000	5	7	0	0	10
1958—Boston	31	20	8	.400	6	4	.667	5	10	2	0	20
1959—Boston	32	8	4	.500	6	5	.833	5	4	0	0	13
1960—Boston	26	7	1	.143	0	0	.000	3	8	6	1	2
1961—Boston	33	11	2	.182	0	0	.000	6	8	2	0	4
1962—Boston	31	13	4	.308	4	3	.750	4	6	2	0	11
1963—Boston	25	11	4	.364	0	0	.000	5	8	1	0	8
Totals	...	158	52	.329	51	43	.843	78	86	27	2	147

COLLEGIATE COACHING RECORD

SEA.	CLUB	W.	L.	PCT.	SEA.	CLUB	W.	L.	PCT.
1963-64—	Boston College	10	11	.455	1967-69—	Boston College	17	8	.680
1964-65—	Boston College	22	7	.759	1968-69—	Boston College	24	4	.857
1965-66—	Boston College	21	5	.808		Totals (6 seasons)	117	38	.755
1966-67—	Boston College	23	3	.885					

NOTE: Cousy guided Boston College to NIT in 1965, 1966 and 1969 and to NCAA Tournament in 1967 and 1968.

NBA COACHING RECORD

		REGULAR SEASON				PLAYOFFS	
SEA.	CLUB	W.	L.	PCT.	POS.	W.	L.
1969-70—	Cincinnati	36	46	.439	5	...	...
1970-71—	Cincinnati	33	49	.402	3	...	...
1971-72—	Cincinnati	30	52	.366	3	...	...
1972-73—	K.C.-Omaha	36	46	.439	4	...	...
1973-74—	K.C.-Omaha	6	16	.375	...	...	...
	Totals (5 seasons)	141	209	.403		...	...

Elected to Naismith Memorial Basketball Hall of Fame, 1970 . . . . Named to NBA 25th Anniversary All-Time Team, 1980 . . . . NBA Most Valuable Player, 1957 . . . . Named to NBA All-Star First Team, 1952, 1953, 1954, 1955, 1956, 1957, 1958, 1959, 1960, 1961 . . . . NBA All-Star Second Team, 1962 and 1963 . . . . Holds NBA record for most assists in one half, 19, vs. Minneapolis, February 27, 1959 . . . Shares NBA record for most assists in one quarter, 12, vs. Minneapolis, February 27, 1959 . . . . Holds NBA playoff game records for most free-throw attempts, 32, and most free throws made, 30, vs. Syracuse, March 21, 1953 . . . . Shares NBA playoff game record for most assists, 19, vs. St. Louis, April 9, 1958, and vs. Minneapolis, April 7, 1959 . . . . Shares NBA championship series record for most assists in one half, 10, vs. St. Louis, April 9, 1957 vs. Minneapolis, April 7, 1959, and vs. Minneapolis, April 9, 1959 . . . . Holds NBA championship series record for most assists in one quarter, 8, vs. St. Louis, April 9, 1957 . . . . NBA All-Star Game MVP, 1954 and 1957 . . . . Shares NBA All-Star Game records for most career assists, 86; most assists in one half, 8, in 1952, and most assists in one quarter, 6, in 1952 . . . . Member of the NBA championship teams, 1957, 1959, 1960, 1961, 1962, 1963 . . . . Led NBA in assists, 1953, 1954, 1955, 1956, 1957, 1958, 1959, 1960 . . . . Named to THE SPORTING NEWS All-America First Team, 1950 . . . . Named to THE SPORTING NEWS All-America Second Team, 1949 . . . . Member of NCAA championship team, 1947 . . . . Commissioner of American Soccer League, 1975 through mid-1980 season.

These statistics courtesy of The Sporting News.

WILLIAM FENTON RUSSEL (Bill)

Born February 12, 1934 at Monroe, La.   Height 6:10.   Weight 220.
High School—Oakland, Calif, McClymonds.
College—University of San Francisco, San Francisco, Calif.
Drafted by Boston on first round, 1956. (Boston traded Ed Macauley and Cliff Hagan to St. Louis for its first-round choice, April 29, 1956.)

—COLLEGIATE RECORD—

YEAR	G.	MIN.	FGA	FGM	PCT.	FTA	FTM	PCT.	REB.	PTS.	AVG.
52-53†	23	...	...	...	...	...	...	...	...	461	20.0
53-54	21	...	309	150	.485	212	117	.552	403	417	19.9
54-55	29	...	423	229	.541	278	164	.590	594	622	21.4
55-56	29	...	480	246	.513	212	105	.495	609	597	20.6
Varsity Totals	79	...	1212	625	.516	702	386	.550	1606	1636	20.7

NBA REGULAR SEASON RECORD

SEA.—TEAM	G.	MIN.	FGA	FGM	PCT.	FTA	FTM	PCT.	REB.	AST.	PF	DISQ.	PTS.	AVG.
56-57—Boston	48	1695	649	277	.427	309	152	.492	943	88	143	2	706	14.7
57-58—Boston	69	2640	1032	456	.442	443	230	.519	1564	202	181	2	1142	16.6
58-59—Boston	70	2979	997	456	.457	428	256	.598	1612	222	161	3	1168	16.7
59-60—Boston	74	3146	1189	555	.467	392	240	.612	1778	277	210	0	1350	18.2
60-61—Boston	78	3458	1250	532	.426	469	258	.550	1868	268	155	0	1322	16.9
61-62—Boston	76	3433	1258	575	.457	481	286	.594	1790	341	207	3	1436	18.9
62-63—Boston	78	3500	1182	511	.432	517	287	.555	1843	348	189	1	1309	16.8
63-64—Boston	78	3482	1077	466	.433	429	236	.550	1930	370	190	0	1168	15.0
64-65—Boston	78	3466	980	429	.438	426	244	.573	1878	410	204	1	1102	14.1
65-66—Boston	78	3386	943	391	.415	405	223	.551	1779	371	221	4	1005	12.9
66-67—Boston	81	3297	870	395	.454	467	285	.610	1700	472	258	4	1075	13.4
67-68—Boston	78	2953	858	365	.425	460	247	.537	1451	357	242	2	977	12.5
68-69—Boston	77	3291	645	279	.433	388	204	.526	1484	374	231	2	762	9.9
Totals	963	40726	12930	5687	.440	5614	3148	.561	21620	4100	2592	24	14522	15.1

NBA PLAYOFF RECORD

SEA.—TEAM	G.	MIN.	FGA	FGM	PCT.	FTA	FTM	PCT.	REB.	AST.	PF	DISQ.	PTS.	AVG.
56-57—Boston	10	409	148	54	.365	61	31	.508	244	32	41	1	139	13.9
57-58—Boston	9	355	133	48	.361	66	40	.606	221	24	24	0	136	15.1
58-59—Boston	11	496	159	65	.409	67	41	.612	305	40	28	1	171	15.5
59-60—Boston	13	572	206	94	.456	75	53	.707	336	38	38	1	241	18.5
60-61—Boston	10	462	171	73	.427	86	45	.523	299	48	24	0	191	19.1
61-62—Boston	14	672	253	116	.458	113	82	.726	370	70	49	0	314	22.4
62-63—Boston	15	617	212	96	.453	109	72	.661	326	66	36	0	264	20.3
63-64—Boston	10	451	132	47	.356	67	37	.552	272	44	33	0	131	13.1
64-65—Boston	12	561	150	79	.527	76	40	.526	302	76	43	2	198	16.5
65-66—Boston	17	814	261	124	.475	123	76	.618	428	85	60	0	324	19.1
66-67—Boston	9	390	86	31	.360	52	33	.635	198	50	32	1	95	10.6
67-68—Boston	19	869	242	99	.409	130	76	.585	434	99	73	1	274	14.4
68-69—Boston	18	829	182	77	.423	81	41	.506	369	98	65	1	195	10.8
Totals	165	7497	2335	1003	.430	1106	667	.603	4104	770	546	8	2673	16.2

NBA ALL-STAR GAME RECORD

SEASON—TEAM	MIN.	FGA	FGM	PCT.	FTA	FTM	PCT.	REB.	AST.	PF	DISQ.	PTS.
1958—Boston	26	12	5	.417	3	1	.333	11	2	5	0	11
1959—Boston	27	10	3	.300	1	1	1.000	9	1	4	0	7
1960—Boston	27	7	3	.429	2	0	.000	8	3	1	0	6
1961—Boston	28	15	9	.600	8	6	.750	11	1	2	0	24
1962—Boston	27	12	5	.417	3	2	.667	12	2	2	0	12
1963—Boston	37	14	8	.571	4	3	.750	24	5	3	0	19
1964—Boston	42	13	6	.462	2	1	.500	21	5	4	0	13
1965—Boston	33	12	7	.583	9	3	.333	13	2	6	1	17
1966—Boston	23	6	1	.167	0	0	.000	10	5	2	0	2
1967—Boston	22	2	1	.500	0	0	.000	5	8	2	0	2
1968—Boston	23	4	2	.500	0	0	.000	9	3	5	0	4
1969—Boston	28	4	1	.250	2	1	.500	6	2	1	0	3
Totals	343	111	51	.459	34	18	.529	139	39	37	1	120

WILLIAM FENTON RUSSELL (Bill) (Cont.)

NBA COACHING RECORD

SEA. CLUB	REGULAR SEASON			PLAYOFFS		
	W.	L.	PCT.	POS.	W.	L.
1966-67—Boston	60	21	.741	2	4	5
1967-68—Boston	54	28	.659	2	12	7
1968-69—Boston	48	34	.585	4	12	6
1973-74—Seattle	36	46	.439	3	...	...
1974-75—Seattle	43	39	.524	2	4	5
1975-76—Seattle	43	39	.524	2	2	4
1976-77—Seattle	40	42	.488	4	...	...
Totals (7 seasons)	324	249	.565		34	37

Selected as "Greatest Player in the History of the NBA" by Professional Basketball Writers' Association of America, 1980 . . . . Elected to Naismith Memorial Basketball Hall of Fame, 1974 . . . . Named to NBA 25th and 35th Anniversary All-Time Teams, 1970 and 1980 . . . . NBA Most Valuable Player, 1958, 1961, 1962, 1963, 1965, ... Named to NBA All-Star First Team, 1959, 1963, 1965 . . . . NBA All-Star Second Team, 1958, 1960, 1961, 1962, 1964, 1966, 1967, 1968 . . . . NBA All-Defensive First Team, 1969 . . . . Holds NBA record for most rebounds in one half, 32, vs. Philadelphia, November 16, 1957 . . . NBA all-time playoff leader in rebounds and personal fouls. . . . Holds NBA championship series game record for most rebounds, 40, vs. St. Louis, March 29, 1960, and vs. Los Angeles, April 18, 1962 . . . . Holds NBA playoff record for most rebounds in one quarter, 19, vs. Los Angeles, April 18, 1962 . . . . NBA All-Star Game MVP, 1963 . . . . Member of NBA championship teams, 1957, 1959, 1960, 1961, 1962, 1963, 1964, 1965, 1966, 1968 (also coach), 1969 . . . Led NBA in rebounding, 1957, 1958, 1964, 1965 . . . . NCAA Tournament Most Outstanding Player, 1955 . . . . Member of NCAA championship teams, 1955 and 1956 . . . . Member of U.S. Olympic team, 1956 . . . . One of only seven players to average over 20 points and 20 rebounds per game during NCAA career.

These statistics courtesy of The Sporting News.

JOHN HAVLICEK (Hondo)

Born April 8, 1940 at Martins Ferry, O. Height 6: 05. Weight 205.
High School—Bridgeport, O. College—Ohio State University, Columbus, O.
Drafted by Boston on first round, 1962.

—COLLEGIATE RECORD—

YEAR	G.	MIN.	FGA	FGM	PCT.	FTA	FTM	PCT.	REB.	PTS.	AVG.
58-59†	....	....	....	....	....	....	....	....	....	341	12.2
59-60	28	....	312	144	.462	74	53	.716	205	407	14.5
60-61	28	....	321	173	.539	87	61	.701	244	475	17.0
61-62	28	....	377	196	.520	109	83	.761	271	475	14.6
Varsity Totals	84	....	1010	513	.508	270	197	.730	720	1223	

NOTE: The 1958-59 Ohio State freshman team did not play an intercollegiate schedule.

NBA REGULAR SEASON RECORD

SEA.—TEAM	G.	MIN.	FGA	FGM	PCT.	FTA	FTM	PCT.	REB.	AST.	PF	DISQ.	PTS.	AVG.
62-63—Boston	80	2200	1085	483	.445	239	174	.728	534	179	189	2	1140	14.3
63-64—Boston	80	2587	1535	640	.417	422	315	.746	428	238	227	1	1595	19.9
64-65—Boston	75	2169	1420	570	.401	316	235	.744	371	199	200	2	1375	18.3
65-66—Boston	71	2175	1328	530	.399	349	274	.785	423	210	158	1	1334	18.8
66-67—Boston	81	2602	1540	684	.444	441	365	.828	532	278	210	0	1733	12.4
67-68—Boston	82	2921	1551	666	.429	453	368	.812	546	384	237	2	1700	20.7
68-69—Boston	82	3174	1709	692	.405	496	387	.780	570	441	247	0	1771	21.6
69-70—Boston	81	3369	1585	736	.464	578	488	.844	635	550	211	1	1960	24.2
70-71—Boston	81	3678	1982	892	.450	677	554	.818	730	607	200	0	2338	28.9
71-72—Boston	82	3698	1957	897	.458	549	458	.834	672	614	183	1	2252	27.5
72-73—Boston	80	3367	1704	766	.450	431	370	.858	567	529	195	1	1902	23.8

JOHN HAVLICEK (Hondo) (Cont.)

SEA.–TEAM	G.	MIN.	FGA	FGM	PCT.	FTA	FTM	PCT.	—Rebounds— OFF.	DEF.	TOT.	AST.	PF	DQ.	STL.	BLK.	PTS.	AVG.
73-74—Boston	76	3091	1502	685	.456	416	346	.832	138	349	487	447	196	1	95	32	1716	22.6
74-75—Boston	82	3132	1411	642	.455	332	289	.870	154	330	484	432	231	2	110	16	1573	19.2
75-76—Boston	76	2598	1121	504	.450	333	281	.844	116	198	314	278	204	1	97	29	1289	17.0
76-77—Boston	79	2913	1283	580	.452	288	235	.816	109	273	382	400	208	4	84	18	1395	17.7
77-78—Boston	82	2797	1217	546	.449	269	230	.855	93	239	332	328	185	2	90	22	1322	16.1
Totals	1270	46471	23930	10513	.439	6589	5369	.815			8007	6114	3281	21	476	117	26395	20.8

NBA PLAYOFF RECORD

SEA.–TEAM	G.	MIN.	FGA	FGM	PCT.	FTA	FTM	PCT.	REB.	AST.	PF	DISQ.	PTS.	AVG.
62-63—Boston	11	254	125	56	.448	27	18	.667	53	17	28	1	130	11.8
63-64—Boston	10	289	159	61	.384	44	35	.795	43	32	26	0	157	15.7
64-65—Boston	12	405	250	88	.352	55	46	.836	88	29	44	1	222	18.5
65-66—Boston	17	719	374	153	.409	113	95	.841	154	70	69	2	401	23.6
66-67—Boston	9	330	212	95	.448	71	57	.803	73	28	30	0	247	27.4
67-68—Boston	19	862	407	184	.452	151	125	.828	164	142	67	1	493	25.9
68-69—Boston	18	850	382	170	.445	138	118	.855	179	100	58	2	458	25.4
71-72—Boston	11	517	235	108	.460	99	85	.859	92	70	35	1	301	27.4
72-73—Boston	12	479	235	112	.477	74	61	.824	62	65	24	0	285	23.8

SEA.–TEAM	G.	MIN.	FGA	FGM	PCT.	FTA	FTM	PCT.	—Rebounds— OFF.	DEF.	TOT.	AST.	PF	DQ.	ST.	BLK.	PTS.	AVG.
73-74—Boston	18	811	411	199	.484	101	89	.881	28	88	116	108	43	0	24	6	487	27.1
74-75—Boston	11	464	192	83	.432	76	66	.868	18	39	57	51	38	1	16	1	232	21.1
75-76—Boston	15	505	180	80	.444	47	38	.809	18	38	56	51	22	0	12	5	198	13.2
76-77—Boston	9	375	167	62	.371	50	41	.820	15	34	49	62	33	0	8	4	165	18.3
Totals	172	6860	3329	1451	.436	1046	874	.836			1186	825	517	9	60	16	3776	22.0

NBA ALL-STAR GAME RECORD

SEASON–TEAM	MIN.	FGA	FGM	PCT.	FTA	FTM	PCT.	REB.	AST.	PF	DISQ.	PTS.
1966—Boston	25	16	6	.375	6	6	1.000	6	1	2	0	18
1967—Boston	17	14	7	.500	0	0	.000	2	1	1	0	14
1968—Boston	22	15	9	.600	11	8	.727	5	4	0	0	26
1969—Boston	31	14	6	.429	2	2	1.000	7	2	2	0	14
1970—Boston	29	15	7	.467	3	3	1.000	5	7	2	0	17
1971—Boston	24	12	6	.500	0	0	.000	3	2	3	0	12
1972—Boston	24	13	5	.385	5	5	1.000	3	2	2	0	15
1973—Boston	22	10	6	.600	5	2	.400	3	5	1	0	14

SEASON–TEAM	MIN.	FGA	FGM	PCT.	FTA	FTM	PCT.	—Rebounds—			Ast.	PF	DQ.	STL.	BLK.	PTS.
								OFF.	DEF.	TOT.						
1974—Boston	18	10	5	.500	2	0	.000	0	0	0	2	2	0	1	0	10
1975—Boston	31	12	7	.583	2	2	1.000	1	5	6	1	2	0	2	0	16
1976—Boston	21	10	3	.300	3	3	1.000	1	1	2	2	0	0	1	0	9
1977—Boston	17	5	2	.400	0	0	.000	0	1	1	1	1	0	0	0	4
1978—Boston	22	8	5	.625	0	0	.000	0	3	3	1	2	0	0	0	10
Totals	303	154	74	.481	41	31	.756			46	31	20	0	4	0	179

Named to NBA 35th Anniversary All-Time Team, 1980 . . . . NBA All-Star First Team, 1971, 1972, 1973, 1974 . . . . NBA All-Star Second Team, 1964, 1966, 1968, 1969, 1970, 1975, 1976 . . . . NBA All-Defensive First Team, 1972, 1973, 1974, 1975, 1976 . . . . NBA All-Defensive Second Team, 1969, 1970, 1971 . . . . NBA Playoff MVP, 1974 . . . . NBA all-time leader in regular-season games, playoff games and regular-season field-goal attempts . . . . Shares NBA playoff game record for most field goals made, 24, vs. Atlanta, April 1, 1973 . . . . Holds NBA championship series record for most points in overtime periods, 9, vs. Milwaukee, May 10, 1974 . . . . Shares NBA championship series record for most field goals made in one quarter, 8, vs. San Francisco, April 18, 1964 . . . . Shares NBA All-Star Game record for most games played, 13 . . . . Member of NBA championship teams, 1963, 1964, 1965, 1966, 1968, 1969, 1974, 1976 . . . . Selected by Cleveland Browns on seventh round of 1962 NFL draft . . . . Named to THE SPORTING NEWS All-America Second Team, 1962 . . . . Member of NCAA championship team, 1960.

These statistics courtesy of The Sporting News.

DAVID WILLIAM COWENS (Dave)

Born October 25, 1948 at Newport, Ky.   Height 6:09.   Weight 230.
High School—Newport, Ky., Catholic.
College—Florida State University, Tallahassee, Fla.
Drafted by Boston on first round, 1970 (4th pick).

—COLLEGIATE RECORD—

YEAR	G.	MIN.	FGA	FGM	PCT.	FTA	FTM	PCT.	REB.	PTS.	AVG.
66-67	18	....	208	105	.505	90	49	.544	357	259	14.4
67-68	27	....	383	206	.538	131	96	.733	456	508	18.8
68-69	25	....	384	202	.526	164	104	.634	437	508	20.3
69-70	26	....	355	174	.490	169	115	.680	447	463	17.8
Varsity Totals	78	....	1122	582	.519	464	315	.679	1340	1479	19.0

NBA REGULAR SEASON RECORD

SEA.—TEAM	G.	MIN.	FGA	FGM	PCT.	FTA	FTM	PCT.	REB.	AST.	PF	DISQ.	PTS.	AVG.
70-71—Boston	81	3076	1302	550	.422	373	273	.732	1216	228	350	15	1373	17.0
71-72—Boston	79	3186	1357	657	.484	243	175	.720	1203	245	314	10	1489	18.8
72-73—Boston	82	3425	1637	740	.452	262	204	.779	1329	333	311	7	1684	20.5

SEA.—TEAM	G.	MIN.	FGA	FGM	PCT.	FTA	FTM	PCT.	—Rebounds—			AST.	PF	DQ.	STL.	BLK.	PTS.	AVG.
									OFF.	DEF.	TOT.							
73-74—Boston	80	3352	1475	645	.437	274	228	.832	264	993	1257	354	294	7	95	101	1518	19.0
74-75—Boston	65	2632	1199	569	.475	244	191	.783	229	729	958	296	243	7	87	73	1329	20.4
75-76—Boston	78	3101	1305	611	.468	340	257	.756	335	911	1246	325	314	10	94	71	1479	19.0
76-77—Boston	50	1888	756	328	.434	198	162	.818	147	550	697	248	181	7	46	49	818	16.4
77-78—Boston	77	3215	1220	598	.490	284	239	.842	248	830	1078	351	297	5	102	67	1435	18.6
78-79—Boston	68	2517	1010	488	.483	187	151	.807	152	500	652	242	263	16	76	51	1127	16.6
79-80—Boston	66	2159	932	422	.453	122	95	.779	126	408	534	206	216	2	69	61	940	14.2
Totals	726	28551	12193	5608	.460	2527	1975	.782			10170	2828	2783	86	569	473	13192	18.2

Three-Point Field Goals: 1979-80, 1-for-12 (.083).

NBA PLAYOFF RECORD

SEA.–TEAM	G.	MIN.	FGA	FGM	PCT.	FTA	FTM	PCT.	REB.	AST.	PF	DISQ.	PTS.	AVG.
71-72—Boston	11	441	156	71	.455	47	28	.596	152	33	50	2	170	15.5
72-73—Boston	13	598	273	129	.473	41	27	.659	216	48	54	2	285	21.9

SEA.–TEAM	G.	MIN.	FGA	FGM	PCT.	FTA	FTM	PCT.	—Rebounds—			AST.	PF	DQ.	ST.	BLK.	PTS.	AVG.
									OFF.	DEF.	TOT.							
73-74—Boston	18	772	370	161	.435	59	47	.797	60	180	240	66	85	2	21	17	269	20.5
74-75—Boston	11	479	236	101	.428	26	23	.885	49	132	181	46	50	2	18	6	225	20.5
75-76—Boston	18	798	341	156	.457	87	66	.759	87	209	296	83	85	4	22	13	378	21.0
76-77—Boston	9	379	148	66	.446	22	17	.773	29	105	134	36	37	3	8	13	149	16.6
79-80—Boston	9	301	103	49	.476	11	10	.909	18	48	66	21	37	0	9	7	108	12.0
Totals	89	3768	1627	733	.451	293	218	.744			1285	333	398	15	78	56	1684	18.9

Three-Point Field Goals: 1979-80, 0-for-2.

NBA ALL-STAR GAME RECORD

SEASON–TEAM	MIN.	FGA	FGM	PCT.	FTA	FTM	PCT.	REB.	AST.	PF	DISQ.	PTS.
1972—Boston	32	12	5	.417	5	4	.800	20	1	4	0	14
1973—Boston	30	15	7	.467	1	1	1.000	13	1	2	0	15

SEASON–TEAM	MIN.	FGA	FGM	PCT.	FTA	FTM	PCT.	—Rebounds—			AST.	PF	DQ.	STL.	BLK.	PTS.
								OFF.	DEF.	TOT.						
1974—Boston	26	10	5	.500	3	1	.333	6	6	12	1	6	0	0	1	11
1975—Boston	15	7	3	.429	0	0	.000	0	6	6	3	4	0	1	0	6
1976—Boston	23	13	6	.462	5	4	.800	8	8	16	1	3	0	1	0	16
1977—Boston	Selected—Injured, Did Not Play															
1978—Boston	28	9	7	.778	0	0	.000	6	8	14	5	5	0	2	0	14
Totals	154	66	33	.500	14	10	.714			81	12	21	0	4	1	76

DAVID WILLIAM COWENS (Dave) (Cont.)

NBA COACHING RECORD

		REGULAR SEASON			PLAYOFFS	
Sea.	Club	W.	L.	Pct.	Pos.	W.	L.
1978-79—Boston		27	41	.397	5	....	....

NBA Most Valuable Player, 1973 . . . . Named to NBA All-Star Second Team, 1973, 1975, 1976 . . . . NBA All-Defensive First Team, 1976 . . . . NBA All-Defensive Second Team, 1975 and 1980 . . . . NBA Co-Rookie of the Year, 1971 . . . . NBA All-Rookie Team, 1971 . . . . NBA All-Star Game MVP, 1973 . . . . Member of the NBA championship teams, 1974 and 1976 . . . . Named to THE SPORTING NEWS All-America Second Team, 1970.

These statistics courtesy of The Sporting News.

ROBERT GORDON ORR
(Bobby)

Born, Parry Sound, Ont., March 20, 1948.
Defense. Shoots left. 6', 199 lbs.
Last amateur club: Oshawa Generals (Jrs.).

REGULAR SCHEDULE   PLAYOFFS

SEASON	CLUB	GP	G	A	TP	PIM	GP	G	A	TP	PIM
1966-67ab	Boston	61	13	28	41	102	....	....	....	....	....
1967-68cd	Boston	46	11	20	31	63	4	0	2	2	2
1968-69cd	Boston	67	21	43	64	133	10	1	7	8	10
1969-70cdefg	Boston	76	33	°87	°120	125	14	9	11	20	14
1970-71cdfhj	Boston	78	37	°102	139	91	7	5	7	12	25
1971-72cdfgkl	Boston	76	37	°80	117	106	15	5	°19	°24	19
1972-73cd	Boston	63	29	72	101	99	5	1	1	2	7
1973-74cd	Boston	74	32	°90	122	82	16	4	°14	18	28
1974-75cdem	Boston	80	46	°89	°135	101	3	1	5	6	2
1975-76	Boston	10	5	13	18	22	.... .	....	....	....	....
1978-79	Chicago	6	2	2	2	0	....	....	....	....	....
NHL Totals		657	270	645	915	949	74	26	66	92	107

a Won Calder Memorial Trophy.
b Second All-Star Team (defense).
c Won James Norris Memorial Trophy.
d First All-Star Team (defense).
e Won Art Ross Trophy.
f Won Hart Trophy.
g Won Conn Smythe Trophy.

h NHL record for assists in regular season.
i NHL record for points in regular season by a defenseman.
j Won Lou Marsh Trophy as Top Canadian Athlete.
k NHL record for assists in playoffs.
l NHL record for points in playoffs by a defenseman.
m NHL record for goals in regular season by a defenseman.
  Signed by Chicago as a free agent, June 24, 1976.

MILTON CONRAD SCHMIDT
(Milt)

Born, Kitchener, Ont., March 5, 1918.
Center. Shoots left. 5' 11", 180 lbs.
Last amateur club: Kitchener, Ont.
(Juniors).

REGULAR SCHEDULE   PLAYOFFS

SEASON	CLUB	LEA.	GP	G	A	TP	PIM	GP	G	A	TP	PIM
1936-37	Providence	IAHL	23	8	1	9	12	....	....	....	....	....
1936-37	Boston	NHL	x	2	8	10	15	x	0	0	0	0
1937-38	Boston	NHL	x	13	14	27	15	x	0	0	0	0
1938-39	Boston	NHL	x	15	17	32	13	12	3	3	6	2
1939-40	Boston	NHL	48	22	°30	°52	37	6	0	0	0	0
1940-41	Boston	NHL	45	13	25	38	23	11	5	6	°11	9
1941-42	Boston	NHL	36	14	21	35	34	....	....	....	....	....
1942-43, 43-44, 44-45			(Canadian Armed Forces)									
1945-46	Boston	NHL	48	13	18	31	21	10	3	5	8	2
1946-47	Boston	NHL	59	27	35	62	40	5	3	1	4	4
1947-48	Boston	NHL	33	9	17	26	28	5	2	5	7	2
1948-49	Boston	NHL	44	10	22	32	25	4	0	2	2	8
1949-50	Boston	NHL	68	19	22	41	41	....	....	....	....	....
1950-51a	Boston	NHL	62	22	39	61	33	6	0	1	1	7
1951-52	Boston	NHL	69	21	29	50	57	7	2	1	3	0
1952-53	Boston	NHL	68	11	23	34	30	10	5	1	6	6
1953-54	Boston	NHL	62	14	18	32	28	4	1	0	1	20
1954-55	Boston	NHL	23	4	8	12	26	....	....	....	....	....
Career Totals			688	237	347	584	478	80	24	25	49	60

a Won Hart Trophy (NHL's Most Valuable Player Award).

PHILIP ANTHONY ESPOSITO
(Phil)

Born, Sault Ste. Marie, Ont., February 20, 1942.
Center. Shoots left. 6'1", 205 lbs.
Last amateur club: St. Catherines Teepees (Jrs.).

			REGULAR SCHEDULE					PLAYOFFS				
SEASON	CLUB	LEA	GP	G	A	TP	PIM	GP	G	A	TP	PIM
1961-62	Sault Ste. Marie	EPHL	6	0	3	3	2	....	....	....	....	....
1962-63	St. Louis	EPHL	71	36	54	90	51	....	....	....	....	....
1963-64	St. Louis	CPHL	43	26	54	80	65	....	....	....	....	....
1963-64	Chicago	NHL	27	3	2	5	2	4	0	0	0	0
1964-65	Chicago	NHL	70	23	32	55	44	13	3	3	6	15
1965-66	Chicago	NHL	69	27	26	53	49	6	1	1	2	2
1966-67	Chicago	NHL	69	21	40	61	40	6	0	0	0	7
1967-68a	Boston	NHL	74	35	°49	84	21	4	0	3	3	0
1968-69bcd	Boston	NHL	74	49	°77	°126	79	10	°8	°10	°18	8
1969-70b	Boston	NHL	76	°43	56	°99	50	14	°13	°14	°27	16
1970-71bcgh	Boston	NHL	78	°76	76	°152	71	7	3	7	10	6
1971-72bc	Boston	NHL	76	°66	67	°133	76	15	°9	15	°24	24
1972-73bc	Boston	NHL	78	°55	°75	°130	87	2	0	1	1	2
1973-74bcdh	Boston	NHL	78	°68	77	°145	58	16	9	5	14	25
1974-75a	Boston	NHL	79	°61	66	127	62	3	4	1	5	0
1975-76	Boston	NHL	12	6	10	16	8	....	....	....	....	....
	N.Y. Rangers	NHL	62	29	38	67	28	....	....	....	....	....
1976-77	N.Y. Rangers	NHL	80	34	46	80	52	....	....	....	....	....
1977-78	N.Y. Rangers	NHL	79	38	43	81	53	3	0	1	1	5
1978-79	N.Y. Rangers	NHL	80	42	36	78	37	18	8	12	20	20
1979-80	N.Y. Rangers	NHL	80	34	44	78	73	9	3	3	6	8
1980-81	N.Y. Rangers	NHL	41	7	13	20	20	....	....	....	....	....
	NHL Totals		1282	717	873	1590	910	130	61	76	137	138

a Second All-Star (center).
b First All-Star Team (center).
c Won Art Ross Trophy.
d Won Hart Trophy.

g NHL record for goals in regular season.
h Won Lester B. Pearson Award.
i Won Lester Patrick Award.

Traded to Boston by Chicago with Ken Hodge and Fred Stanfield for Gilles Marotte, Pit Martin and Jack Norris, May 15, 1967. Traded to NY Rangers by Boston with Carol Vadnais for Brad Park, Jean Ratelle and Joe Zanussi, November 7, 1975.

EDWARD WILLIAM SHORE
(Eddie)

Defenseman
b. St. Qu'Appelle-Cupar, Sask., Nov. 25, 1902

SEASON	CLUB	GP	G	A	PTS	PLAYOFFS	CLUB	GP	G	A	PTS
1926-27	Boston	—	12	6	18	1926-27	Boston	—	1	1	2
1927-28	Boston	—	11	6	17	1927-28	Boston	—	0	0	0
1928-29	Boston	—	12	7	19	1928-29	Boston	—	1	1	2
1929-30	Boston	—	12	19	31	1929-30	Boston	—	1	0	1
1930-31	Boston	—	15	16	31	1930-31	Boston	—	2	1	3
1931-32	Boston	—	9	13	22	1932-33	Boston	—	0	1	1
1932-33	Boston	—	8	27	35	1934-35	Boston	—	0	1	1
1933-34	Boston	—	2	10	12	1935-36	Boston	—	1	1	2
1934-35	Boston	—	7	26	33	1937-38	Boston	—	0	1	1
1935-36	Boston	—	3	16	19	1938-39	Boston	—	0	4	4
1936-37	Boston	—	3	1	4	1939-40	New York A	—	0	2	2
1937-38	Boston	—	3	14	17						
1938-39	Boston	—	4	14	18						
1939-40	Bos-NY A	—	4	4	8						
	Totals	—	105	179	284		Totals	—	6	13	19

(Rocco Francis Marchegiano)
(Brockton Blockbuster)

ROCKY MARCIANO

Born, September 1, 1923, Brockton, Mass.
Nationality, Italian-American. Weight 184 pounds.
Height, 5 ft, 11 ins.
Managed by Gene Caggiano. Later by Al Weill.

1947

Mar. 17	Lee Epperson, Holyoke	KO	3

1948

July 12	Harry Balzerian, Providence	KO	1
July 19	John Edwards, Providence	KO	1
Aug. 9	Bobby Quinn, Providence	KO	3
Aug. 23	Eddie Ross, Providence	KO	1
Aug. 30	Jimmy Weeks, Providence	KO	1
Sept. 13	Jerry Jackson, Providence	KO	1
Sept. 20	Bill Hardeman, Providence	KO	1
Sept. 30	Gil Cardione, Wash., D. C.	KO	1
Oct. 4	Bob Jefferson, Providence	KO	2
Nov. 29	Patrick Connolly, Providence	KO	1
Dec. 14	Gilley Ferron, Philadelphia	KO	2

1949

Mar. 21	Johnny Pretzie, Providence	KO	5
Mar. 28	Artie Donato, Providence	KO	1
Apr. 11	James Walls, Providence	KO	3
May 2	Jimmy Evans, Providence	KO	3
May 23	Don Mogard, Providence	W	10
July 18	Harry Haft, Providence	KO	3
Aug. 16	Pete Louthis, New Bedford	KO	3
Sept. 26	Tommy DiGiorgio, Providence	KO	4
Oct. 10	Ted Lowry, Providence	W	10
Nov. 7	Joe Domonic, Providence	KO	2
Dec. 2	Pat Richards, New York	KO	2
Dec. 19	Phil Muscato, Providence	KO	5
Dec. 30	Carmine Vingo, New York	KO	6

1950

Mar. 24	Roland LaStarza, New York	W	10
June 5	Eldridge Eatman, Providence	KO	3
July 10	Gino Buonvino, Boston	KO	10
Sept. 18	Johnny Shkor, Providence	KO	6
Nov. 13	Ted Lowry, Providence	W	10
Dec. 18	Bill Wilson, Providence	KO	1

1951

Jan. 29	Keene Simmons, Providence	KO	8
Mar. 20	Harold Mitchell, Hartford	KO	2
Mar. 26	Art Henri, Providence	KO	9
Apr. 30	Red Applegate, Providence	W	10
July 12	Rex Layne, N. Y.	KO	6
Aug. 27	Freddie Beshore, Boston	KO	4
Oct. 26	Joe Louis, N. Y.	KO	8

ROCKY MARCIANO (Cont.)

1952

Feb. 13	Lee Savold, Philadelphia	KO	6
Apr. 21	Gino Buonvino, Providence	KO	2
May 12	Bernie Reynolds, Providence	KO	3
July 28	Harry Matthews, New York	KO	2
Sept. 23	Jersey Joe Walcott, Phila.	KO	13

(Won World Heavyweight Title)

1953

May 15	Jersey Joe Walcott, Chicago (Title Bout)	KO	1
Sept. 24	Roland La Starza, New York (Title Bout)	KO	11

1954

June 17	Ezzard Charles, New York (Title Bout)	W	15
Sept. 17	Ezzard Charles, New York (Title Bout)	KO	8

1955

May 16	Don Cockell, San Francisco (Title Bout)	KO	9
Sept. 21	Archie Moore, New York (Title Bout)	KO	9

1956

Announced retirement as undefeated world heavyweight champion, April 27, 1956.
Elected to Boxing Hall of Fame, 1959.

TB	KO	WD	WF	D	LD	LF	KOBY	ND	NC
49	43	6	0	0	0	0	0	0	0

JOHN A. KELLEY (Johnny)   John Kelley was born September 6, 1907.

BOSTON MARATHON RECORD

YEAR	PLACE	TIME	YEAR	PLACE	TIME
1928	D.N.F.°		1955	24th	2:45:22
1932	D.N.F		1956	D.N.F.	
1933	37th	2:50:00	1957	13th	2:53:00
1934	2nd	2:36:06	1958	9th	2:52:12
1935	1st	2:32:07	1959	23rd	2:47:52
1936	5th	2:38:49	1960	19th	2:44:39
1937	2nd	2:39:00	1961	17th	2:44:53
1938	3rd	2:37:34	1962	25th	2:44:36
1939	13th	2:41:03	1963	84th	3:14:00
1940	2nd	2:32:03	1964	48th	2:49:14
1941	2nd	2:31:26	1965	59th	2:48:00
1942	5th	2:40:00	1966	59th	2:55:00
1943	2nd	2:30:00	1967	135th	3:13:00
1944	2nd	2:32:02	1969	186th	3:05:02
1945	1st	2:30:40	1970	163rd	3:03:00
1946	2nd	2:31:27	1971	977th°°	3:45:47
1947	13th	2:40:00	1972	890th°°	3:35:12
1948	4th	2:37:46	1973	1105th°°	3:35:02
1949	4th	2:33:07	1974	1266th	3:24:10
1950	5th	2:43:45	1975	1247th°°	3:26:00
1951	6th	2:39:09	1976	1525th°°	3:28:00
1952	12th	3:04:59	1977	2312th°°	3:32:22
1953	7th	2:32:46	1978	2325th°°	3:32:17
1954	16th	2:50:25	1979	3577th°°	3:45:12
1954	16th	2:50:25	1980	3444th°°	3:35:21
			1981	°°	4:01:25
			1982	°°	4:01:18

°D.N.F. means did not finish. °°Estimated finish.

We are indebted to John A. Kelley, Jerry Nason, Will Cloney and Prof. John Lucas for their assistance in compiling this chart.

WILLIAM RODGERS (Bill)

Birth date: 12-23-47
Birthplace: Hartford, Connecticut
Height: 5'9"
Weight: 128 lbs.
College: Wesleyan, B.A., Boston College, M.A.

NATIONAL CHAMPIONSHIPS

20Km Road—1st Place—1973—1:03:58
30Km—1st Place—1976—1:29:04 (unofficial world record)

BEST ROAD RACE MARKS

1978—10Km—28:36
1977—20Km—1:00:24
1977—30Km—1:29:04
1978—½ Marathon—1:03:08
1979—30Km—1:31:50—American record
    on the track
1979—25Km—1:14:12—world record
    on the track

COMPLETE MARATHON RECORD

Terminology:
PR—Personal Record
AR—American Record
DNF—Did Not Finish
°—200 meters short

	MARATHON	DATE	PLACE	TIME	LOCATION
1.	Boston	4/16/73	DNF		Boston, Mass.
2.	Bay State	10/28/73	1	2:28:12	Framingham, Mass.
3.	Boston	4/15/74	14	2:19:34	Boston, Mass.
4.	New York City	9/29/74	5	2:36:00	New York, N.Y.
5.	Philadelphia	12/1/74	1	2:21:57	Philadelphia, Pa.
6.	Boston	4/21/75	1AR	2:09:55	Boston, Mass.
7.	Enschede	8/30/75	DNF		Holland
8.	Fukuoka	12/7/75	3	2:11:26	Japan
9.	U.S. Olympic Trial	5/22/76	2	2:11:58	Eugene, Oregon
10.	Olympic	7/31/76	40	2:25:14	Montreal, Canada
11.	New York City	10/24/76	1	2:10:10	New York, N.Y.
12.	°Sado Island	11/7/76	1	2:08:23	Japan
13.	Baltimore	12/5/76	1	2:14:22	Baltimore, Md.
14.	Kyoto	2/13/77	1	2:14:26	Japan
15.	Boston	4/18/77	DNF		Boston, Mass.
16.	Amsterdam	5/21/77	1	2:12:47	Holland
17.	Waynesboro	10/8/77	1	2:25:12	Waynesboro, Va.
18.	New York City	10/23/77	1	2:11:28	New York, N.Y.
19.	Fukuoka	12/4/77	1	2:10:55	Japan
20.	Boston	4/17/78	1	2:10:13	Boston, Mass.
21.	New York City	10/22/78	1	2:12:12	New York, N.Y.
22.	Fukuoka	12/3/78	6	2:12:51	Japan
23.	Boston	4/16/79	1AR PR	2:09:27	Boston, Mass.
24.	Montreal	8/26/79	15	2:22:12	Montreal, Canada
25.	New York City	10/21/79	1	2:11:42	New York, N.Y.
26.	Boston	1980	1	2:12:11	Boston, Mass.
27.	Boston	1981	3	2:10:34	Boston, Mass.
28.	Boston	1982	4	2:12:13	Boston, Mass.

INDEX

INDEX